Techniques For Writing: Composition

Milton Wohl

California State University ● Fresno

Revised Edition

NEWBURY HOUSE PUBLISHERS, INC.
ROWLEY, MASSACHUSETTS 01969
ROWLEY ● LONDON ● TOKYO

1985

Library of Congress Cataloging in Publication Data

Wohl, Milton.
   Techniques for writing, composition.

   "Volume 2."
   Continues the author's Preparation for writing:
grammar.
   1. English language--Text-books for foreigners.
2. English language--Rhetoric.   I. Title.
PE1128.W755   428'.2'4   78-646
ISBN 0-88377-107-1

Cover design by Cynthia Crowley.

NEWBURY HOUSE PUBLISHERS, INC.

Language Science
Language Teaching
Language Learning

ROWLEY, MASSACHUSETTS 01969

Revised edition: September 1985

Printed in the U.S.A.   6   5   4   3   2

For My Wife, Yadira,
and the Memory of Ruth M. Romero

PREFACE TO THE REVISED EDITION

This revised edition was initially motivated by the author's desire to improve and expand the section on paraphrase. If paraphrase is the logical counterpart of reading comprehension, as some of us believe, then perhaps paraphrasing does stimulate cognitive language processing. Currently there is considerable talk about "writing as process" as opposed to "writing as product." In the revised section on paraphrasing I have tried to address myself to the former.

The examples and exercises for paraphrase are not only greater in number but become increasingly difficult and challenging as one works through that section.

A new unit (6) on business communication has been added. This unit presents authentic samples of business letters and illustrates current practices in the business world. While this addition may be appropriate only for the more advanced writer, others may find it instructive as well as challenging.

This revision also includes a change in the sequence of the units. What was unit 3 in the original edition is now unit 1. What *were* units 1 and 2 are now units 2 and 3, respectively. And a few topics were switched from one unit to another.

Although the author feels there is some logic to this new arrangement, the instructor is urged to introduce each unit in the order that best meets the needs of his or her students. As a matter of fact, the instructor is encouraged to work with parts of more than one unit in a single class hour.

In addition to these changes, exercises have been added and expanded, and new topics have been introduced. It is hoped that these changes and additions will make *Techniques for Writing: Composition* a more valuable contribution to mastery of the writing process.

Milton Wohl
California State University, Fresno
October 1984

PREFACE TO THE FIRST EDITION*

Like its companion text *Preparation for Writing: Grammar* this book is intended for high intermediate and advanced students of English as a second language. Its main objective is to prepare its users for the kind of formal and informal writing expected of college freshmen.

Good writing assumes correct grammar. However, in the experience of this writer, students rarely enter a composition class without wide gaps in their control of English syntax. The instructor cannot ignore the fact that many students still do not handle tense and aspect correctly and have a difficult time with determiners. *Preparation* is designed to remedy this situation. With its pretests and answer key, *Preparation* is well suited for reference and self-study by the students, with some supervision by the teacher. *Preparation* included blanks for writing in answers. Because of the greater length of most writing assignments in the present book, write-in blanks have been omitted.

Units 1 to 5 (Sections A and B) are designed to get students started in writing by easy stages, terminating in the writing of complete essays. Units 10 to 14 (Sections F and G) have a more specialized function and serve to prepare students for the kind of skills needed for term papers and technical writing.

It is recommended that class discussion precede most writing assignments to familiarize the students with appropriate vocabulary and to stimulate their creative powers. This procedure will help the student in developing and organizing his (or her) ideas when he (or she) sits down to write.

*The unit numbering in the first edition of this book has been changed in this new edition.

An answer key for many of the exercises has been provided. In some exercises in which alternative responses are possible, sample answers are given. In addition, there is a complete answer key for the punctuation exercises.

Following the answer key is a very brief section called "Notes to the Instructor." While these few pages are far from being a detailed teacher's manual, these very brief comments and suggestions may be helpful to the teacher.

Lacking the long experience with and exposure to the language enjoyed by the native speaker, the second-language learner is at a distinct disadvantage. The latter does not possess the large bundle of techniques and alternate ways of expression available to the native speaker. He lacks the flexibility of expression that native speakers possess. The inclusion of certain exercises in this text is for the purpose of narrowing this gap.

Like *Preparation,* this book has been based on the needs demonstrated by students of various language and cultural backgrounds. It is the author's hope that this material will prove useful in this most challenging task—that of helping others to improve their writing skills.

Milton Wohl
California State University, Fresno

THANKS TO ...

The author would like to extend his thanks to Esther Kellas and the heirs of Ruth M. Romero for their kind permission to include here the work on capitalization, apostrophe, and italics. He also wishes to express his appreciation to the following individuals who contributed in various ways to the development of this text:

To the anonymous readers for their criticism and comments.

To June McKay, University of California, Berkeley, for her encouragement over the years.

To Tom Lovik, Peggy McCurdy, and Rita Wong, English for Foreign Students, University of California, Berkeley, for their valuable comments and suggestions.

To Bill Choate, Edison High School, for his comments and suggestions after reading a preliminary draft of this book.

To Edward Gammon, colleague and friend, for his helpful criticism and continuing encouragement.

To the rest of my colleagues in the Department of Linguistics, for their forbearance in answering my many questions.

To my daughter Elaine, for the drawings in Unit 10.

To Elsie Taylor, for her creative typing of the manuscript.

To Clarice Crockett, for her patience in unwittingly serving as a native-speaker informant.

To Newbury House editors for their constructive help.

But any errors or deficiencies that may remain are the fault of the author.

Milton Wohl
California State University, Fresno

ACKNOWLEDGMENTS

The author wishes to express his appreciation to the following authors, publishers, and individuals for their permission to reprint excerpts from copyrighted (and some not copyrighted) materials:

The Associated Press for "Divorce Barriers Crumble before Changes in Laws" (1975) by G.A. Fitzgerald.

The Daily Collegian, California State University, Fresno, for "Socialism for Black Africa" (March 21, 1975) by Mokwugo Okoye; and for "Wounded Knee: Broken Treaties and Lives" (March 23, 1973) by Gary Alexander.

Carl N. Degler for "Revolution without Ideology: The Changing Place of Women in America," *DAEDALUS,* Vol. 93, No. 2.

Robert Y. Fuchigami for his Letter to the Editor, *The California Professor* (1969).

Harper & Row for *Stride Toward Freedom: The Montgomery Story* (1958) by Martin Luther King, Jr.

F. Andrew Hart for the excerpt from his letter to the Editor, *The Fresno Bee* (1974).

McGraw-Hill Book Co. for *Social Statistics* (1972) by Hubert M. Blalock, Jr., and for "The contributions of psychological theory and educational research to the teaching of foreign languages," by John B. Carroll, in *Trends in Language Teaching,* A. Valdman, ed. (1966).

The National Observer, copyright Dow Jones & Co., Inc., for "Let 'Em Starve" (March 29, 1975) by Michael T. Malloy; for "For Whom the Decibel Tolls" (Nov. 11, 1972) by Barbara J. Katz; and for the news article by A. Gribbin (April 21, 1973).

Plenum Publishing Corporation for "Effects of Sex Hormones on Cognitive Style in Rats and Men" by John L.M. Dawson in *Behavior Genetics,* Vol. 2, No. 1 (March 1972).

G.P. Putnam's Sons, copyright 1974, for *The Ultimate Triumph* by Ruth Freeman Soloman.

Rodale Press, Inc., *Prevention Magazine,* for "Table Talk: How to Enjoy Vegetables" (March 1972) by Shelagh Jones; for "Vitamin D—Sunshine to Swallow in Winter" (February 1973) by Michael Clark; and for "Can Vegetarians Get Complete Protein Nourishment" (March 1973).

Saturday Review Corporation for editorials from *Saturday Review of Education* (March, 1973) and *Saturday Review World* (October 23, 1973); and for "The Perils and Potentials of a Watery Planet" by Capt. Jacques Cousteau, in *Saturday Review World* (August 24, 1974) (with permission of The Cousteau Society, Inc.).

Science (American Association for the Advancement of Science) and Professor B.F. Skinner for "Teaching Machines" by B.F. Skinner in *Science,* Vol. 128, pp. 969-977 (October 24, 1958).

Simon & Schuster, Inc., for "Science and Human Life" by Bertrand Russell in *What Is Science,* J.R. Newman, ed. (1955).

Straw Hat Restaurant Corporation, for permission to reproduce their advertisement.

Xerox Education Publications, Xerox Corp., for "The Bermuda Triangle: What's Happening?" by Lewis K. Parker, *Read* (October 1, 1975).

CONTENTS

Techniques For Writing: Composition

SECTION
A

Making a Start in Writing

UNIT 1   THE PARAGRAPH

Introduction

Good writing parallels good speech. A speaker or writer presents and develops a number of points, arguments, or ideas. And if these statements all relate to a single theme and are presented in a logical order, a unified speech or piece of writing results.

In almost all kinds of writing the basic structural unit is the paragraph—a sequence of sentences organized around a single idea; a group of related sentences which, when logically and sequentially arranged, explain and develop a particular idea.

If one can write a good paragraph, he or she can write a good essay. A paragraph is like an essay in miniature. But before one is able to write a good essay, he or she must first be able to write a good paragraph. The paragraph is basic to all good writing.

A characteristically weak paragraph is one which lacks details and is short in length. While it is true that a paragraph will sometimes consist of a short, simple sentence, this is usually reserved for introductory or closing paragraphs. A common fault of beginning writers is their use of tiny, underdeveloped paragraphs—paragraphs lacking details and specific examples. Except for those cases already noted, a good paragraph should be of some length; it should be well nourished with lots of details, examples, and "for-instances." While a good paragraph does contain some generalizations and abstractions, it should be supported by concrete, specific details and examples.

In addition to length, another characteristic of a good paragraph is unity. A unified paragraph can be compared to a single cell—the fundamental structural unit of plant and animal life. A cell consists of a nucleus (the controlling idea) and protoplasm (details and examples) on which the nucleus depends to sustain itself. In the same way, the controlling idea of a paragraph sustains itself with concrete examples and vivid details.

Indentation, Line Skipping, and Paragraph Recognition

A convention of writing is to skip a line and indent a few spaces when beginning a new paragraph. In modern usage, however, many writers do not indent, relying on line skipping alone to signal the start of a new paragraph. (Not indenting after a chapter or major section heading in a book is a common practice as, for example, in this book.) This marking of paragraphs serves to guide the reader as to the structural organization intended by the writer.

However, mere indentation or line skipping does not of itself create a new paragraph. The distinctiveness of one paragraph as compared to another should be self-evident. It should be easy to see where one paragraph ends and the next begins, just as one can see single cells under a microscope.

Recognizing paragraphs

We have stated that paragraph divisions ought to be easily recognizable without the formal signals of line skipping or indentation. The beginning of a new paragraph is usually made apparent through the use of certain indicators: a shift in focus; a change of tense or time period; expressions of contrast or comparison (in contrast, on the other hand, etc.); and other devices used for transition.

Exercises for paragraph recognition

The following selections have been run together without benefit of line skipping or indentation. To see whether you can pick out each new paragraph, write a capital *P* wherever you think a new paragraph begins.

Of course, there may be other correct answers; that is, there may be reasons for dividing the paragraphs differently. After you have completed each selection, you may compare your effort with that of the original author by consulting the answer key.

Exercise 1   The following short article appeared in a school newspaper in support of a candidate for Student Body President. Write a capital *P* wherever you think a new paragraph begins. (The author had four paragraphs.)

For Smith

Tom Smith has all the attributes of a good Student Body President. He is a moderate, with proven ability to speak with all sides on the divisive issues which confront this college. His opponent in today's election, Bill Jones, cannot do this—at least his voting record of the past and his recent actions do not give the indication that he would. To get down to specific cases, Jones is too provincial in his outlook. If he wins the election, he will owe too many political debts to his supporters in the Agriculture Department to be an effective representative of the entire student body. Jones is overly optimistic to think he can work with all groups on campus. As an Ag major and a leader in the School of Agriculture, Jones is tied ideologically to the students of that school only. Smith's voting record as College Union Senator-at-Large has been progressive. It was Smith who explored and recommended the need for construction of a new college union. He has continuously supported the Educational Opportunity Program and other programs which serve the needs of providing a broader education.

Exercise 2   Write a capital *P* wherever you think a new paragraph begins. The author had three paragraphs.

Every society feels the need for an ideal for its collective goals; contemporary civilization, which no longer sees life as a God-ordained, unalterable entity but as something in a state of perpetual change, is critical of itself because of some self-assigned ends that it never succeeds in attaining. And individuals no longer regard the position they occupy in society as definitive—as if there were no other life save the one they lead on this earth. They attach vital importance to the political and economic regime that controls their lives. The question for us in Africa is which, if any, of the many "isms" of our time is best suited for our needs at this time. Is it possible to evolve something entirely new to serve our ends? A possible answer is given by secular ideology which, as the ideology of the State, is held up as the highest embodiment of truth. Unfortunately for modern man, whose most obvious instrument of progress is science and technology, the language of science and technology and productivity does not warm the heart, even if it is intellectually convincing. But when the demands and goals of science are expressed in the learning of an ideology, everything is altered. Now, it is no longer a matter of working or producing, but of building socialism, a great nation, or of creating a new kind of man in a new kind of Great Society.

Exercise 3   This author had three paragraphs for the following text material. Put a large *P* where you think a new paragraph should begin.

Will machines replace teachers? On the contrary, they are capital equipment to be used by teachers to save time and labor. In assigning certain mechanizable functions to machines, the teacher emerges in his proper role as an indispensable human being. He may teach more students than heretofore, but he will do so in fewer hours and with fewer burdensome chores. The role of the teacher may well be changed, for machine instruction will affect several traditional practices. Students may continue to be grouped in "grades" or "classes," but it will be possible for each to proceed at his own level, advancing as rapidly as he can. The other kind of "grade" will also change its meaning. In traditional practice the grade C means that a student has a smattering of a whole course. But if machine instruction assures mastery at every stage, a grade will be useful only in showing *how far* a student has gone. The grade C might mean only that he is halfway through a course. Differences in ability raise other questions. A program designed for the slowest student in the school system will probably not seriously delay the fast student, who will be free to progress at his own speed. If this does not prove to be the case, programs can be constructed at two or more levels, and students can be shifted from one to the other as performances dictate.

Sequence and Coherence

A writer of any language tries to arrange his sentences in a way that allows the reader to follow the ideas presented easily. If the writer arranges his sentences so that they make sense to the reader, such writing is said to be logical and coherent; that is, the sentences follow one another in a way that makes it easy for the reader to get the message intended by the writer. Thus, *coherence* can be defined as *the orderly progression of facts and ideas arranged in a logical sequence.*

The purpose of the following exercises is to test whether you can take a set of related sentences and put them in a logical order so as to make the paragraph well unified and coherent. After you have given your best effort, you may compare your results with those of the original authors by consulting the answer key.

Hint: The most general statement is usually the one that begins the paragraph.

Exercise 4   Create a coherent paragraph by arranging the sentences in a logical order. Put the number of each sentence in its appropriate blank space.

_____   _____   _____   _____   _____   _____

1.   In these rural areas 70 percent of the available agricultural land suffers from dryness and lack of irrigation.
2.   As a result, the crops are usually marginal with hardly enough production to feed the farmer's family.
3.   The first fact to consider is that over 60 percent of the population live in rural communities.
4.   In my country, one of the most urgent problems facing the government today relates to agriculture.
5.   And without irrigation, agricultural production is wholly dependent on the uncertain rainfall.
6.   To understand the nature of this problem one has to look at some of the facts.

Exercise 5   Arrange the sentences below in a logical order by putting the number of each sentence in the appropriate blank space.

Buddhism

_____   _____   _____   _____   _____

1.   This new religion was so strict and exacting that not even an image of the Buddha was permitted in its places of worship.
2.   He had come to the island as a Buddhist missionary in order to preach a new religion—Buddhism.

3. And it was not long before Buddhism spread throughout the island and was adopted as the national religion.
4. In 307 B.C. the son of the great Indian emperor Asoka came to Sri Lanka, the island country formerly called Ceylon.
5. Despite these strict demands the people took to his new religion with great zeal.

Exercise 6   Write the number of each sentence in one of the blank spaces so as to arrange the sentences in a logical sequence.

Nonviolent Resistance

(This is a middle paragraph [not a beginning one] from the writings of Martin Luther King, Jr., used by permission.)

_____   _____   _____   _____   _____

1. This is why Gandhi often said that if cowardice is the only alternative to violence, it is better to fight.
2. If one uses this method because he is afraid or merely because he lacks the instruments of violence, he is not truly nonviolent.
3. He made this statement conscious of the fact there is always another alternative;
4. First of all, it must be emphasized that nonviolent resistance is not a method for cowards; it does resist.
5. there is the way of nonviolent resistance.

Exercise 7   Arrange the sentences below in a logical sequence. First decide in which paragraph each sentence belongs. Then arrange the sentences of each paragraph in a logical order by writing the number of each in the appropriate blank space.

"Some Thoughts on Competition"

Paragraph I
For many Americans competition is a fundamental principle of life.

_____   _____   _____   _____   _____

Paragraph II
If we are to have a humane society, we shall have to rid ourselves of much of the competitiveness that now dominates our every action and decision.

_____   _____   _____   _____

1. At times this spirit becomes so strong it prompts some people to refer to our society as a "dog-eat-dog world."
2. In our own society we are just beginning to face the hard fact that some of us will have to settle for less if all of us are to have a reasonable existence.
3. In fact, some of us place this principle high up on the scale of American values.
4. Even our scholastic grading system encourages competition among our students.
5. On the world scene the overriding fact is the misery of 75 percent of the world's people while the few enjoy great luxury.
6. In the schools, our faith in the value of competition provides support for our commitment to interscholastic sports.
7. In the years ahead, the belief that competition brings about the greatest good for the greatest number will be increasingly questioned.
8. The only possible answer to the dangers of this unequal distribution of wealth lies in greater cooperation among nations.
9. Outside the schools, the spirit of competition has become firmly entrenched in our social life as well as in the business world.

A Note on Transition

The professional writer knows how to write sentences and paragraphs that seem to flow along smoothly, in a logical sequence, without the necessity for specific transition words or expressions. The beginning writer, however, usually finds it helpful to employ these words and expressions in order to achieve good transition between sentences and paragraphs. (See Sentence Adverbials, Unit 3.) In addition to the use of sentence adverbials, however, the repetition of key words and the use of time expressions are often useful transition techniques. Note, for example, the need for transition between the following two sentences:

And after my eight months of training in Agricultural Mechanics in the U.S., I will return to my home country. One day I hope to design and build my own house.

The last sentence "sticks out like a sore thumb." There is a need to somehow relate it to the previous sentence. The introduction of a time expression would seem to be helpful in this case. Note the following:

With added transition:

And after my eight months of training in Agricultural Mechanics in the U.S., I will return to my home country. And *in the more distant future* I hope to one day design and build my own house.

Thus, the use of transitional devices can help the beginning writer achieve unity and coherence in his or her writing. Other useful techniques to provide transition will be discussed in Unit 4.

Mini-research Report

Instructions: With reference to the city or metropolitan area you are now living in, collect data on the items listed below. Then organize your data into a unified, coherent essay using as many of the data as you can. (See sample report following.)

Fact Sheet on the _____ Metropolitan Area.
    Location:
    Climate:
    Population:
    Principal minority groups:
    Business and industry:
    Chief products or services:
    Educational institutions:
    Cultural institutions or organizations:
    Nearby recreational facilities:
    Transportation facilities:

Sample mini-research report

The Fresno Metropolitan Area
by Hebe Hu

Fresno, a central California city, is located in the San Joaquin valley, midway between Los Angeles and San Francisco. The summer weather is hot and dry, with an average temperature in July and August of 87 degrees. Cold and damp winter weather brings an average temperature of 48 degrees in January and February.

Since the climate is suitable for growing certain crops, Fresno produces agricultural products such as grapes, raisins, figs, oranges, apricots, cotton, and a few others.

In addition to agriculture, there are some industries such as light manufacturing and food processing. State highway 99, which passes through the city, and the Union Pacific and Santa Fe railroads have helped Fresno to become a shipping and distribution center for food products.

In 1970 the population of Fresno was 350,000, but it has been increasing in recent years, reaching 385,000 last year. Besides the main population group, which is Anglo-Saxon, there are ethnic minorities including Armenians, Blacks, Chicanos, Chinese, American Indians (called "native Americans"), and Japanese.

As for educational facilities, there are fifty-eight elementary schools, thirteen junior highs, six high schools, and three institutions of higher learning including Fresno State University, Fresno City College, and Reedley College.

The cultural needs of Fresno are supplied by a Symphony Orchestra, Community Theatre, Art center, and many branches of the County Library. As to the recreational areas, these include Woodward Park, Roeding Park and Zoo, Lake Millerton, and Kearney Park.

The city is still growing, and it is expected that Fresno will continue to grow and prosper in the near future.

Topic Sentence

Ideally, each paragraph of an essay ought to treat one, and only one, aspect of the central theme. As an aid in achieving this kind of single-mindedness many writers employ a key sentence which states the main idea of the paragraph. Such a sentence is known as a *topic sentence.*

A good topic sentence narrows the focus and points to one particular aspect of the overall theme. Such a sentence represents the key phrase of that paragraph. In a single statement (or sometimes a question) the writer lets the reader know what the paragraph is about; consequently, the topic sentence usually represents the most general statement of the paragraph.

While it is true that many good writers do not employ a topic sentence in every paragraph they write, the use of such a sentence is a valuable technique for the less experienced student. The use of a topic sentence forces the writer to decide what the main point of the paragraph will be. At the same time it serves as a guide which may help the writer avoid sentences that are not relevant to the main point of the paragraph.

The topic sentence occurs most frequently at the beginning of a paragraph; it may, however, occur in the middle or even at or near the end. When the topic sentence does occur at the end, it serves to summarize the preceding sentences and to conclude the paragraph.

It has just been pointed out that although the most usual place for the topic sentence is at the beginning of a paragraph, it sometimes occurs elsewhere.

Can you pick out the topic sentence in each of the following examples?

Topic sentence recognition

Example 1

It is often difficult to get the general public to fully understand what the right to strike means. This right is one of the most important gains that the labor movement has been able to obtain for the American worker. The exercise of this fundamental right has often caused a great deal of bitterness between labor and management. However, if the unions were not permitted this action, their position in collective bargaining would be greatly weakened.

Example 2

It was a bright and beautiful day when the plane landed at Orly Airport in Paris, France. After passing through Customs and picking up my two pieces of luggage, I started off on my great adventure. This was to be my first trip abroad—alone. Previously I had always gone with my mother, who was always very protective; but now I was on my own, with no one around to prevent my mistakes or check my impulses.

Example 3

The majority of the student body could care less about athletics in general. We students already have to pay for athletics through our registration fees each semester. Now we are being asked to pay even more to build a stadium for a small number of super-stars to display their athletic prowess. I urge the student body to vote against the proposed assessment for a new stadium.

Example 4

Corporate agriculture has an unfair tax advantage over the family farmer. Large corporations are able to enjoy numerous tax breaks not available to the small farmer.

Consequently, the family farmer pays a far higher percentage of his farm income in taxes than does his corporate counterpart. In 1970, for example, with profits of $78 million, Amtecko Corporation paid no federal income tax, but rather had a federal income tax credit of $20 million.

Example 5

Looking around this small metropolis in the heart of a fertile valley, one sees vineyards, fruit orchards, olive groves, and even fields of cotton. The land stretches out flat for miles and miles, like a giant tapeworm unraveled. And on a clear day one can see the beautifully rugged mountain peaks of the high Sierras to the east and north. The lofty mountains seem so close, as if one had only to reach out his hand to touch them. I must admit that what I like most about this quiet little city is its magnificent natural scenery.

Read each of the following paragraphs carefully. Then select, from among the sentences listed below, that which you think would be the most appropriate topic sentence for the paragraph. If you are not satisfied with any of the choices you might try writing your own topic sentence.

Selection 1

_____. The number of inhabitants on this planet has already reached four billion. If the present growth rate remains unchecked, the world's population may very well double in the next 30 to 35 years. Such a situation may bring about starvation, poverty, and serious health problems.

Topic sentence choice:
   a. It is predicted that the world will face serious health problems in the next 30 to 35 years.
   b. One of the most important problems the world will have to face in the near future is the rapid growth of its human population.
   c. The world's human population has been growing rapidly in recent years.

Selection 2

_____.Arriving in the land below the Rio Grande River, the Spanish conquistador Hernando Cortez was surprised to see the local inhabitants raising crops that included avocados, corn, garlic and nuts. Onions, tomatoes, chile peppers, and pumpkins were also grown in the rich soil. Irrigation systems were employed in some of the drier regions. The Aztec farmers were skillful in creating terraced gardens to make the most of the rainfall and to minimize soil erosion. There is evidence that they employed crop rotation as well as natural fertilizers to enhance the production of their farm products.

a. The Aztecs of Mexico were a nation of accomplished farmers.
b. Hernando Cortez discovered farming in Mexico.
c. Mexico is blessed with rich farmland and an abundance of food products.

Selection 3

_____ . Mental depression or melancholy is a serious psychiatric condition which is seemingly without rational explanation. Severe cases may lead to suicide, one of the commonest causes of death worldwide. One group of psychologists claim that the depression derives primarily from psychological causes, including upbringing, family, and job success. A growing number of scientists disagree, pointing to a variety of suspicious chemical or other physical features of the environment.

a. Suicide is a leading cause of death worldwide.
b. Severe depression often leads to suicide.
c. Mental depression is a common phenomenon, but psychologists and scientists do not agree as to its cause.

Exercise 8   The topic sentence of each of the following paragraphs has been omitted. After a careful reading, write an appropriate topic sentence for each. Then compare your effort with that of the original author. (See Answer Key.)

1. ____(topic sentence)____. At the age of twelve, Jack had already chosen his future career. His father had urged him to follow in his footsteps and become a lawyer, but Jack had other ideas. While still in high school Jack began to make enquiries about Harvard Medical School. He knew there were several obstacles to be overcome and that it would take a long time and a lot of hard work. But Jack never wavered in his choice of profession.

2. (Complete the last line and have it serve as the topic sentence.) Factories closed down and many businesses went bankrupt. The cheap restaurants were empty. The air was filled with the smell of fear. The number of burglaries and petty thefts increased. The homeless, the hungry, the miserable gathered aimlessly on sidewalks or waited in bread lines. And children begged openly in the streets. New York City was _____ .

3. _____(topic sentence)_____ . Japan, a country in the capitalist camp, has been strongly influenced by modern western society. It has been striving to build a highly industrialized nation with a strong domestic and overseas commerce. China, on the other hand, has been engaged in reconstructing man's view of life and forging new cultural concepts. In a word, whereas China thinks about and highly values a moral society, Japan has admiration for a material one.

Developing Paragraphs from Topic Sentences

Some students can write a well-unified paragraph without following any formal steps or using formal techniques such as a topic sentence. And this is all to the good. After all, the important thing is to produce a good paragraph; how you go about achieving this result is up to you, the writer. No doubt, one can achieve the same objective in a variety of ways. However, if you would like to try a step-by-step plan for writing a unified paragraph, here are some suggestions:

One way to develop a paragraph.

1. Choose a general topic of interest to you. (For example, marriage customs in my country; the population explosion, etc.)
2. Narrow down the topic. Select one aspect of the topic and decide what your main point is. Then write your tentative topic sentence.
3. Write down a few facts, beliefs and/or opinions that are directly related to your topic sentence—details that will help to support or explain it.
4. Take a second look at your tentative topic sentence. Does it express the main idea? Show it to a friend for his reaction. Revise as you think necessary.
5. Using the facts and ideas from step 3, develop the topic sentence into a full paragraph. This is your first draft.
6. Think about unity as you read what you have written. Revise as necessary and then write your final draft.

Exercise 9   Complete each of the following unfinished sentences so as to make a good topic sentence. Then add four or five additional sentences to make a unified paragraph.

1. I have always wanted to know . . .
2. The one thing I like best about traveling is . . .
3. When I get married . . .
4. For me, the main purpose of marriage is . . .
5. If I were to suddenly become rich I would . . .
6. For me, the most interesting place to visit, had I enough time and money, would be . . .
7. The one thing that gives me the most pleasure these days is . . .
8. Of all the different occupations and professions in the world today, the one job I would really enjoy would be working as a . . .
9. The person I most admire in today's world is . . .
10. For me, the most important thing in life is . . .
11. The first thing I am going to do when I land on the moon is . . .
12. My most positive personality trait is . . .

Exercise 10   Write a one-paragraph summary of a current news event from a newspaper or magazine. Choose an appropriate topic sentence to present the main idea. Then add a few more sentences giving some details to round out the paragraph. (For help in paraphrasing, see Unit 13.)

Editing the Finished Product

The final step in completing a piece of writing is *editing*. Editing is the checking of one's written work for various faults and making last-minute changes and corrections. One should be on the lookout for faulty parallelism, spelling, and punctuation as well as for run-on sentences and other matters. But students of English as a second language must also check their writing for basic grammatical errors—errors regarding which they know the rules but slip up in the application of these rules. Basic grammatical errors include the improper use of tense and aspect, agreement, articles, word order, and other small but important details.

However, it is often difficult to see these basic grammatical faults in one's own writing. We are so intent on the content that we fail to notice certain details of form. We should try to "step back" and take an objective look at our work, as if seeing it for the first time. One suggestion is for students to exchange papers before they are submitted to the instructor and check for these basic grammatical errors which detract so much from one's writing. Perhaps noticing faults in our neighbor's paper will make us more aware of our own shortcomings.

Here are some sentences and larger selections for you to practice your editing skills on. They contain quite a few basic grammatical errors. See if you can find them all. (Exercise 14 has to do with poor style and punctuation.)

Exercise 11
1. The west coast, which are wide and sandy, is different from other side of island.
2. This include the holidays of Easter and New Years.
3. The street are fill with people hurrying to pay visit to friend.
4. Sun-Moon Lake, which is Taiwan's leading holiday resort, it is occupied by local people.
5. But most the tourist like to have few pictures taken with natives.
6. As all we know, the petroleum is not renewable resource.
7. The farmer have to get the best use out of the land.
8. Anyone wants to find a place of total relaxation should go there.
9. The tourists come to my country to visiting different part of the country.
10. It is one of the best attraction for the tourists.
11. Vast numbers of tourist come to visit every years.
12. Some student are force to drop out school.
13. The world must find solution for it's oil shortage.
14. I saw on TV many building in the city was destroyed.
15. Because of the increase in the price of oil, the cost of fertilizer, which it also uses a lot of energy in the manufacturing process, have also gone up.
16. Today, it is hard to afford for some countries the new, higher prices.
17. In other word, the world needs an energy source, is ecologically good for environment, yet economical to exploit.
18. This new invention can convert sunlight in electricity or the sea tides in some kind of the usable energy.
19. I truly enjoy helping people, to care for them, and to make them happy.
20. Of course the middle class has fewer problem compare to lower class.

Exercise 12
(1) One of the newest building on campus is library. (2) Knowing how the library works help us use facilities more efficient. (3) The library offer everything most student need, and the people who works there are

very helpful. (4) This make the students easy to study. (5) The study areas, however, which are suppose to be quiet place, seems to generate a lot of talking by student. (6) I like to read in music library because is so quiet. (7) For the student who want to know what had happened in year he or she born, there is old newspapers to look at.

(8) Another of the service offer by the library is Reserved Book Room. (9) It offers some others services such as copiers and typewriter. (10) All of this typewriters are the modern one. (11) I also heard that the new library will contains a new computer system for checking out book in the future.

(12) The students have free access to the stacks and are allow to look at any of the periodical they wish. (13) The Public Affairs section contain various kind of materials, such as books, pamphlet, and magazines.

(14) The new library contain a number of book written in the 15th century. (15) There is also a lot of instructional materials that covers grades K through 12. (16) I cannot go into more detail to describe library facilities because that would takes too long.

(17) All in all, I think the new library is a well-organize and quiet place to study.

Exercise 13
(1) After World War II, divorce rate has increased in many country in the world. (2) But divorce rate seems to be increasing more rapid in the U.S. than in other country. (3) The divorce problem is one of the most serious social problem facing society today.

(4) One of the reasons for this condition is the current laws which makes easy to divide the family. (5) I feel that if parents live with their married children, divorce rate would go down.

(6) Another of reasons for the high American divorce rate that American women have that much more freedom than women in others countries. (7) If we compare the attitude toward the divorce in my country with that of United States, we find big difference between two countries. (8) In my country, Korea, there is a stigma, bad feeling, toward anyone who is divorce person. (9) Also, married people have passive attitude toward divorce, especially women, more passive than Korean male.

Exercise 14
a. Today, the world continues to use more and more oil despite its high price, but as we all know, petroleum is not a renewable resource,

and one day in the future we will run out of this energy source, and that day may not be very far off.

b. I asked José whether he had many friends and whether it was easy for him to find a friend, and how did he select his friends, he told me it was hard to find a good friend these days, but he said he didn't have enemies so he supposed that all people would be his friends, and he told me that in the past he had little difficulty in his dealings with other people.

Wh- Phrases in Topic Sentences

In example 1, on page 10, we saw the phrase "what the right to strike means" occurring as part of a topic sentence. Phrases of this kind, that is, phrases beginning with the question words *what, where, when, why, how, how often* (and a few others), are often used as titles for short articles and essays. Here are some examples:

1a. ***Why** I am a Vegetarian.*
1b. ***How** I Found Peace and Happiness on a Dairy Farm.*
1c. ***What** to Look for When Buying a House.*
1d. ***When** Not to Buy Stocks.*

Phrases of this kind also function as subjects or as object/complements, as illustrated in the following:

As Subjects
2a. ***Who killed that bear** is a mystery.*
2b. ***Whom the Democrats will select as their candidate** cannot be predicted.*
2c. ***Where all the money goes** cannot be explained.*
2d. ***How important this new regulation will be** is not known.*

As Object/Complements
3a. *We will never know **who killed that bear**.*
3b. *One cannot predict **whom the Democrats will select as their candidate**.*
3c. *No one can explain **where all the money goes**.*
3d. *No one knows **how important this new regulation will be**.*

An important note on word order
Although these phrases contain question words (*whom, what,* etc.),

they occur in *statement* word order, not interrogative word order. To clarify, observe the following chart and note the differences:

WORD ORDER COMPARISON

Statement word order	Interrogative word order
Someone sees Mary.	Does Tom see someone?
Who sees Mary?	Whom does Tom see?
. . . whom he saw	Whom did he see?
. . . who she is	Who is she?
. . . what that is	What is that?
. . . what he wants	What does he want?
. . . where he went	Where did he go?

Sentences containing *wh-* phrases of this kind are sometimes used as topic sentences for paragraphs, as has already been illustrated. But before asking you to write more paragraphs, perhaps you should practice writing sentences containing *wh-* phrases as subject or as object/complement.

Exercise 15   **Subject.** Substitute an appropriate question word for the word(s) inside the bracket and combine into a single sentence.

Examples: a.   Mary told [someone]. (it) is beside the point.
Whom Mary told is beside the point.
b.   The world will live in peace [sometime]. (it) cannot be predicted.
When the world will live in peace cannot be predicted.

1.   John has written [something]. (it) is only his opinion.
2.   The money comes from [somewhere]. (it) is not my problem.
3.   The workers are demanding [something]. (it) is the right to strike.
4.   The farmers want more land [for a reason]. (it) is not the main issue.
5.   A young person should take [someone's] advice. (it) is not an easy question to answer.
6.   Jones was able to win the election [by . . .]. (it) is a very interesting question.
7.   One should consult the dictionary [this] often. (it) depends on the individual.

8.   That project will require [a certain amount of] time. (it) will depend on several factors.

Exercise 16   **Object/complement.** Substitute an appropriate *wh*-word for the word(s) inside the brackets and combine into a single sentence. Follow the examples:

Examples: a.   It is difficult to know (it). [something] makes students happy.
                    It is difficult to know what makes students happy.
               b.   I cannot tell you (it). The committee chose [someone].
                    I cannot tell you whom the committee chose.

1.   We still don't know (it). [something] caused all the excitement.
2.   I don't remember (it). The secretary told [someone].
3.   He asked if I knew (it). The right to strike means [something].
4.   We must decide (it). We want to purchase [a certain] typewriter.
5.   We can only guess (it). The consequences of overpopulation will be [something].
6.   We are often asked to explain (it). We want a good education [for a reason].
7.   Most people do not realize (it). The entrance exam is [that] difficult.
8.   We must find (it) out. The best opportunities lie [somewhere].
9.   No one seems to realize (it). The situation is really [that] serious.
10. We all have different ideas as to (it). Being successful in life means [something].

Now that you have developed skill in composing these sentences (and getting the word order correct), try putting it to use in the following assignment.

Writing Assignment
   Develop a topic sentence using the phrases listed below as subject or as object/complement. Then expand the topic sentence into a medium-sized paragraph. If you prefer you may make up your own *wh*- phrases. A sample paragraph is given for your guidance.

Sample paragraph

Why I Like to Watch Football Games

People often ask me why I like to watch football games. For me, football is one of the most exciting spectator sports. I enjoy seeing the crunch of bodies as the opposing linemen battle each other every time the ball is snapped. I love to watch the backfield men in motion as they execute their elaborate plays. And I thrill to see a successful running play or a well-executed touchdown pass to the end zone. There is nothing quite so exciting as a well-played, hard-fought football game.

1. how to put an end to poverty (war) (hunger)
2. what profession or occupation a young person should choose
3. what being successful in life means to me
4. how to choose the right marriage partner
5. why I would (not) want to live on a small South Sea island
6. what the consequences of a population explosion will be
7. where to spend the perfect honeymoon
8. why I (do) (don't) believe in divorce
9. why it is dangerous to sleep under a standing elephant
10. how I became friendly with a rattlesnake

Reported Speech*

In everyday situations we are often called upon to recall a conversation we have heard or participated in. Sometimes we may choose to repeat the exact words used by the speaker: *And John said, "Get out of here before I. . . . "* At other times, especially in more formal situations, we report what was said without using the exact words of the speaker. This is known as *reported speech.* In this type of speech, or writing, we often shift to a later tense, especially if some time has elapsed between the actual telling and the reporting of same. For example, something said in present tense is often reported using past tense, as in the following examples:

---

*For work on paraphrase see Unit 13.

Actual Speech	*Reported Speech*

"Hello. My name is Jones."   He said his name was Jones.

"I have a headache. I want to go   She said she had a headache
home."   and wanted to go home.

The purpose of the following exercises is to practice converting actual speech into reported speech. Be sure to rewrite questions in statement word order, using an appropriate tense. Follow the examples.

Exercise 17

Examples: a.   Tom: "Mary, will you marry me?" (asked)
                 Tom asked Mary whether she would marry him.
          b.   Henry: "I will help if you need me." (stated)
                 Henry stated he would help if I needed him.

1. Mr. Hall: "I am in complete sympathy with your position." (told me)
2. Janos: "I don't like to work in the chemistry lab on weekends." (was saying)
3. Two students: "We can't complete our assignment on time." (told me)
4. Mr. Scott: "I am very satisfied with the result." (indicated)
5. Clerk: "You have to fill out the application form in duplicate." (told me)
6. Susie: "I have the flu and I won't be going to class today." (telephoned to say)
7. Thief: "Yes, I admit it. I stole the apple pies." (admitted)
8. Suspect: "I didn't do it. I swear I am innocent." (denied)
9. Judge: "Mr. King, are you willing to testify in the case?" (asked)
10. Instructor: "Richard, why did you drop my course?" (demanded to know)
11. Principal: "Miss Smith, are your students well behaved?" (asked)
12. Teacher: "Do you students want to have your test at a later time?" (asked)
13. Advisor: "Why did you choose history as your major?" (wanted to know)

The following examples show how a conversation might be reported in a somewhat formal manner.

Actual Speech	*Reported Speech*
Me: "Jack, what do you think of abortion?" Jack: "I am definitely against it. It is against nature."	When I asked Jack what he thought of abortion he replied that he was definitely against it because it was against nature.
Me: "Aren't there certain circumstances under which abortions are needed? There may be medical and psychological reasons which make abortions truly necessary."	I asked him whether there weren't certain circumstances under which abortions were needed. I told him there might be medical and psychological reasons which made abortions truly necessary.
Jack: "Do you think it is morally right to put an end to a human life? Does anyone have the right to make that decision?"	Then Jack asked whether I thought it was morally right to put an end to a human life, and whether anyone had the right to make that decision.
Me: "I believe that every life is sacred, but I think that the woman should have a choice in the matter. An unwanted child can mean physical hardship and mental depression, especially for an unmarried mother."	I replied that although I believed that every life was sacred I thought that the woman should have a choice in the matter. I also pointed out that an unwanted child can mean physical hardship as well as mental depression, especially for an unmarried woman.
Jack: "Well I agree there may be some circumstances in which abortion is justified, but in general I am still against it."	At this point Jack agreed there might be some circumstances in which abortion was justified, but that in general he was still against it.

Exercise 18   Retell (orally) the following conversation using correct patterns of reported speech. Do not use the exact words of the speakers. Be sure to report all questions in statement word order, using an appropriate tense.

(The day after my arrival in San Francisco I boarded a plane for Los Angeles. A moment later a tall, friendly looking man sat down beside me. This was our conversation:)

Man: "Hello. Where are you headed?"
—   "I'm going to Los Angeles."
Man: "Do you have friends there?"
—   "No, I don't. I'm going to study at the University."
Man: "I notice you have an accent. Where are you from?"
—   "I'm from a small town in _____."
Man: "Have you been in the U.S. very long?"
—   "I just arrived here yesterday. Haven't you noticed my English is not very good?"
Man: "On the contrary, for someone who has only been here one day, your English is very good."
—   "Thank you. You are very kind."
Man: "No, I mean that sincerely. I wish I could speak another language as well as you speak English."

Exercise 19   The following is a conversation that took place between two friends of college age. Recount their conversation in reported speech. All questions are to be reported in statement word order.

Al: "I just read in the paper that the number of divorces in this country is increasing greatly."
Tom: "I'm not surprised. That only proves that the present institution of marriage is a foolish anachronism."
Al: "How can you say such a thing? Don't you believe in marriage?"
Tom: "No, I don't. I think marriage is just an empty ceremony, without any real meaning. A marriage certificate is just a piece of paper."
Al: "Tom! I'm really shocked. Do you actually *approve* of two people living together without being legally married?"
Tom: "Well, I'm not prejudiced. If there is a serious commitment between the two—if there is an honest whole-person relationship—then I believe it is all right."
Al: "I have to disagree with you, Tom. Society would not have retained marriage all these years if it were not a good and necessary institution. I'm sorry, Tom, but what you are saying is morally wrong."

Exercise 20   Using reported speech, recount a conversation that you recently had with someone. The conversation may be among more than two people.

Exercise 21   Think up six to eight questions on a topic of interest to you, possibly a controversial one. Interview someone using these questions as the basis. Then write up the results of your interview using reported speech. You will probably want to use sentences like, *When asked why he was (was not) in favor of* _____ , *my subject replied that . . .*

SECTION
B

Toward Mature Writing

UNIT 2   RELATIVE CLAUSES

Introduction

While most people would agree that the basic unit of any composition is logically the paragraph, we cannot ignore the fact that paragraphs are made up of sentences. Since our aim in this text is to produce well-formed, mature writing, we will begin by considering how simple sentences are combined to form longer, more complex ones.

Complex sentences are most commonly formed through the use of relative clauses and coordination. The proper use of these two processes can help us avoid an overly simple style. We will also put them to use in a later section on technical writing. For now, we will begin by taking a look at relative clauses and their use.

Relative Clauses Defined

Relative clauses are extremely common in both spoken and written English. A relative clause is a sentence which is slightly modified and then combined with another sentence. Relative clauses can usually be recognized by the presence of relative pronouns—words like *who, whom, that, which* and others—which we will call *wh-* words.

Let us observe some simple examples of relative clauses and how they are formed.

a.   I met a man. The man knows your sister.
             who   → *I met a man who knows your sister.*

b.   I know a girl. The girl won the contest.
             that   → *I know the girl that won the contest.*

c.   I met a woman. Bill married the woman.
                    whom   → *I met the woman whom Bill married.*

d.   Tom received a letter. The letter upset him.
             which   → *Tom received a letter which upset him.*

e.   I know a student. The student's uncle is a judge.
             whose   → *I know the student whose uncle is a judge.*

f.   I spoke to a man. The police had found the man's car.
                         whose car
      I spoke to the man whose car the police had found.

Exercise 1   Combine into a single sentence using an appropriate *wh-* word. Follow the examples.

Examples: a.   I saw a man. The man killed a bear.
                        I saw the man who (that) killed the bear.
              b.   I met a girl. I went to school with the girl's brother.
                        I met a girl whose brother I went to school with.

1.   I met the man. The man came to visit your family.
2.   I bought that new book. Everyone is talking about the book.
3.   I went to see an eye doctor. You recommended an eye doctor.
4.   My cousin drove up in a new car. The car cost $6,000.
5.   I have a friend. The friend thinks that Mary is nice looking.
6.   Did you talk to your friend? Your friend's uncle is a lawyer.
7.   That is Mrs. Brown. John is engaged to Mrs. Brown's daughter.

8.   Let's ask Mr. Hall. Everyone has confidence in Mr. Hall.
9.   Helen was grateful to Mr. King. Helen had taken Mr. King's advice.
10. The prize was awarded to Professor Dunce. Professor Dunce's ideas on microbiology are revolutionary.

Exercise 2   Write five original sentences similar to those illustrated above. Include at least one example each of *which* and *whose.*

Deletion of *Wh-* Words in Relative Clauses

When can words like *that, who(m)* or *which* be omitted?
   Observe the following ungrammatical sentences:

   #*The man killed the bear was Tom Brown.*[1]
   #*He wrote a novel describes the suffering of the poor.*

The above two sentences are not grammatical because the relative pronouns *that* (or *who*) and *which* were left out.
   Observe when the relative pronouns may be deleted and when they may not, in the following sentences:

Relative as subject	Relative as object
He's the man **that** saw Mary.	He's the man (that) Mary saw.
	He's the man Mary saw.
She's the girl **who** married Tom.	She's the girl (whom) Tom married.
	She's the girl Tom married.
That's the book **which** cost $6.00.	That's the book (which) you bought.
	That's the book you bought.

Comments: 1.   The relatives *that, whom,* and *which* may be deleted when functioning as object.

2.   These relatives cannot be deleted when functioning as subject.

---

[1] The symbol # placed at the beginning of a sentence means that what follows is ungrammatical or in some way strange or non-English.

Now that you have studied the above, let us see whether you can put this knowledge to use by doing the following exercise:

Exercise 3   If the *wh-* word can be omitted, put parentheses around it. If the *wh-* word cannot be omitted, underline it.

Examples: a.   He's the man that Mary saw.
He's the man (that) Mary saw.
b.   He's the man that saw Mary.
*He's the man **that** saw Mary.*

1.   That is the nation that Russia invaded.
2.   That is the nation that invaded Russia.
3.   That is the baby that the President kissed.
4.   She is the girl whom I met at the bookstore.
5.   We saw the bear that killed the hunter.
6.   Mr. Wilson is the kind of scholar whom we all admire.
7.   That is the kind of predicament which all of us try to avoid.
8.   Have you read the book that has caused all the controversy?
9.   These are the suggestions that the committee made.
10.   I did not understand the explanation that he gave me.
11.   I spoke to the man who received all the applications.
12.   The invading armies destroyed many art treasures which the people had so highly valued.
13.   I refer to the historical novel which won the Pulitzer Prize in 1960.
14.   Henry visited the tiny central American country that produces some of the best coffee in the world.
15.   We are pleased to enclose the educational materials which you requested.
16.   We saw many hills in the area which are quite high and very dry.
17.   He is the philosopher whom I got my inspiration from.
18.   The large river which flows down to the Gulf of Thailand is the Chao Phya.

You have probably noticed how the relative pronoun *that* often substitutes for *who, whom* or *which.* This substitution, however, is *not* permitted in all cases. Observe the following two categories:

A.   Restrictive clauses[2]

My uncle $\begin{Bmatrix} \textbf{who} \\ \textbf{that} \end{Bmatrix}$ lives in Detroit bought a new car.

The man $\begin{Bmatrix} \textbf{whom} \\ \textbf{that} \end{Bmatrix}$ I met yesterday is a friend of yours.

The old house $\begin{Bmatrix} \textbf{which} \\ \textbf{that} \end{Bmatrix}$ Bill likes is up for sale.

B.   Nonrestrictive clauses

My uncle Joe, **who lives in** Detroit, bought a new car.
Bill Brown, **whom** I met yesterday, is a friend of yours.
Mr. Smith's old house, **which** Bill likes very much, is up
    for sale.

Comments: 1.   In category A (restrictive clauses) *that* can substitute for *who, whom,* or *which.*
2.   In category B (nonrestrictive clauses) *that* cannot
be used.

Exercise 4   Read the following sentences aloud. Put parentheses
around the relative pronoun if the word *that* can be substituted.
Underline the relative pronoun if it cannot.

Examples: a.   *The man (whom) you talked to is a well-known*
psychiatrist.
b.   *Mrs. Jones, who saw the thief, called the police.*

1.   Dr. Johnson, who is an avid fisherman, is coming for a visit next
week.
2.   The telephone operator whom I called said your phone was
disconnected.
3.   Mrs. Miller's oldest son Richard, whom she is so proud of, is
home for a visit.

[2]For an explanation of restrictive/nonrestrictive clauses see *Preparation for
Writing,* companion volume to the present book.

4.   The daughter who lives in Boston came for a visit.
5.   People who smoke a lot may be endangering their health.
6.   The people whom John told you about want to buy a house.
7.   People who are willing to listen to unfounded rumors should not be allowed on this committee.
8.   College students, who are often faced with financial problems, should be aided in finding summer employment.
9.   Submarine duty is not for the man who does not know how to get along with other people.
10.   The man whom you spoke to did not have the correct information.

Wh- Adverbials for Time and Place

Normal word order. (A reminder)

Subject	Predicate		
Mr. Brown /	takes his wife /	to Paris /	in the spring.
		(place)	(time)

Observe the *wh-* adverbials that substitute for *place* and *time*:

1.   *The newlyweds went to Paris **where** they spent their honeymoon.*

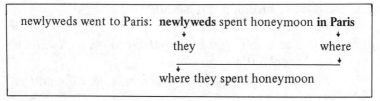

2.   *Farmers plant wheat in the spring **when** the earth is warm and moist.*

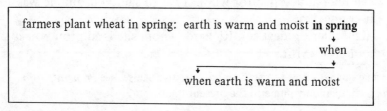

3. *The meeting will be held at 3 PM at which time[3] you will receive further information.*

```
meeting held at 3 PM:  you receive information at 3 PM
                                                    ↓
                                          at which time
                                                    ↓
                       ↓
                       at which time you receive information
```

Exercise 5   Combine into one sentence. Substitute an appropriate *wh-* form for the *time* or *place* adverbial.

Examples: The newlyweds went to Paris. They spent their
                   honeymoon *in Paris.*
                   The newlyweds went to Paris where they spent their
                   honeymoon.
                   Come to the meeting tomorrow at 3 PM. You will
                   receive further information *at that time.*
                   Come to the meeting tomorrow at 3 PM, at which
                   time you will receive further information.

1. Farmers plant their vegetable gardens in the spring. The earth is
    warm and moist *at that time.*
2. The Johnson family moved to California. The father soon found
    a job *there.*
3. I am going to have my appendix removed on December 31.
    Everyone will be celebrating New Year's Eve *on that day.*
4. Mr. King likes living in Florida. He can go fishing *there* when-
    ever he wants to.
5. Many foreign students go to study in California. They can enjoy
    the warm climate *in California.*
6. Mr. Sato will return to Japan in 1982. He will have earned his
    degree by *that* time.
7. How wonderful it is to visit Japan in April. The cherry blossoms
    are in full bloom *in April.*
8. It is difficult to travel there in April and May. The monsoon rains
    fall during *that* time.
9. It is fascinating to shop at that open market. One can find a
    great variety of tropical fruits *at the market.*
10. The hydrogen chloride solution was heated to 210 degrees. At
    this point the solution exploded.

---

[3]*When* is the informal equivalent of *at which time.*

UNIT 3   COORDINATION

Avoiding Overly Simple Sentences

In an attempt to write simply and to avoid grammatical errors students sometimes write so-called baby sentences in their early attempts at writing. The following paragraph is an example:

> *I grew up in Chia Yi. Chia Yi is a nice little town. Everyone is peace-loving and friendly there. The town is located in the southern part of Taiwan. Taiwan is the island which was formerly known as Formosa.*

Combining sentences through the use of relative clauses eliminates much repetition. Note the following changes:

First revision

> *I grew up in Chia Yi.* which ~~Chia Yi~~ *is a nice little town. Everyone is peace-loving and friendly* where ~~there~~. *The town is located in the southern part of Taiwan.* which ~~Taiwan~~ *is the island which was formerly known as Formosa.*

> *I grew up in Chia Yi, (which is) a nice little town where everyone is peace-loving and friendly. The town is located in the southern part of Taiwan, (which is) the island (which was) formerly known as Formosa.*

Final revision

> *I grew up in Chia Yi, a nice little town where everyone is peace-loving and friendly. The town is located in the southern part of Taiwan, the island formerly known as Formosa.*

> or,

> *Chia Yi, where I grew up, is a nice . . .*

Exercises in sentence combining. Combine each group of sentences into a complex sentence. Use *wh-* words like *which, where,* and *when* as appropriate. Punctuate properly.

Exercise 1
I have always wanted to visit the city of Paris.
I have heard so much about Paris.
Everyone falls in love in Paris, especially in the spring.
And in the spring, the flowers are in bloom and romance is in the air.

Exercise 2
Last night I spoke on the phone with my cousin Janos.
Janos plans to stay in Colorado until next June.
Janos is currently attending college in Colorado.
Janos hopes to graduate in Engineering next June.

Exercise 3
My friend Enrique is going to show some slides of his country.
Enrique is a foreign student from Bolivia.
Bolivia is a landlocked nation in South America.
Bolivia shares a common border with Chile and Peru.

Exercise 4   The following consists of several short, overly simple
sentences. Make this writing more concise by combining two or more
short sentences into one longer one.

In India, the national soup is called *curry*. It is a hot, spicy dish that
looks like stew. Curry is made from beans—black beans, white beans,
and some others. I cannot remember the names of the others.

To us, curry is good, tasteful food. People from my country love it.
Curry is very hot and spicy. Many people are only used to rather
bland foods. These people refuse to eat curry. They are unable to
appreciate its exotic flavor.

Overuse of *and*

Beginning writers often have difficulty combining sentences and
coordinating sentence parts. We are all familiar with the use of *and* as a
connector of multiple items. But the fact is that many beginning writers
use too many *and*s in a single sentence. Note the following sentence,
which is grammatically acceptable but stylistically unsatisfactory:

The climate in this area is very favorable for agricultural products, especially such
items as grapes, citrus fruits, peaches *and* almonds *and* commercial crops like cotton.

We can take care of this difficulty by using other connectives to replace the second *and*, as follows:

The climate in this area is very favorable for agricultural products, especially such items as grapes, citrus fruits, peaches, and almonds, *as well as* commercial crops like cotton.

Other common connectives that can be used to replace *and* are:

besides	*mixed with, together with*
in addition to	*not only . . . but (also)*
plus	

Here are a few examples:

1. John is a busy man. He works in an office and in a department store on weekends, *in addition to* attending night school four times a week.
2. Dentists tell us to brush our teeth daily and to beware of plaque, a sticky film made up mostly of bacteria *mixed with* saliva and debris.
3. This fragile globe, the planet Earth, is *not only* running out of natural gas and petroleum, *but* will soon face a shortage of clean air and pure water as well.

Exercise 5   Rewrite each sentence to reduce the use of *and*. Replace the *and* in bold type with the connective in parentheses at the end of each item. Do not repeat the sentence in brackets at the beginning of each item, which is given only to provide context. Verbs following *besides* and *in addition to* must use the "ing" form. Follow the examples.

1. [Children have fun at the seashore.] They like to run and play on the beach **and** splash around in the water. (as well as)
    *They like to run and play on the beach **as well as** splash around in the water.*
2. [Bill is a big help to his mother.] He works in the house and helps take care of his little brother **and** (also) goes to school full time. (in addition to)
    *He works in the house and helps take care of his little brother and sister **in addition to** going to school full time.*
3. [Mrs. Smith has a new maid.] The maid washes the dishes and cleans the kitchen and bathrooms **and** (also) takes care of the baby. (besides)

4. [I highly recommend Miss Adams for the position.] She is a good teacher and scholar **and** (also) an excellent administrator. (as well as)

5. [What are the effects of war?] War stimulates the production of arms and other war materials **and** also helps to increase the number of young widows. (not only . . . but)

6. [Mr. Brown is in trouble.] He falsified some checks and other documents **and** cheated on his income tax. (besides)

7. [We just moved into an unfurnished apartment.] We appreciate the money and furniture you lent us **and** the moral support you have given us. (as well as)

8. [Helen is very active.] She enjoys playing basketball and other sports **and** playing in a small jazz band. (as well as)

9. [The secretary, who is male, works hard.] He types letters and invoices **and** runs errands from time to time. (in addition to)

10. [There is a new method for applying fertilizer.] The old method was inefficient and caused much waste and loss of time **and** also added to the farmer's production cost. (not only . . . but)

11. [The city has many profitable industries.] These industries manufacture petrochemical products, such as plastics and butane rubber, **and** oil refinery pumps and other machinery. (along with)

12. [Mr. Jones has an enormous library collection.] It comprises literally thousands of current books and magazines **and** numerous rare books and manuscripts. (plus)

Dependent (Subordinating) Conjunctions

Certain connecting words, called *conjunctions,* serve to unite two clauses, as follows:

Clause 1	← Conjunction →	Clause 2
I bought two of them	**because**	the price was so low.

The second clause is usually called subordinate or dependent. Some of the most common dependent or subordinating conjunctions are:

because	if	before
since	provided (that)	after
inasmuch as	whether (or not)	when
so (as) long as		
	once[4]	whereas[5]
although		
even though	no matter $\begin{cases} \text{what} \\ \text{where} \\ \text{how} \end{cases}$	
		so that
unless		in order that
until		now that

The above connectives function as grammatical bridges. The conjunction and its clause is (grammatically) dependent on the other (main) clause; it cannot occur alone.

The following sentences illustrate the use (and meaning) of some of the most common dependent conjunctions:

1. *We decided to disband the organization **because** there were so few members.*
2. *The students will go on a picnic **if** the weather is favorable.*
3. ***Unless** there is an objection, we will now take a vote.*
4. *Susie cannot manage to gain weight **although** she eats heartily.*
5. *California residents pay in-state fees **whereas** nonresidents must pay out-of-state fees.*
6. ***Once** a man has lost his pride, everything else seems unimportant.*
7. ***Inasmuch as** Henrietta made the suggestion, we will appoint her chairperson.*
8. *Miss Johnson will teach this class **until** the regular teacher returns from the hospital.*
9. *The funds never seem to be enough **no matter how much** money is allowed for this purpose.*
10. ***Now that** the hunting season is at hand, many sportsmen are cleaning and oiling their lethal weapons.*
11. ***As long as** a man retains his pride, he can hold his head up high.*

---

[4]*Once* means *from the moment that.*

[5]*While* is often used as an informal equivalent of *whereas,* e.g., *The mortgage on the house in the city was paid up in 1969, while the mortgage on the mountain cabin was not paid off until 1975.*

12. *This copy is sent to you **in order that** you may consider it for adoption in your class.*
13. ***Since** everyone is here, let us begin the meeting.*
14. ***Before** you can be admitted to this school, you must take the TOEFL test.*
15. ***After** you finish your shopping, stop by the post office for some stamps.*

Exercise 6   The purpose of this exercise is to test your knowledge of the above listed dependent conjunctions. Complete each of the following so as to make a logical, meaningful sentence. Your completed sentence should illustrate that you well understand the meaning of each conjunction.

Example: I can't go to that restaurant with you *because . . .*
             I can't go to that restaurant with you because I have no money.

1.   I won't be able to buy that bicycle *unless . . .*
2.   *Even though* I need a bicycle badly, I . . .
3.   *Although* such an act is not illegal, it . . .
4.   I would be willing to go with you, *provided . . .*
5.   You have to pay a fee *in order to . . .*
6.   The government is building more schools *so that . . .*
7.   History 10 is an easy course, *whereas . . .*
8.   *Once* you have passed the exam, you . . .
9.   *As much as* I would like to, I cannot . . .
10. *Inasmuch as* you made the suggestion, . . .
11. I am unable to give you the money, *no matter how . . .*
12. *No matter what* John has told you, . . .

As you may have noticed, dependent (subordinate) clauses are often transposed to the front position. Putting the conjunction first adds emphasis to the idea that one thing is dependent on another. For example, the sentence

*I bought three of them **because** the price was so low.*

can be transposed and punctuated as follows:

***Because** the price was so low, I bought three of them.*

Exercise 7 Transpose the dependent clause to front position and punctuate, as in the above example.

1. We cannot agree to your proposal *because* we are opposed to violence.
2. I shall assume you are no longer interested *unless* I hear from you soon.
3. You should drop the course *if* you are unable to attend regularly.
4. I assume that John is no longer interested *inasmuch as* I have not heard from him.
5. Why don't we drop the matter *as long as* no one suffered any injury.
6. We shall continue to uphold the freedom of speech *no matter how often* we are punished for our beliefs.
7. Unfortunately, a man is apt to encounter prejudice *no matter where* he goes.
8. All our soldiers can return to peaceful occupations *now that* the war has ended.
9. I will send this letter to the president *provided* you are all in agreement.
10. Acoustic phonetics is a branch of physics *whereas* articulatory phonetics is covered in physiology.
11. I will defend your right of free speech *although* I disagree with your position.
12. We agreed to meet with Mr. Smith *so that* we might keep the channels of communication open.
13. One must know the culture of the people *in order to* understand whatever happens in Latin America.
14. You will realize how important a good bibliography is *once* you have written a research paper yourself.

Dependent conjunctions:
fragmentation through faulty punctuation

When there are clauses beginning with a dependent conjunction a student will sometimes split his words into two sentences through faulty punctuation. This creates an ungrammatical unit called a *fragment.* For example, many composition teachers become distressed when they see the following:

> *The students are very unhappy about these conditions. #Because it is very difficult to enter the national university.*

But by simply changing the punctuation we get a proper sentence as follows:

> *The students are very unhappy about these conditions because it is . . .*

Exercise 8   The following "sentences" are the kind that make teachers turn grey prematurely. Rewrite these "sentences" in correct form by correcting the punctuation. Then reverse the clauses, as in the example.

Example: I plan to major in music. #Unless my father tells me otherwise.
   a.   *I plan to major in music unless my father tells me otherwise.*
   b.   *Unless my father tells me otherwise, I plan to major in music.*

1.   I never liked to study mathematics. #Until I took a math class from Mr. Digit.
2.   I couldn't get a plane reservation for the day I wanted. #Because all the seats were sold out.
3.   When I was fifteen I took a job in a supermarket. #In order to earn a little extra money for my education.
4.   I couldn't enter the university as I had wanted to. #Even though I passed the entrance exam with a high score.
5.   I am not going to speak to Nancy again. #Since it was she who caused me to get into trouble.
6.   Billions of aerosol spray cans are endangering our lives. #Because ozone is being depleted from the earth's atmosphere.

Conjunctions: one too many

We have seen that dependent conjunctions are used in conjoining sentences. However, in combining any two sentences we must be careful to use only one of these connectors; students sometimes put in two conjunctions where only one is permitted. Consequently, it tries the patience of composition teachers to see an incorrect sentence like the following:

#Although it was hard at first, **but** I got used to reading English textbooks after a while.

Exercise 9   The following sentences contain one too many conjunctions. Eliminate one of them and then read aloud (or write) your corrected sentence.

1.   #Although the woman called for help, yet no one came to her rescue.
2.   #Even though we waited for two hours, but the bus never came.
3.   #As much as I would like to please you, but I can't say "yes."
4.   #Because I didn't want to disobey my parents, so I entered that school.
5.   #Although I was invited to the party, but I decided not to go.
6.   #While Germany has a large agricultural area, whereas Switzerland has only a small land area suitable for growing food.
7.   #Because I wanted an opportunity to learn more, so I decided to go abroad.
8.   #Although I was learning a lot in my job, yet I felt I could learn more by returning to school.
9.   # Because the island was once ruled by England, therefore the language of the Bay Islanders is English.
10.   # Although it doesn't happen in every case, but most foreign students often feel lonely in the United States.

Subordination vs. Coordination

We have just been looking at subordinating (dependent) conjunctions such as *although, because, unless,* etc. You are also familiar with another set of connecting words, namely, *and, or,* and *but,* which are called coordinating conjunctions.

Students sometimes mistakenly think the words *although* and *but* have the same meaning. While it is true that both words do express *contrast,* there *is* a distinction.

Words like *but* are used to connect clauses of equal importance, as can be seen in the following examples:

John went swimming, **and** Bill went to the movies.
You can pay for it now, **or** you can charge it.
The boys like to watch football, **but** the girls are bored by the game.

Unlike the above conjunctions, however, clauses joined by subord-
inators like *although, because*, etc., do not relate to each other in the
same way; that is, they do not signal this relationship of equality.
Rather than joining two ideas of equal importance, these connecting
words subordinate one to another; they create a main (principal)
clause and a subordinate one. For more on principal and subordinate
clauses, see Unit 11.

Having Plus Past Participle

We have just seen that a common way to combine two sentences is to
use a subordinating conjunction. For example, the following

1. *I had looked up the word in the dictionary*
    (and)
2. *I was sure of the spelling*

can be combined in various ways:

    a. *Since I had looked up the word in the dictionary, I was
    sure of the spelling.*
    b. *Because I had looked up the word in the dictionary, I . . .*
    c. *Due to the fact that I had looked up the word in the
    dictionary, I . . .*

However, if the two sentences being combined have the same subject
and the first sentence is in past tense, they can be combined more
concisely, as follows:

    d. *Having looked up the word in the dictionary, I was sure
    of the spelling.*

This construction implies a causal relationship between the two clauses
(note *because* in sentence b above). The use of *having* plus a past
participle also means that one event or state occurred prior to the
other. Here are further examples of this construction with the underlying sentences in parentheses:

1. (Jack has lived here all his life. Jack knows the city well.)
    Having lived here all his life, Jack knows the city well.

2. (We have been deceived before. We decided to proceed cautiously.)

   Having been deceived before, we decided to proceed cautiously.

3. (Jaime had never seen the ocean before. Jaime was thrilled by the huge expanse of water.)

   Never having seen the ocean before, Jaime was thrilled by the huge expanse of water.

Note: The use of *having* plus past participle to combine sentences is a useful technique in writing concise sentences.

Exercise 10   Combine the following sets of sentences. Follow the example.

Example: (I had asked the professor. I was sure of the answer.)
   Having asked the professor, I was sure of the answer.

1. (Susie had studied hard. Susie was confident she would pass the exam.)
2. (Mary had been disappointed in the past. Mary now distrusts all young men.)
3. (The lawyer had been promised a large fee. The lawyer agreed to take the case.)
4. (The new president had been elected by a huge majority. The new president took office amidst a great deal of optimism.)
5. (The doctor had done everything medically possible to save the patient. The doctor went home for a well-deserved rest.)
6. (The police detective had checked the records. The police detective knew the accused man was telling the truth.)
7. (Tom had witnessed such mob scenes before. Tom quickly walked away from the scene of violence.)
8. (Bob had studied Russian for two years before going abroad. Bob was able to defend himself in the language fairly well.)
9. (I have never lived near the ocean. I was thrilled by the thought of a trip to the seashore.)
10. (I had not eaten for two days. I began gulping down the food as fast as I could.)
11. (We had not written ahead for reservations. We were happy to learn there were rooms available for us.)

12. (Richard had not notified his wife of his early return. Richard was not sure she would be at home.)
13. (We have seen the mountainous terrain of the country. We can now understand why agriculture is at best only marginal.)

Sentence Adverbials (Connectors)

A sentence in an essay often bears a close relationship to a preceding one. To show this relationship, words like *however, consequently*, etc., are used to refer back to the previous sentence. Such words act as a *semantic bridge to connect two ideas*. They also mark the *transition from one sentence to another*. Such words are called *sentence adverbials* or *sentence connectors*.

> *This country is faced with many serious social problems;* **however,** *some people are more concerned with political questions.*

> *The floods had damaged many bridges;* **consequently,** *all trains were running late.*

Sentence adverbials and other connecting words can be grouped into semantic categories. Connecting words which are not true sentence adverbials are enclosed in parentheses.

Group A Words which indicate *addition*:

also	moreover
besides	furthermore
in addition	(and)

John speaks the language well; **moreover,** *he has an excellent knowledge of the culture.*

Group B Words which indicate *contrast*:

however	(but)
nevertheless	(yet)
nonetheless	(still)

Mary's parents do not approve of the man she intends to marry; **however,** *they do not plan to oppose the marriage.*

Group C   Words which indicate *conclusion* or *result*:

therefore	accordingly
consequently	hence
thus	(as a result)

Tuition charges and other fees have mounted steadily; **consequently,** *many students are forced to seek part-time employment.*

Group D   Words to make analogies:

(similarly)	(in the same way)
(in like manner)	(likewise)

A society which values excellence in sports will turn out good athletes. **Similarly,** *a society that holds education in high esteem will produce outstanding educators.*

Sentence adverbials may be preceded by either a semicolon or a period. In the former case, the semicolon acts as a *grammatical bridge.*

> *The floods had damaged the bridges;* **consequently,** . . .
> *The floods had damaged the bridges.* **Consequently,** . . .

Since these sentence connectors function like adverbs, they enjoy great flexibility of position and may occur in initial, medial, or final position.

> **Consequently,** *all trains were running late.*
> *All trains,* **consequently,** *were running late.*
> *All trains were running late,* **consequently.**

Connectors such as *but, yet, still* (all the ones in parentheses above) are not true sentence adverbials and do not have the same flexibility. When they are used as adverbials, *but, yet,* and *still* occur only in initial position and are preceded by a period.

> *Robert has an easy time in his math classes. But not all of us can be that fortunate.*

Exercise 11   Complete the second sentence with a logical idea to demonstrate you understand the meaning of the connector.

1.   The man was arrested for speeding and for driving under the influence of alcohol. Consequently, . . .

2. It is evident that this plan has certain weaknesses; nevertheless, . . .
3. A farmer tries to increase the productivity of his farm. In like manner, . . .
4. The city needs more money to meet its financial obligations. The City Council, accordingly, . . .
5. The city does not have enough money to pay its employees. Furthermore, . . .
6. The evidence against the accused man was substantial. The jury, however, . . .

Exercise 12 Rewrite the second sentence, varying the position of the sentence adverbial, as in the example, and punctuate accordingly.

Example: John was very unhappy in his job; *consequently,* he decided to resign his position.
*He decided, **consequently**, to resign his position.*

1. John is a good man to send because he speaks the language; *furthermore,* he understands the psychology of the people.
2. The people will eventually have to face up to the country's many social problems. *However,* the average citizen is unwilling to become involved.
3. The president would not accede to the demands of the students; *consequently,* the peaceful demonstrations and protests continued.
4. The football coach was not on speaking terms with most of the players; *therefore,* team morale was rather low.
5. Mitosis is a dynamic process which progresses from start to finish without any stops; *nonetheless,* there are certain characteristic stages which are recognized by biologists.
6. We ought to have a meeting to review the functions of the committees and the responsibilities of the chairman. *Moreover,* I should think that someone might even discuss the techniques of running a meeting.
7. It is essential that last year's Executive Committee remain in office until such time as new elections can be held. *Accordingly,* I am directing the Executive Committee to continue its legal responsibilities until further notice.
8. The Company agreed to reinstate the two workers, and the union called off the strike; the problem was *thus* solved.

UNIT 4   SOME MATTERS OF STYLE

Introduction

Some aspects of writing have more to do with *style* than with grammatical correctness. For example, the choice of one word over another, say *utilize* instead of the simpler verb *use,* is determined by how formal or informal the writer wishes to be. Likewise the use of one grammatical form as opposed to another also relates to the degree of formality desired by the writer. There are other stylistic choices the writer makes when he creates a piece of writing. (See Unit 9.) We will now take up a few of these matters of style, beginning with colloquial language.

Colloquial vs. Formal Language

Students of English ought to be aware of the difference between formal written English and colloquial language. Colloquial language is informal, everyday speech or writing. It is used in conversation and in informal talks as well as in personal letters and notes.

Colloquial writing is characterized by the frequent use of contractions such as *I've, he's, I'm, it's,* and other reduced forms. Perhaps the most obvious difference between these two language styles lies in the choice of vocabulary. Compare the following:

Colloquial, informal	*Formal, written*
I spanked the kids.	I punished the children.
He works pretty hard.	He works very hard (*or* diligently).
So I flunked the course.	Consequently I failed the course.
I asked my boss if . . .	I asked my employer whether . . .
He's kind of (sort of) famous.	He is rather (somewhat) famous.
Lots of people do that.	A great many people do that.
Don't get mad, now.	Do not become angry.
Anyway, I'll . . .	In any event, I will . . .
Right now, I am . . .	At present, I am . . .
And now here comes the funny part.	What happened next was rather strange (or comical).
The last class I took was really neat.	The last class I took was very good.

Colloquial language also shows itself in syntax. Unfortunately the boundary between colloquial and formal is not always clear-cut; not all writers would agree on every point. With this qualification, here are a few examples of colloquial syntax contrasted with their formal equivalents:

Colloquial	*Formal*
He wanted to know if...	He wished to know whether...
Like I mentioned before...	As I mentioned previously...
Winston tastes good, like a cigarette should.	Winston tastes good, as a cigarette should.
He acted like he didn't know.	He acted as if (though) he did not know.
I wanted to learn English to where people could easily understand me when I spoke.	I wanted to learn English to the point that people could easily understand me when I spoke.

Word Order Differences

Another aspect of language which distinguishes colloquial from formal writing is word order. Observe the following differences in word order:

1a. *Colloquial*
    This scene you will never be able to forget.
1b. *Formal*
    You will never be able to forget this scene.
    This scene is one you will never be able to forget.
2a. *Colloquial*
    All of these activities you can do all year round.
2b. *Formal*
    One can do all of these activities all year round.
    All of these activities can be done all year round.
3a. *Colloquial*
    Those people who are against nuclear energy we can blame for the high cost of electricity.
3b. *Formal*
    We can blame those who are against nuclear energy for the high cost of electricity.
    Those who are against nuclear energy can be blamed for the high cost of electricity.

It is suggested that colloquial language be avoided in formal written English. On the other hand, one should not be overzealous in the use of very formal language, especially in cases where simpler, less formal vocabulary or syntax would be more appropriate. Appropriateness is probably the key word. We must remember that colloquial language is perfectly good language; everyone uses it, from kings and presidents on down. Colloquial language, whether spoken or written, is informal language which we use in everyday situations—language which we could not do without. Colloquial language, of course, is not to be confused with slang.

How can the beginning writer distinguish colloquial from formal language? By reading and being exposed to a great deal of formal language one should be able to get a feeling for these differences.

Parallelism

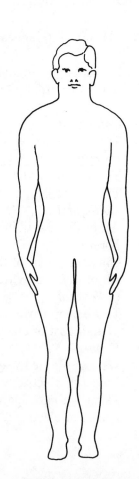

If our brothers are oppressed,
then we are oppressed.
If they hunger, we hunger.
If their freedom is taken away,
our freedom is not secure.
                    . . . Stephen Vincent Benet

The human form is a good example of symmetry.[1] That is, the parts are evenly matched—
two ears, two eyes, two nostrils, two arms, two
legs, etc. The quotation from Benet above
illustrates symmetry of language forms. We
call this *parallelism.*

---

[1]Symmetry: an exact correspondence between the opposite halves of a figure, form, etc., on either side of an axis or center.

The human form is symmetrical; it shows harmony of form resulting from proper balance of the parts. So too, good writing demands balance, not only in the composition as a whole but in individual sentences as well. This harmony of form is known as *parallelism.*

Grammatical parallelism requires the use of like grammatical structures within the same phrase. This would include categories such as tense, aspect, and number (singular/plural) as well as the same grammatical form or part of speech. In other words, a series of qualities or actions should be expressed in like grammatical forms—nouns with nouns, adjectives with adjectives, adverbials with adverbials, and verb forms with verb forms of the same type.

To place unlike grammatical forms close together, within the same phrase or clause, is considered poor form, if not ungrammatical. This placing together of unlike grammatical elements can be called *faulty parallelism.*

A. Here are some examples of faulty parallelism with suggestions for improvement:

1. *Susie liked swimming, tennis and ~~to play~~ volleyball.*
2. *The Red Cross performs many useful services, such as help-*

    coping

    ing war veterans and ~~to cope~~ with natural disasters.
3. *Women come together and do useful things such as learning*

    taking

    to cook and sew, or∧first aid courses.
4. *The area remains poor because of an unsuitable climate and*

    a lack of

    ~~lacking~~ *sufficient farm lands.*

B. Here are some positive examples of writing which employ parallelism properly—parallelism which lends style and adds balance to the sentences. See if you can locate the parts that are parallel.

1. *Bill Clark's death saddens us, but his life also holds a message. He was approaching his eighty-first birthday when he died. For him, age was not an excuse to stop doing, but a treasure to be enjoyed. It was not a time to spend waiting, but a time to spend learning, living, and using the special talents and abilities that exist in all of us.*

2. *Having read theater critic Bill Nelson's assault on the Ph.D. degree, I suspect that he is not much of a critic; I know he is not much of a scholar.*

3. *This time we are not asking, just thanking. In all candor, we will ask again in the future because we will need your help and will continue to need it until hunger becomes a thing of the past.*

4. *We observe today not a victory of party but a celebration of freedom, symbolizing an end as well as a beginning, signifying renewal as well as change. . . .*
    Let every nation know, whether it wishes us well or ill, that we shall pay any price, bear any burden, meet any hardship, support any friend, oppose any foe to assure the survival and the success of liberty.
    (From John F. Kennedy's Inaugural Speech, January 1961.)

Exercise 1   The following sentences suffer from faulty parallelism. Modify each sentence by matching the grammatical units so as to correct the faulty parallelism.

Example: *The people in my town are friendly, cheerful, and hard*

working.

^ ~~workers~~.

The people in my town are friendly, cheerful, and hard working.

1. There is a Japanese proverb which says, "Three hours mean success; five hours mean to fail."
2. My friends and I like to swim, play ping pong, and taking walks.
3. Harry not only studies hard, but he is a football player as well.
4. I enjoy my Music Appreciation class most of all because it requires no study—only to enjoy music.
5. After my graduation from high school and I passed the entrance exam I became a freshman at Taiwan University.
6. The librarian explained how to check out books, how to use the card catalog, and where we could find certain information.
7. I watched the girls playing basketball and the boys laugh and make remarks.
8. Is it not better for China and the United States to be friendly rather than enemies?

9. Money can give us happiness and enjoy our life.
10. The main purpose of marriage is to establish a family system which contributes to stabilize and a prosperous society.
11. The jury found the defendant guilty, and the man was sentenced to four years in jail by the judge.
12. Because of his money-saving idea, the grateful company made George a vice-president, and he was also given a substantial salary increase.

The run-on sentence

An occasional weakness among beginning writers is one traditionally called the *run-on* sentence. The fault lies in the writer's eagerness to say many things at once. In the process he often uses *and* and *but* too frequently in connecting his ideas. The result is a composition of very poor style.

Here is an example of an actual sentence written by a foreign student studying in the United States.

> *I could not really speak English very well at the time but I went to take the entrance exam at City College anyway but I failed and they rejected me so I went back to night school and the next semester I took the test again and I passed.*

With just a few changes the above could be made much more acceptable. Observe the same "sentence" with minor revisions.

> *Although I could not really speak English very well at the time, I went to take the entrance exam at City College anyway. I failed and they rejected me; consequently, I went back to night school. The next semester I took the test again and I passed.*

Exercise 2   Rewrite the following run-on sentence to make it stylistically more pleasing. You may add words, change the punctuation, and make other minor changes as appropriate.

> I got my Associate in Science degree there and I transferred here to State College and this is my second semester and my major right now is Industrial Technology but I guess I will be changing to Construction Engineering and hopefully I will finish up in two more years and then go back to my country and seek employment there.

*That Troublemaker **because***
In addition to the overuse of *and* and *but*, another connective that often causes trouble is the word *because*. *Because* is a much used, almost essential connective, which, when used in proper balance, causes no difficulty. However, when this connective is attached to a clause which is already fairly long, an awkward sentence may result, as in the following example:

> *There are several things I do not care for in this city, but the one thing I am most unhappy about is the poor public transportation system **because** in my home country, Japan, transportation by bus, subway, and train is very good, always available, and convenient to one's destination.*

The above is considered a run-on sentence; it is too long, somewhat awkward, and consequently in poor style. This fault can be easily remedied by dividing the sentence into two and using deliberate repetition, as follows:

Revised:

> *There are several things I do not care for in this city, but the one thing I am most unhappy about is the poor public transportation system. **I am unhappy with the system** because in my home country, Japan, transportation by bus, subway, and train is very good, always available, and convenient to one's destination.*

Deliberate Repetition: A Transition Technique

Although good writers tend to avoid unnecessary repetition, the repeating of a word or phrase is often done deliberately. For one thing, this deliberate repetition serves as an excellent transition device to relate two sentences or two paragraphs.

Deliberate repetition can be used to divide a sentence in places other than before the word *because*. Here is an example:

Original:

> *I do not believe in being a vegetarian because meat, eggs, and some dairy products, such as milk and cheese, are required for a balanced diet, which allows people to remain physically fit and thus capable of doing their jobs more efficiently.*

Revised:

> *I do not believe in being a vegetarian because meat, eggs, and some dairy products, such as milk and cheese, are required for a balanced diet. Such **a balanced diet** allows people to remain physically fit. . . .*

Nor is the use of repetition limited to sentences with *because*. As a matter of fact this technique can be used with most sentences which might otherwise become overly long. Here is an example:

Original:

> *The classrooms for education courses were usually very crowded, and even in our major subjects there were large numbers of students huddled together in one room, especially in the Educational Psychology class where there was only one instructor for over 200 students.*

Revised:

> *The classrooms for education courses were usually very crowded, and even in our major subjects there were large numbers of students huddled together in one room. **This crowded condition** was especially true in the Educational Psychology class where there was only one instructor for over 200 students.*

Deliberate repetition is often employed merely as a linking device instead of using a conjunction or two separate sentences. Here are some examples:

    a. *Mr. Brown is a wonderful, generous man—**a man** who is not only understanding but who is very considerate of other people's feelings.*

    b. *A proper attitude is most important in order for two people to achieve a beautiful and stable marriage—**a marriage** filled with love and happiness.*

    c. *With the help of good soil and a mild climate, many important crops thrive in the valley—**crops** such as grapes, oranges, lemons, and cotton.*

Deliberate repetition is also used as a rhetorical device to achieve a dramatic effect, or sometimes just for emphasis. Note the following example:

Many citizens are not fully aware of the objectives of the early education program. Early schooling wants to provide children of all social classes with increased common experiences. Not every child has had a book read to him or has seen a filmstrip. Not every child has held a rabbit, seen an egg hatch, or watched a plant grow from a seed. And not every child has painted a picture or worked with clay. Indeed, a good basis for a child's future education lies in the array of varied experiences he has had.

Breakdown by Enumeration

Of course, repetition is not the only way to break down an awkward sentence into smaller units. In the following example we avoid the use of *because* altogether:

Original:

When I was a young and eager high school student in my country, I frankly wanted to become an English teacher because I was very much interested in American literature and because I was also good at writing compositions in English.

Revised:

When I was a young and eager high school student in my country, I frankly wanted to become an English teacher for two reasons: First, I was very much interested in American literature, and second, I was also good at writing compositions in English.

Exercises   Divide each of the following into two sentences, using some kind of repetition or other transition device.

Exercise 3a

The weather in this town is a little on the hot side, but this is not to say it is uncomfortable because although the temperature is quite high the humidity remains low, making things quite bearable.

Exercise 3b

For me, the most interesting place to visit, had I enough time and money, would be that fascinating country, Spain, because I have

always wanted to meet Spanish people, eat Spanish food, and enjoy
Spanish culture firsthand.

Exercise 3c
I ask you now, is that fair? I say no! Because that would mean we are
paying tax twice for the same item. (The last part is ungrammatical.)

Exercise 3d
I like my father very much and I hope that someday, somehow, I can
help to solve his problems, even though it gets harder each day
because his health is not the best and also because he is getting older.

Exercise 3e
Even if I cannot get admitted to medical school I will still continue
my education and try to find a major which relates closely with people
so that I can work directly with both children and adults in order to
teach them what I will have learned from my studies.

Exercise 3f
Most people would agree that knowing the language of the country
one is traveling through can certainly make things easier, less
worrisome, and more enjoyable for the tourist because he or she will
be able to speak directly with the people to find out about their
customs and traditions, as well as their religious beliefs.

Exercise 3g
This city has many problems such as pollution, heavy traffic jams,
and other calamities, but I would still like to remain here as long as I
can because I think it is one of the most exciting cities I have ever lived
in.

Eliminating Connectors

Another way to remedy a run-on sentence is to eliminate the
connector entirely. This is often done by good writers, provided the
connection between the two sentences is fairly obvious. Here is an
example.

> *I wouldn't want to live anywhere else but in this city, where there
> is a sense of vitality and constant change. Because you do not have
> the burden of your past, and tradition has been swept away.*

Exercise 4

Go back to Exercises 3a to 3g. Try omitting the connectors altogether and dividing each sentence in an appropriate place, using correct punctuation. After you have done this, decide which form you prefer, with or without the connector.

The *-Ing* Transformation

Much mature writing is characterized by conciseness—a type of writing which uses a minimum of words without omitting essential meaning. One common way of shortening is to combine two sentences with identical noun phrases into one through use of the *-ing* transformation illustrated below.

> *Mr. Brown arrived ten minutes later. He wore a black hat.* →
> *Mr. Brown arrived ten minutes later **wearing** a black hat.*

You will note that in addition to deleting the noun phrase *he,* tense is also omitted. (The *-ing* form by itself has no tense.)

Exercise 5   Oral Practice. Combine each of the following pairs into a single sentence using the *-ing* transformation.

Example: The musicians strolled into the room. They were playing
soft music. →
*The musicians strolled into the room **playing** soft music.*

1. Helen proudly showed us her highly prized letter from the White House. It bore the president's signature.
2. The president arrived at the airport. He smiled and waved to the waiting crowd.
3. Bill wrote a letter to the registrar. The letter asked for information on admission requirements.
4. Bill received a phone call from the registrar. The phone call directed him to report to the Dean's Office.
5. Robert anxiously made a long distance phone call. He asked his parents to send him some money.
6. I have this morning sent a letter to the Secretary of State. I have informed him that I will resign my office as of noon tomorrow.
7. Mr. Byrnes has resigned his post as prime minister. Mr. Byrnes has designated Mr. Wilson as acting prime minister.

The *-ing* transformation is also frequently applied to relative clauses to achieve a more concise style, as shown in the following illustration:

    1a. *Tom Brown wrote two novels. The novels describe life on an Indian reservation.* ➔

    2a. *Tom Brown wrote two novels* **which describe** *life on an Indian reservation.* ➔

    3a. *Tom Brown wrote two novels* **describing** *life on an Indian reservation.*

It may be helpful for us, as students of writing, to run through the above process with a few more sentences.

Exercise 6   Combine each set of sentences in two ways: First, combine using a relative clause; then apply the *-ing* transformation.

Example: Bill wrote a letter. The letter asked for information. ➔
      a)   *Bill wrote a letter* **which asked** *for information.* ➔
      b)   *Bill wrote a letter* **asking** *for information.*

1. The student council passed a resolution. The resolution condemns the action of the president.
2. Professor Chomsky developed a new theory of language. The theory states that every sentence has a deep structure.
3. I was advised of the committee's recommendation. The recommendation urged the Graduate School to reconsider my application.
4. I have written a letter to the Secretary of State. The letter directs him to break diplomatic relations with that nation.
5. The governor issued a proclamation. The proclamation states that Thanksgiving will be celebrated on the fourth Thursday in November.
6. The government passed a new law. The law requires the universities to charge higher tuition.
7. Some children are denied candy by mothers. These mothers wish to protect them from getting cavities.
8. Overweight people should keep a diary. The diary will list all the food they eat during the day.
9. Doctors who treat overweight people are trying out a new technique. The technique eliminates the need for crash dieting.

The normal position for adverbial phrases is at the end of a sentence; however, for reasons of emphasis or of style the adverbial phrase is often shifted to the front. Note these examples:

1. *We conclude that John is innocent* **when we look at the evidence.**
   When we look at the evidence, *we conclude that John is innocent.*
2. *Mary tripped and fell* **while she was getting out of the car.**
   While Mary was getting out of the car, *she tripped and fell.*

With the adverbial phrase in front position, and provided the subjects of both clauses are the same, we can delete the first subject and put the verb in the *-ing* form. Observe the following examples:

1. *While Mary was getting out of the car, she tripped and fell.*
   While getting out of the car, Mary tripped and fell.
   Getting out of the car, Mary tripped and fell.
2. *When we look at the evidence, we conclude that John is innocent.*
   Looking at the evidence, we conclude that John is innocent.
3. *Before we went to the concert, John and I stopped off for coffee.*
   Before going to the concert, John and I stopped off for coffee.
4. *After he had studied math for five years, Bill finally graduated.*
   After studying math for five years, Bill finally graduated.

Notes: a. *while* may be deleted; *when* **must** be deleted.
           b. *after* and *before* cannot be deleted.

Exercise 7   Apply the *-ing* transformation wherever possible.

Example: When we looked at the evidence, we found that Tom was innocent.
             Looking at the evidence, we found that Tom was innocent.

1. While Frank was driving along the highway, Frank hit a bump in the road.
2. Before I go home, I usually unplug the fan.

3. When the jailer looked into the cellblock, the jailer saw that the prisoners had escaped.
4. Before Helen agreed to get married, Tom had bought an engagement ring.
5. Before Tom pays the bill, Tom would like to have a detailed invoice.
6. After Mary saw the doctor, Mary began to feel more at ease.
7. After I graduated from high school, I went to work for an insurance company.
8. While the astronauts were traveling to the moon, the astronauts were kept busy with photographic chores.
9. After one measures the specific gravity of the fluid, one looks at the chart.
10. When we looked in the dictionary, we discovered the source of our difference.
11. While Mary was getting into the taxi, Helen tripped and fell down.
12. When we noticed the man's exhausted condition, Tom and I offered to give him a ride.

The Passive Construction

Even though most writing manuals advise students to avoid the passive in their writing, it is an important construction of the English language. The following sentences contrast the passive with the active form to which it is related:

Active	*Passive*
People hold meetings in the church.	Meetings **are held** in the church.
Someone is circulating a petition.	A petition **is being** circulated.
The people elected Snoopy president.	Snoopy **was elected** president.

Writing manuals and composition teachers constantly advise students to use the active form whenever possible—that the active construction is generally preferred over the passive. And with good reason, for the passive often makes for somewhat awkward or "bulky" writing. The active construction effects a simpler, more direct writing style than the passive. This can be illustrated by the following made-up (fictitious) examples:

Passive: *The problem is known by everyone, but the solution is known only by a few people.*

Active: *Everyone knows the problem, but only a few people know the solution.*

Passive: *The problem was given up on by the scientists.*

Active: *The scientists gave up on the problem.*

Note: The active constructions above use a short, simple verb form. Thus the active form does seem simpler and more direct than the passive.

Exercise 8 The following passive sentences are judged to be awkward or in poor style. Change each sentence to the active form and then decide for yourself which construction you like better. Where no agent is indicated, make one up.

1. Many ways to solve this problem have been found by scientists.
2. With more cooperation among countries, an end could be put to hunger and poverty.
3. Being able to solve the economic problems of its people is looked forward to by every government.
4. I wish an end could be put to all the fighting and violence now going on.
5. It has been declared by the governor that sacrifices will have to be made by the people.
6. It was reported by the fire chief that the big fire had been caused by spontaneous combustion.

Appropriate use of the passive construction

Despite all the recommendations to avoid it, however, the passive construction enjoys high frequency of use in both spoken and written English. In technical writing, for example, it is used quite frequently. And there are other occasions when the passive seems especially appropriate for the purpose at hand. Observe the following passive sentences:

1. *It **is hoped** that all of this can **be accomplished** in the near future.*
2. *A meeting **was held** at the school last week to discuss the problem.*

3. *Disperse or you will **be arrested**. You have **been warned!***
4. *Dr. Jones has **been nominated** for the science award.*
5. *The Nobel Prize **was established** to promote peace.*
6. *It has **been demonstrated** that this procedure works well.*

The reasons for the use of the passive may be summarized as follows:

The passive construction is used
1. when the identity of the subject (agent) is either unknown or unimportant. (Note the indefinite pronouns used in the preceding examples of the active form.)
2. when one wants to give emphasis to the object of the active sentence. (The front shifting of the noun phrase effects a change of focus. Front position lends emphasis to the transposed noun phrase.)

In addition, it is occasionally stylistically convenient to use a passive construction instead of an active one. For instance, the following is *not* acceptable:

> #*Walking down the street, a large flower pot hit John on the head.*

The above is an example of improper grammar known as a *dangling modifier.* Because of its position in the sentence, we are led to believe that *the large flower pot* was walking down the street, which is, of course, absurd. But by using a passive construction we can avoid the dangling modifier effect. Note the same sentence in the passive:

> *Walking down the street, John was hit on the head by a large flower pot.*

For a second example let us compare a sentence in its active and passive form:

Active: *Someone promptly reported the accident which occurred on the beach in the early morning to the U.S. Coast Guard.*

Passive: *The accident which occurred on the beach in the early morning **was** promptly **reported** to the U.S. Coast Guard.*

For a final example compare the following two versions of a sentence:

Active: *By allowing monkeys to live among the afflicted trees, scientists are controlling the orange fungus disease, which*

> *attacks young coffee trees during the rainy season, in a novel way.*
>
> Passive: *The orange fungus disease, which attacks young coffee trees during the rainy season, **is being controlled** by scientists in a novel way by allowing monkeys to live among the afflicted trees.*

Note: The passive form allows the adverbial phrase *in a novel way* to follow the verb *control* more closely. While there are other ways of improving stylistically awkward sentences, the use of the passive is sometimes a good solution.

Exercise 9   Transform each sentence into its corresponding passive form. Omit the *by + agent* noun phrase.

Example: One generally prefers the active form in writing.
　　　　　　 The active form is generally preferred in writing.

1.   Someone may have stolen the car.
2.   Congress repealed that law in 1947
3.   Someone sent out the letter on May 15.
4.   The people have overthrown the military government.
5.   Everyone has known these facts for a long time.
6.   They are distributing the new chemistry journal to most college libraries.
7.   One can detect a note of pessimism in Mr. Wilson's article.
8.   One cannot deny a man's right to a good education.
9.   A construction company built the new low-cost housing development six months ago.
10.   No one can leave anything in the exhibit hall.
11.   The government gives students the choice of staying in school or joining the army.
12.   In our system of justice a man is innocent until someone proves him guilty.
13.   The government expects all citizens to be scrupulously honest in filling out their income tax declarations.
14.   Someone has to do something about the high divorce rate.
15.   The college requests all students to notify the Student Records Office of any change in schedules.
16.   In 1790, they did not consider the United States a world power.

17. The U.S.A adopted its Constitution in 1792.
18. They have tabulated the election results.
19. We do not allow smoking in this room.
20. The law prohibits parking in this area.

Problems of Pronoun Reference

Double reference

Pronouns like *it* and *them* are substitute words which replace a noun or noun phrase. Simple enough. But notice the error (marked with an *X*) in the following clause:

> This is ***a difficult subject*** *for me to write about* X̶ *because . . .*

In sentences like the above, a pronoun cannot be used in the same clause in which the noun or noun phrase itself occurs. This can be called an error of *double reference.*

Exercise 10 The following sentences contain errors of double reference. Mark an *X* through the pronoun that must be omitted and circle the noun or noun phrase which it duplicates, as in the example.

Example: (That Cadillac) *is too expensive for Janos to buy* X̶

1. #These articles on poetry are too difficult for us to read them.
2. #That is the sales company that I used to work for it.
3. #Medicine is the career that I am most interested in it.
4. #That bicycle that Linda uses it to ride to school is very expensive.
5. #My country has lots of oil which we sell it to other countries.
6. #Those errors which you wrote them down are all due to carelessness.
7. #Those lawyers whom my brother knows them are very successful.
8. #We saw some large stone statues and other things that people have legends about them.
9. #When I arrived at the office, they had already sold the tickets that I wanted them.
10. #I have some other reasons which I don't have time to mention them.

11.   #Hossein will never be happy, even if he had all the money he
       needed it.

The pronoun *it* often functions as a grammatical object, as in the
following sequence:

1.   *Steve got married; I still can't believe **it**.*

This information can be stated another way:

2.   *I still can't believe **that Steve got married**.*

Note: The pronoun *it* replaces the clause *that Steve got married*.
Beginning writers sometimes make the mistake of writing both the
pronoun *it* and the clause it refers to, as in the following example:

3.   *#We should bear **it** in mind that there is an energy shortage.*

This sentence can be corrected by omitting *it*:

4.   *We should bear ✗ in mind that . . .*

or by changing to the passive:

5.   *It should be borne in mind that . . .*

Exercise 11   Mark an *X* through the pronoun that must be omitted
and circle the clause which it duplicates. Follow the example.

Example: *I can't believe ✗ (that it was really serious.)*

1.   Linda denied it that she was in love with Tom.
2.   We all resented it that we were not notified.
3.   Kathy would not admit it that she was wrong.
4.   I can't imagine it that our team won the game.
5.   The thing which I dislike it the most is the heavy traffic.
6.   I doubt it that the situation will improve.
7.   It is well to keep it in mind that there are many people who
      seldom laugh.

Duplication of subject or object

The following (incorrect) sentence illustrates a common fault in
writing—that of grammatical redundancy:

> #*According to the Education Association, **they** found that Greensville was the only school to require that test.*

Because the pronoun *they* is redundant, the sentence is considered to be in poor style, if not ungrammatical. The faulty sentence can be corrected in two ways:

1a. *The Education Association found that Greensville was . . .*
      or,
1b. *According to the Education Association, Greensville was . . .*

A slightly different error occurs in the following sentence:

> #*In my culture, a seventy-two-year-old person is generally considered that he or she is too old to work.*

The sentence can be corrected in several ways:

2a. *In my culture, a seventy-two-year-old person is generally considered (to be) too old to work.*
2b. *We generally consider that a seventy-two-year-old person is too old to work.* (Active)
2c. *It is generally considered that a seventy-two-year-old person is too old to work.* (Passive)

Exercise 12   The following sentences contain ungrammatical duplication of a pronoun. Modify each sentence so as to correct the fault. Follow the example.

Example: #*To look at a full moon ̶i̶t̶ will bring bad luck.*
              To look at a full moon will bring . . .

1.   #People who believe in superstitions they are silly.
2.   #Designing a bridge it requires skill and talent.
3.   #We have many female doctors that they are just as competent as male physicians.
4.   #Under this new policy only the students which they have passed the English test will be promoted.
5.   #I discovered some basic differences which I thought they were important.
6.   #Anyone who wishes to buy a handgun he can do so very easily.
7.   #Most of the foreign students they have a difficult time getting used to the food.

8.   #The problems we face in education these are caused by the over-crowded conditions.
9.   #There has been a rise in the price of fertilizer, which it uses energy for its production.
10. #Over half the people in the world today they are hungry or undernourished.

Ambiguity

Uncertainty of reference sometimes arises when there is more than one noun or noun phrase to which the pronoun can refer. When there are two or more possible interpretations of something, we are said to have *ambiguity*. In speech we can be less precise in our use of language; if there are any uncertainties or ambiguities we can always ask the speaker to explain more fully. But in writing we must be certain that our meaning is clear and unambiguous. For example, in the following sentence the pronoun *her* can refer to either Mrs. Jones or Mrs. Smith.

> *Mrs. Jones went to talk with Mrs. Smith because her husband was fooling around with another woman.*

The referent of *her* is ambiguous in this case. We can avoid this ambiguity by writing, *Mrs. Jones, whose husband was fooling . . .* or, *Mrs. Jones went to talk with Mrs. Smith, whose husband was . . .* as the case may be. The important point here is that the writer must be certain his pronoun referents are clear and unambiguous.

Vague or unclear reference

With the exception of impersonal expressions such as *It seems to me* and *It is obvious that . . .* , the pronoun *it* should have a clear, precise referent; that is, the thing or condition to which the word *it* refers should be clear to the reader. Note the following:

Clear, Precise:
1.   *I bought a new book and I like it.*

Vague, Imprecise:
  2.   *The public knows that when candidates promise too much they won't be able to fulfill **it**.*

In sentence 2 above it would be better to say *their promises* or *their pledges* in place of *it*, even though the use of these phrases may seem a bit repetitious. Otherwise, the reader has only a vague idea of what the pronoun *it* refers to.

In addition to the pronoun *it*, the substitute words *here* and *there* are sometimes also used imprecisely:

  3.   *I worked in a factory in New York City for two years, but I wasn't very happy **there**.*

Does *there* refer to New York City or the factory?

Exercise 13   Circle the vague word and substitute a more precise expression. Follow the example.

Example: *Some business people are against antipollution laws if*

these laws

   ⓘ∧*will cost them more money.*

1.   The peacock's brightly colored tail, which is not much help in flying, makes it easily recognizable.
2.   My friend is not married at present, nor does he plan on it in the near future.
3.   Here also serves as a shipping center for fresh vegetables.
4.   The government is concerned with the increase of crime and pollution and is taking steps to solve it.
5.   Social life in my country is not the same as it is in Europe or the U.S.A. because the culture there is quite different.
6.   Many of these factories dump several tons of chemicals, oil, and detergents into the lake; some people in the area even claim they can taste it in their drinking water.
7.   In the past, some companies exploited the workers; they did not care whether it was immoral, but only whether it was illegal.
8.   The mayor said there was too much crime and corruption in the city and he would take steps to correct it.
9.   Mrs. Brown's left leg is shorter than her right. The doctor says he can correct it through surgery.

It vs. *this*

There is often some confusion in the use of the substitute words *it* and *this*. Note the misuse of *it* in the following:

> *If I were to suddenly become rich, I would enter a really good university. It is because I am convinced that . . .*

Rather than using *it*, the proper substitute word is *this*. The substitute word *this* is more appropriate when referring to large grammatical structures such as a complete clause or sentence. In general the word *this* has a broader reference than the word *it*, and is usually less specific. The substitute word *this* is usually taken to mean: *this fact, this idea*, or *this situation*.

Exercise 14   Most (but not all) of the following sentences use *it* in places where *this* is more appropriate. Change *it* to *this*, or vice versa, wherever appropriate.

Example: *When I woke up this morning I was feeling quite ill.*

This
~~*It*~~ *made me decide to call the doctor.*

1. In this life one cannot completely refrain from loving or hating because it is the nature of the human being.
2. Yesterday I bought a really good book. It cost almost ten dollars.
3. I like the people here because they are friendly and sympathetic toward me. There are many reasons for it.
4. When traveling away from home it is often difficult to find an inexpensive restaurant with food to one's liking. Students studying abroad usually find it to be a major problem.
5. At the airport I found everyone to be friendly and helpful. It surprised me because I had been told something different.
6. When I got off the plane in Paris I began to feel nervous and all alone. It was the beginning of my first trip abroad.
7. I would like to go to medical school and become a surgeon. It has always been my goal in life.

It vs. *there*

The words *it* and *there* also function as empty lexical units in
expressions like *It is difficult to . . .* and *There is a saying that. . . .*
These empty lexical units make only vague reference to a noun or
phrase, but they do function as grammatical subjects. Students of
English as a second language sometimes confuse these two words, as
can be seen in the following examples:

> #*It is no doubt that women have an important role in society.*
> #*There doesn't matter whether the worker is male or female.*

Exercise 15   It and *there* are confused in most, but not all, of the
following sentences. Make the necessary changes and read the corrected
sentences aloud.

Example: ~~*It is*~~   *There are*   *many times I feel homesick.*

1.   It is many people who only care about themselves.
2.   It is a page missing from this magazine.
3.   There must be a better way to do this tedious job.
4.   It is amazing how much food is wasted because of spoilage.
5.   It is no good reason for this kind of behavior.
6.   It remains many problems to be solved, especially in the cities.
7.   It remains to be seen whether conditions will improve in the
     future.
8.   It is a big difference between daytime and nighttime tempera-
     tures.
9.   There is doubtful that Mr. King will return to his job.
10. It is no doubt that curiosity motivates scientists to explore other
     planets.
11. It has to be a citizen's complaint before the police can take any
     action.
12. There cannot be denied that Hossein is a good worker.
13. It is still a long ways to go before we can achieve economic
     equality.
14. There is still questionable whether Linda is well qualified for
     this job.
15. It cannot be denied that practice makes perfect.

Noun Substitutes: . . . and many others

A few others—some others—many others
Others is a common noun subsitute, but its use sometimes causes problems. Observe the following grammatical and ungrammatical sentences:

1. *For the help I received I wish to thank Tom, Mary, and many others.*
2. *#At the store we bought coffee, sugar, potatoes, and a few others.*
3. *#I went to the zoo and saw some monkeys, lions, tigers, and many others.*
4. *#Playing tennis and going swimming are lots of fun. Others are not so rewarding.*
5. *#We ordered some inexpensive merchandise—toys, games, and some others.*
6. *During my vacation I read a lot of books—"Gone with the Wind," "Paradise Lost," and some others.*

Sentences 1 and 6 are perfectly grammatical, but sentences 2 through 5 sound "funny" and non-English. The reasons for this are as follows:

---

1. Unless otherwise specified, the noun substitute *others* is taken to mean "other people" (as in example 1), but not things or animals.
2. The word *others* can only refer to nonhuman nouns when the referent noun is expressly stated (as in example 6).
3. The referent must be a plural count noun that includes all the items enumerated; it cannot be noncount (note example 5).

Faulty sentences 2 through 5 can be put right by using adjective-noun construction, as follows:

2. *...sugar, potatoes, and a few other* **items.**
3. *...lions, tigers, and many other* **animals.**
4. *...are lots of fun. Other* **activities** *are not so rewarding.*
5. *...toys, games, and some other* **articles.**

Some of the previous faulty sentences can also be put right by inserting an appropriate count noun. For example:

3. *...and saw a lot of* **animals**—*lions, tigers, and many others.*

4. **Activities** *such as playing tennis and going swimming are lots of fun. Others are not so rewarding.*

Noun Substitutes—*Other*—*others*

Exercise 16 Fill the blank with "other" plus an appropriate noun. Some nouns you may want to use include: *qualities, items, products, traits, places, industries, subjects, supplies, equipment,* and *disasters.*

Example: I bought a hat, some socks, and a few___*other articles*___ .

1. I bought a comb, a new toothbrush, and a few _____
    _____ .

2. They produce cotton, tomatoes, peaches, and a few
    _____ _____ .

3. The company has to buy a bulldozer, a forklift, a water pump, and
    a lot of _____ _____ .

4. We need some spaghetti, flour, sugar, and a few
    _____ _____ .

5. The boys like to play tennis, soccer, football, and several
    _____ _____ .

6. The people suffered through storms, floods, tornadoes, and
    _____ _____ .

7. On our trip we visited New York, Detroit, Chicago, and a few
    _____ _____ .

Exercise 17 Correct the following faulty sentences in two ways, as illustrated in the example. Use the noun in parentheses or another of your choice.

Example: #That is where I buy my sugar, coffee, flour, and many
              others. (food items)
          a. That is where I buy my sugar, coffee, flour, and many
              other *food items.*
          b. That is where I buy my *food items*—sugar, coffee, flour,
              and many others.

1. #I went to buy some bananas, oranges, apples, and some others.
    (fruits)
2. #We bought some ashtrays, dish towels, coffee mugs, and a few
    others. (nice souvenirs)

3. #*Life Magazine, Time, Newsweek*, and many others can be purchased at that newsstand. (interesting magazines)
4. #I have a heavy schedule. I'm taking math, French, history, and a few others. (easy subjects)
5. #That's a good store to buy onions, carrots, lettuce, and many others. (fresh vegetables)
6. #Relaxation includes playing tennis, reading books, watching TV, and a few others. (activities)
7. #The city has automobile factories, steel plants, textile mills, and some others. (industrial facilities)
8. #This region produces vegetables, cherries, cotton, and a few others. (agricultural products)
9. #Nancy is great. She has honesty, integrity, patience, and several others. (good qualities)

Exercise 18   Use *others* when possible. Otherwise use *other* plus noun.

Examples: a.   These textbooks are very expensive. Those __*others*__ are more reasonable.
   b.   Some rice is fluffy-dry. __*Other rice*__ is rather sticky.

1. Some public servants are well paid. _____ are poorly paid.
2. Some merchandise is missing. _____ is damaged.
3. Some equipment is quite expensive. _____ is more reasonable.
4. Some nurses and hospital clerks are very pleased. _____ are not satisfied.
5. Citric acid and sodium chloride are quite harmless. _____ may be more harmful.
6. Catholicism and Protestantism believe in Jesus Christ. _____ do not.
7. Some knowledge can be gained from books. _____ must be gained through experience.
8. These two problems are rather easy. Those _____ are difficult.
9. Some people brought food. _____ helped with the decorations.
10. In Port Stanley, the Falkland Islands, we saw many naval vessels—battleships, cruisers, destroyers, and several _____ .

Redundancy

Very often beginning writers waste words saying the same thing twice. Such a needless repetition of words or phrases is called *redundancy*. Observe the following blatant examples of redundancy:

a. I *also* learned how to survey land in the army *too*.
b. *After* two years *later* I went back to school.

The best way to handle most redundancies is merely to omit one of the words or phrases. But sometimes a more radical change is required. See what you can do to improve the following redundant sentences. The first one is done for you.

Exercise 19

1.   I need more further education.
2.   I am here to complete and finish my education as soon as I can.
3.   I worked out a plan of study at the very beginning of the commencement of school.
4.   My parents always helped me during the time when I was in school.
5.   A crucial factor is the ability of the candidates to be able to relate to people.
6.   One only has to drive no more than one hour to get there.
7.   The capacity of the library accommodates about 1200 students.
8.   To me, I felt it was wrong to do that.
9.   I have a lot to say, but I do not have the knowledge of how to go about it.
10.   I was never taught the way in which to express these ideas.
11.   I went to that meeting for the purpose of getting some information about their organization.
12.   The information enclosed in the letter informed Mrs. Levy that her son was in jail.

UNIT 5   LETTER WRITING

In using spoken language one varies one's register, that is, the choice of particular words, expressions, and sentences, according to the relationship of the speaker to the hearer, according to the degree of seriousness of the subject, according to whether it is a formal or informal situation, and other factors.

Likewise in writing, one uses that degree of formality or informality, seriousness or triviality that is appropriate to the circumstances.

Writing a Personal Letter

There are personal letters and there are personal letters. That is, personal letters also vary in degrees of formality according to how well you know the person you are writing to. A letter to a close friend takes on the feeling of intimacy in addition to that of informality. Here the use of contractions, colloquial expressions, and even slang is permitted, if not required.

Here is a letter from a teen-age girl in California to her cousin in South America.

March 27, 1975

Dear Elisa,

Hi! How have you been? Fine, I hope. School's been out for a week because of the holidays. What have you been doing lately? Say "hello" to everyone for me.

In case you're wondering how our trip to San Francisco went, it was fantastic! The first day we went to Fisherman's Wharf and went into all the amusement theatres and such. For dinner we ate at a restaurant on the beach called Zack's (in Sauselito). That was fun.

The second day we explored all the shops in Ghiradelli Square. Even though we left, our money stayed. Now I have three dozen post cards of San Francisco and no idea what to do with them. Everybody here has seen San Francisco, and I've already sent out post cards to every single person I know living overseas. I guess in my next letter I'll just forward them to you so you can have those oodles and oodles of cards on your hands. You might need them.

Jennifer of late has been very sad over the death of her lady parakeet, Clarice. She made an awful-looking coffin out of a shoe box and dug a grave in the backyard. Too bad Clarice isn't alive to appreciate Jenny's once-in-a-lifetime thoughtfulness. Sometimes I wonder if she cares more for her birds than for me, her sister.

Write me back soon.

Love and kisses,
Elaine (☺)

Writing Assignment
Write a letter to a friend or relative. Your style should be informal.
But informality does *not* mean poor or ungrammatical sentences. Much
good writing is informal.

Writing a "Thank You" Note

It is customary (for some people, but not for all) to write a "thank
you" note in appreciation of a dinner invitation or some other form of
hospitality. A "thank you" note is also frequently written to express
appreciation for a gift. Here is an example:

March 26, 1975

Dear Nancy and Harold,

Just a short note to let you know how much Paul and I enjoyed having dinner
at your house last night. You and Harold are certainly gracious hosts.

We also enjoyed meeting your other guests. It was great fun listening to all
those amusing stories. And the music was great too. All in all we had a nice time.

Thanks again for a super evening.

Maria

Writing Assignment
Write a thank you note to someone who recently showed you some
hospitality, did you a favor, or gave you a gift.

Writing a Letter to the Editor

An interesting part of any newspaper is the section called "Letters to
the Editor," or "Letters from the People," or "Letters from Readers,"
etc. People use this section to make a complaint, to praise someone or
something, to comment on a current issue, or simply to "get something off one's chest." Very often a person will write a letter to the
editor in response to a previous letter, either agreeing or disagreeing
with the first writer.

Writing Assignment
1. Compose a letter to the editor of your local newspaper. Either
    make a complaint about something that is bothering you or write
    in praise of something good happening in your city.

2.   From your local newspaper pick out a letter to the editor that is of interest to you. Then write your own letter in response, expressing either your agreement or disagreement with what was written. Add arguments and details of your own.

Letters From The People

Letters From Readers

Bouquets, Barbs

Editor of The Bee—Sir: How about a bouquet and a couple of barbs for this month's Bee. The good news—Woody's back and his wit and humor help soften the never-ending flow of worldly woes. The next time he takes a vacation how about a few old reruns of his columns?

Now for my complaint. How come you are offering language records in Swahili and not Armenian? More people of Armenian descent live in the valley than anywhere else in California. Armenian language is offered at FSU, City College and the Clovis Adult School and the records would be very helpful to anyone taking these classes, or if you wanted to learn a few words to surprise a friend.

Some people in the Fresno area are bilingual and still don't speak Spanish.

L. K.

Fresno.

Helping The Zoo

Editor of The Bee—Sir: This is a reply to those who are critical of the zoo, and a challenge for them to do something about improving it.

Recently a letter to the editor stated that only about two of the animals at the zoo looked halfway happy. How this was determined is questionable. Since the zoo is run by a well-trained professional staff who have studied every aspect of animal care, I feel that they know what they are doing. Anyone who doubts this has only to go out to the zoo and talk to the people in charge; they are always happy to answer any questions on how the zoo is run.

Although the zoo is adequate for the animals' needs as it is, there is a plan to improve it, and we the public can help. The admission fee has been raised and plans have been made to start raising funds for our new zoo master plan. So for those people who are really concerned about the animals in our zoo here is your opportunity to help. For those who are not able to actively help raise funds, your membership in the Fresno Zoo Society will also help a great deal. The San Diego Zoo grew to what it is today because of its large zoo society membership.

Our zoo has a lot to offer besides being a pleasant place to visit. It has excellent educational value for the children, a conservation program for rare and endangered animals and it is a source of pride for our city. It really deserves your support.

CAROL JONES

Fresno.

UNIT 6   BUSINESS COMMUNICATION

Writing Business Letters

Generally speaking, a business letter is characterized by a serious tone, the use of polite forms, and the use of formal language. One avoids the use of colloquial expressions, slang, and contractions such as *I'll, it's, they're*, and other forms. The following letter, Sample 1, is a reply by a United States senator to one of his constituents. Notice that not a single contraction is used anywhere in the letter. Note also that the tone is serious and that the writer uses a simple "sincerely" in the *complimentary close*, as this part is called. The use of "sincerely" and "sincerely yours" is now very common, even in formal letters.

Sample 1 (*Notes.* The names in the sample letters are fictitious, but otherwise, with one exception, all the letters are authentic. FY stands for Fiscal Year.)

UNITED STATES SENATE
Washington, D.C. 20318
January 22, 1982

Ms. Beverly McDermott
1154 Farris Avenue
Los Altos, California   94022

Dear Ms. McDermott,

Thank you for your letter expressing your support for the International Communication Agency's (ICA) cultural and academic programs, including the Fulbright scholarship program.

I share your concern that the Administration's budget request for academic programs would cut these exchanges by more than 50%. I have long supported these exchange programs as important vehicles to promote better understanding and to improve U.S. relations with foreign countries.

The Senate has proposed that the ICA exchange programs be allocated $101.6 million. But final action on the State Justice and Commerce Departments appropriations bill for FY '82 was not completed due to delay caused by debate on a school prayer amendment. Thus the programs will proceed under the continuing budget resolution at the FY '81 level of $100 million. It is expected that the appropriations bill will come up early in 1982. You can count on me to join in efforts to provide adequate funding for the ICA's cultural and academic programs.

I appreciated having your input on this issue.

Sincerely,

Alan Roberts

Block vs. Indented Style

By far the most common style for business letters today is that called "block style." In this style the left-hand margin is solid; there is no indentation of the first line of each paragraph, as there is in the older indented form. Although the complimentary close most frequently appears on the left, it sometimes appears on the right, and occasionally even in the middle (as in Sample 1 above).

The following letter, Sample 2, represents the older, more traditional indented style. The first line of each paragraph is indented, and the complimentary close invariably occurs to the right of center.

Sample 2.   Letter from a plumbing firm.

DILLARD HARDWARE AND PLUMBING, INC.

March 27, 1958

Arcon Manufacturing Company
120 Cherry Avenue
San Jose, California 94715

Gentlemen:

Our firm is a wholesale house for plumbing supplies. We have become aware of your products through one of our salesmen who has just returned from a business trip. We are particularly interested in your line of lavatory basins in various colors.

We would appreciate it if you would send us a catalog or catalogs illustrating all the products you manufacture here in California.

In addition, we would also appreciate your advising us as to the maximum discount you could allow us on the list price. Should your prices be competitive we would be happy to stock your line of merchandise.

We would be much obliged if you would send us this information as soon as possible.

Thank you for your attention to this matter.

Yours truly,

Jack Smith

Jack Smith
Vice President

Tone and Register

In spoken language one varies his or her tone and register. Tone and register refer to the choice of particular words, expressions, and sentences according to the degree of seriousness, the relationship of the speaker to the hearer, whether the communication is formal or informal, and various other factors.

Likewise in writing, one uses that degree of formality or informality, seriousness or triviality that is appropriate to the circumstances. Here is a business letter by a foreign student studying in the United States to a textbook publisher, also written in the indented style.

Sample 3.   Letter from a student

> 3983 East Shields
> Fresno, California 93726
> November 1, 1976

Newbury House Publishers, Inc.
54 Warehouse Lane
Rowley, Massachusetts 01969

Gentlemen:

I am a student at Fresno State University where I am taking linguistics. I am mainly interested in the approaches to and theories of teaching English as a second language. I would appreciate it if you would send me a catalogue of the books relating to this field.

At present I am studying error analysis and contrastive analysis. I am unable to locate some important books, which are published by your company, at the libraries in this area. I would appreciate it if you could send me the following texts as a rush order:

Burt, Marina K. and Carol Kiparsky, *The Gooficon.*

Schumann, John H. and Nancy Stenson, *New Frontiers in Second Language Learning.*

I will send you a check for these books.

Very truly yours,

Masako Sato

Masako Sato

Two places that should be clues to the degree of formality of a business letter are the *salutation* and the *complimentary close*, already mentioned. The following chart lists the most commonly used salutations and complimentary closes:

Degree of Relationship	*Salutation*	*Complimentary Close*
Very formal, impersonal:	Dear Sir:	Very truly yours,
	Dear Madam:	Yours truly,
	Dear Sirs:	Respectfully,
	Gentlemen:	Cordially yours,
	(Gentlepersons:)	
	Ladies:	
	Mesdames:	
	To whom it may concern:	
Less formal, more personal:	Dear Ms. Jones:	Cordially,
	Dear Mr. Johnson:	Sincerely yours,
	Dear Matt:	Yours sincerely,
	Dear Carolyn:	Sincerely,
Very informal, quite personal:	Hello Hector,	Best regards,
	Hello Pat,	Warmest personal
	Hi Frank,	regards,

Logically the degree of formality of the situation ought to match that of the complimentary close. And of course the degree of formality and personableness varies with the type of business establishment, the motivation of the writer, and whether or not the writer is personally acquainted with the person to whom the letter is addressed. For example, an insurance salesman usually writes a friendly leetter and deals with his prospective clients on a first name basis at the first opportunity. Notice that in the two sample letters below, Jerry Smith writes "Dear Mr. Estrada" in his first communication of August 27 but writes "Dear Tony" in his next letter dated September 10, 1984.

Sample 4.   Letter to a prospective client.

DIAMOND INSURANCE AGENCY, INC.

August 27, 1984

Mr. Tony Estrada
Long Branch Computer Corporation
406 Dickinson
Santa Maria, California   93455

Reference: Commercial Insurance Program

Dear Mr. Estrada:

I have been referred to you by a mutual friend, Mr. Chris Harris, with whom I have worked in the past. Chris mentioned you might be in need of an insurance agent who is capable of handling the commercial insurance package for Long Branch Computer Corporation, and who also has the facilities of providing employee benefits and life, health and accident insurance.

Diamond Insurance in Fresno is an independent insurance agency with the capabilities of providing all your personal and commercial insurance needs. I get over to the Coast area rather often since I have relatives in both San Luis Obispo and Morro Bay and good friends in Santa Maria, so I would be more than happy to arrange a meeting with you on my next visit in your area.

Although I have been unable to contact you on the telephone because of our mutually busy schedules, I will continue to try. Please feel free to give me a call if you have any questions, or if I can be of any service.

Sincerely yours,

Jerry Smith

JS:cll

Sample 5.   Follow-up letter to a prospective client

DIAMOND INSURANCE AGENCY, INC.

September 10, 1984

Mr. Tony Estrada
Director of Program Development
Long Branch Computer Corporation
406 Dickinson
Santa Maria, California   93455

Reference: California Grain and Feed Association
Membership

Dear Tony:

It was our pleasure meeting you and your family this past week. We certainly enjoyed visiting you folks and look forward to seeing you again in the near future.

As I promised, enclosed find an application for membership in the California Grain & Feed Association that I obtained through a friend of mine up here in Fresno, Mr. Howard Jensen, the owner of Central Valley Traders.

We have filled out the appropriate endorsements on the back of the application and it is yours to complete and forward to the Association headquarters in Sacramento, California. This Association membership should benefit Long Branch Computer Corporation and you personally, by bringing you in contact with members of the agricultural community.

Tony, please remember you have an open invitation to visit us in Fresno, and we look forward to you and your family taking us up on that.

Sincerely yours,

Jerry Smith

Jerry Smith

JSS:cll
Enclosures

P.S. I have enclosed a copy of several pages of the C.G.F.A. directory that
    you might be interested in.

Did you notice the highly personal tone of the preceding letter? Note the expression, "you folks" in line 2. Also note the folksy[1] nature of the closing sentence.

---

[1]Folksy: friendly, sociable, neighborly.

In contrast, letters from a lawyer's office are much more serious in tone and more formal in the use of language. As an example, a typical letter to a clerk of the court from one lawyer's office is now addressed to *Gentlepersons* because many of the clerks are women. Whether or not this practice will catch on and spread to other business establishments remains to be seen.

And the most common closing sentence from this lawyer's office is:

Thank you for your courtesy and cooperation in this matter.

Very Truly Yours,

Jonathan Browne

Use of Stock Phrases and Sentences

Each type of business tends to use its own stock of phrases at the end of a letter. In the insurance business, for example, the following endings are very common:

1. If I can be of further assistance, please don't hesitate to call.
2. If you have any questions, please let us know.
3. In the meantime please let us know if we can help.

Some additional stock phrases of general use are:

4. Again, thank you.
5. Thanks again for writing.
6. We shall await an early reply.
7. Thank you for your cooperation.
8. Thank you very much for your prompt consideration of this matter.
9. Thanking you for your early attention to this request, we are ...
10. Your prompt action in this matter will be appreciated.

As for the complimentary close, the most popular, in descending order from formal to informal are:

> *Very Truly Yours,*
> *Sincerely,*
> *Best Regards,*

Recent Innovations in Letter Writing

In the last 20 years several changes have occurred in the form, language, and style of business letters. Among the latest trends is that of omitting the title in the address form. Note the omission of Ms. and Mr. in the following comparison:

Traditional Style	*New Trend*
Ms. Nancy Harwell Vice-President, Marketing Berrison and Company	Nancy Harwell Vice-President, Marketing Berrison and Company
Mr. Robert L. Stone Marketing Representative J. M. Scully, Inc.	Robert L. Stone Marketing Representative J. M. Scully, Inc.

Sample 6

DIAMOND   INSURANCE   AGENCY,   INC.

September 27, 1984

Pat Brady
217 W. Orchard
Fresno, Calif.   93711

Subject: Insurance Program for Lido Restaurant

Hello Pat,

It was my pleasure meeting you last week and I certainly look foward to an opportunity of providing you with a comprehensive restaurant insurance program for your new venture with Mr. Mike Wilson.

The experience we have had at Diamond Insurance providing comprehensive coverages for restaurants is extensive. I have made a note in my file to be in contact with you directly about mid-October so that we may proceed in putting together necessary values, information and deductibles that you would like to consider for your new restaurant insurance program.

In the meantime, if you should have any questions regarding our programs or any questions about insurance in general, please do not hesitate to give me a call.

Best regards,

Jerry Smith

Jerry Smith

JS:ll

P.S. We at Diamond Insurance really look forward to working with you.

Sample 7

June 19, 1984

Mark Jensen
Adjustors Associates
Four Sutton Place, Suite 24
San Francisco, Calif.   94134

Re: Claim – 174 W. Maple Avenue, San Jose

Dear Mark,

It is my understanding that you will be obtaining a $200,000.00 advance against my building and loss of rental income combined in your meeting with the Liberty Mutual adjustor next Thursday in Los Angeles. It is my hope that at that meeting you will be able to finalize the ACV and replacement cost portion of this loss as well as the loss of rental income figure.

Very truly yours,

John W. Kettering

John W. Kettering

Sample 8

Jonathan Waters
27 Circle Drive
San Jose, California 95192

Dear Jonathan Waters:

Congratulations. You have been selected as one of our lucky winners in our Travel-Fare Giveaway contest. All you have to do to claim your valuable prize is to attend a brief sales presentation within the next 30 days.

Please call us at Area Code 215, 814-2300 at your earliest convenience and ask for Sally.

Sincerely,

Mark Peach (signature)

Mark Peach
Sales Representative

In some kinds of business communication no salutation at all is used. Note the next two samples:

Sample 9

MUNICIPAL COURT

CONSOLIDATED
FRESNO JUDICIAL DISTRICT

COUNTY OF FRESNO, STATE OF CALIFORNIA
FRESNO, CALIFORNIA   93724

April 25, 1984

Case: 608220

Smith Helen M
110 W. Sierra
Fresno, CA 93704

I have reviewed your letter and have granted your request to attend Traffic School for dismissal of your citation if you have not previously attended a traffic school as a result of receiving a traffic citation.

In order to attend, you must appear at the Traffic Division between the hours of 8:00 A.M. and 4:00 P.M., Monday through Friday, within ten (10) days of the receipt of this letter. At the time that you do appear, it will be necessary to pay a $10.00 administrative fee.

Thank you very much for your prompt consideration of this matter.

Very truly yours,

Elaine York (signature)

Elaine York
Traffic Refereee

EY:jk

Sample 10

ROYAL   INSURANCE   AGENCY,   INC.

P.O. Box 2166
San Diego, Calif. 94108
Marketing Department

November 23, 1983

Diamond Insurance Agency, Inc.
P.O. Box 2317
Fresno, CA 93742

Attn: Phil

RE: Eagle Printing Press

Phil,

On November 19 you presented me in your office with the Business Guard signed
Solicitation Form. At that time I had agreed to use that as a block of the account
called Eagle Printing Press.

I didn't have a chance to get back to the office that day, but on Monday when I
returned I checked our log just to make sure. At that point and time, much to my
dismay, I found another agent had sent the account in on November 5.

I informed Bill Cowley of the situation Tuesday morning, and mentioned to him that
I would follow up with a letter to you. There is not much else I can do about this. Let's
look forward to the next one.

George Redford
Marketing Representative

GR:jm

Adding P.S. (Postscript)

With a business communication that is essentially a sales letter, a
common practice nowadays is to add a P.S. (postscript) at the very end.
(See Sample 5.)

Here are some typical P.S.'s from an insurance firm:

P.S.   Let us save you money now!
P.S.   Group medical insurance should be reviewed with you annually. May we
       help?
P.S.   We at Diamond Insurance really look forward to working with you.

Clear, Concise, and Courteous (The three C's)

Three general principles of business communication may be stated as
follows:

1.   Make the message clear.
2.   Make the message concise.
3.   Be courteous.

The degree of conciseness and politeness varies, of course, with the
nature of the business at hand. A sales letter, for example, tends to be less
concise than a letter from a finance company asking for payment. A
concise letter avoids unnecessary words and phrases without being
blunt (i.e., very direct). Bluntness is often equated with lack of courtesy.

Efficiency and Economy in Writing Replies

Writing individual personalized letters, although very desirable, is
rather expensive. For this reason companies and corporations like to
keep their correspondence "short and sweet." A common practice
among business firms today is to write a short reply on the bottom, or
even on the back, of the letter they receive. A copy of the letter is made,
and the original is returned to the sender with the reply on the same
sheet. As a matter of fact, some firms request that one write the reply on
the bottom of their letter. In this way, one can examine both the original
letter and the response at a glance. Take note of the following example:

WILSON MANAGEMENT COMPANY
March 4, 1984   COCOA, FLORIDA   32922

RE: DENNIS ELECTRIC - April 1st EXP.

On February 5th, we sent you a follow-up CSR on the above referenced account with a known expiration date of April 1, 1984. As of this date, we have not yet received a submission from your agency on this account.

As you know, the timely gathering and processing of . . .

If, for some reason, you are unable to submit this account, *please briefly explain why at the bottom of this letter* and return it to us immediately in the enclosed envelope.

Thanking you in advance,

Sam Peters

Sam Peters
Broker Services

Mechanization of Correspondence

Generally speaking, one would be well advised to avoid formulas and to write fresh, spontaneous letters with the appropriate degree of personableness and informality. However, because writing individual letters is very time-consuming and costs a company money, many firms have on hand a number of "canned" or already composed messages which their letter writers can draw on in order to write a letter in the shortest possible time.

Another device often used by salespersons is to send a preprinted message instead of a regular note or short letter. A company will have a number of different messages printed up to meet most occasions. Here is an example:

Old Style Politeness: Use of Formal Phrases

Use of polite forms

Over the years traditional business letters have used phrases with *should* and *would* as polite forms—as a way of showing courtesy. Note the following examples:

a. I should hope the enclosed information will be satisfactory.
b. I would appreciate it if we could have your reply before the end of the month.
c. I should be much obliged if you would send me the necessary forms.

Of course, business letters cover a range of formality and politeness. In today's business world there seems to be a trend away from the use of long, formal phrases and sentences and toward the use of simple, more direct ones. Note the following examples of this more direct style:

d. Please send me the necessary forms as soon as possible.
e. Please explain why we have not received your payment.
f. Your MCI telephone service has been terminated for lack of payment.
g. There has been a misunderstanding. Please return the premium the insured has paid you.

In the final analysis, then, one must choose that degree of formality and politeness that is appropriate for a particular business firm. Some may choose to be gentle and diplomatic; others may elect to be concise and straightforward.

Would appreciate plus *it* deletion

The common expression *would appreciate* deserves special attention. Of course, a sentence like *I would appreciate some money* is quite simple and creates no problem. But when *would appreciate* is followed by a phrase, there are two alternatives. For example, the idea that you want someone to come early may be expressed in two ways:

a. *I would appreciate **it if you would come** early.*
    (or)
b. *I would appreciate **your coming** early.*

The phrase *your coming early* represents a nominalization[2] of *you come early*.

Now let us consider the case in which a sentence contains two underlying clauses having the same subject. For example, the following underlying ideas

    a. *I would appreciate* (something)
        (and)
    b. *I hear from you soon*

can be combined and expressed as:

    I would appreciate hearing from you soon.

Note: Since the subject of both clauses is identical, the second *I* is omitted.

Exercise   Combine each pair of sentences in the two ways shown in the example.

Example: I would appreciate it. Send me the information.
           a. *I would appreciate it if you would send me the information.*
           b. *I would appreciate your sending me the information.*

1.   I would appreciate it. Send the samples right away.
2.   I would appreciate it. Can I receive your answer right away?
3.   We would appreciate it. Can he send us the list of names?
4.   We would appreciate it. Can we hear from you soon?
5.   We would appreciate it. Will you allow us to use your name?
6.   We would appreciate it. Can we receive your approval?
7.   We would appreciate it. Please inform us of your decision immediately.
8.   They would appreciate it. Can Mr. Brown help their good cause?
9.   She would appreciate it. Can she hear your opinion?
10.   We would all appreciate it. Will you bear with us for a while?

Writing Assignment 1
Situation: You have just graduated from a college or university. You wish to continue your education on the graduate level.

---

[2]For explanation and drill on nominalizations see *Preparation for Writing*.

Assignment: Write to a university asking for information about programs, the cost of tuition, and the possibility of getting a scholarship. Use formal language. Also, use the expression "would appreciate" plus verbal phrase at least twice.

Be Concise

Conciseness is particularly valued in business communication of all kinds. Of course, one should not go to extremes. One should not be concise at the expense of clarity. The message must remain clear and unambiguous. And blunt or overly direct phrases and sentences can go against the principle of courtesy.

We have only to listen to administrators and others on TV and to observe written communication to realize that many people use a long phrase or sentence where a shorter, more direct one would do just as nicely. For example, most of us are familiar with the phrase "at this point in time," which some people like to use instead of the simpler "presently" or "at present."

Here are some examples of commonly used phrases and their more concise equivalents:

Long Phrase	*More Concise*
a mutual friend of ours	— a mutual friend
first and foremost	— first
to find a solution to	— to solve
I am of the opinion that	— I think that
We take the position that	— We feel (believe)
in accordance with your request	— as you requested
for the purpose of discussing	— to discuss
in the event that we	— if we
in view of the fact that (no harm was done)	— since (no harm was done)
could you give us an explanation as to why	— please explain why

Use of Paraphrase

To use different words to say the same thing is to paraphrase. Paraphrasing can be useful for all kinds of report writing. A good paraphrase should simplify and eliminate redundancy. It often shortens, although that is not the main purpose for using paraphrase. (See Unit 13.) Here are a few examples of sentences which become more concise when paraphrased:

Original	*Paraphrased Version*
We would like to express our appreciation for the help and cooperation you have extended to us in this matter.	We appreciate your help and cooperation.
Should you find yourself in disagreement, please advise us.	If you disagree, please advise.
This is to acknowledge the receipt of your check in the amount of $25.	Thank you for your check for $25.

Writing Assignment 2 (Paraphrasing)
Paraphrase each of the following sentences using simpler, more common words and phrases and less formal sentence constructions. The first one is done for you.

1. We are now using packaging material which is lighter in weight than that used in former times.
   We are now using lightweight packaging.
2. A reduced risk of contamination is also present with our containers, which are disposable.
3. Our sales reports sometimes contain certain information which is of a confidential nature.
4. We would appreciate your prompt compliance with this request.
5. There are many people who do not fully appreciate the value of careful workmanship, but we do.
6. It would not be unreasonable to assume that you have an interest in our products.
7. This new regulation would involve the necessity of our conforming to the requisites of the law.
8. The fact that we face a budget deficit at this point in time is not entirely unexpected although the magnitude of the deficit has proven to be somewhat surprising.
9. It is not uncommon for employees of the company to register complaints regarding the amount of their monthly remuneration.

10. In the future, should the volume or frequency of interoffice communications become a significant impediment to the accomplishment of the normal work activities of company personnel, it may become necessary to limit or curtail such services.

For more practice in paraphrasing, see Unit 13.

Writing Assignment 3
Situation: You are a college student in your senior year and expect to graduate in two months. You are anxious to secure employment in your major field of specialization.

Assignment: Write a letter to a firm of your choice. Your purpose is to try to interest them in you as a possible future employee. You have had only limited work experience, but you have a good educational background, and you are a fast learner. What you lack in experience is balanced by your enthusiasm, your interest in the firm, and your willingness to work hard. Make your letter somewhat general. Say you are attaching your curriculum vitae listing your qualifications in more detail. The use of polite forms is in order for this type of letter.

Writing Assignment 4
Situation: You are the manager of the local office of the Pacific Gas & Electric Company. You have received a letter from an irate customer, Sam Jones, who says he received a notice saying his gas and electricity would be shut off unless his delinquent account was paid up within seven days. He claims his account was fully paid up. He also threatens you with talk of seeing a lawyer. Upon checking, you find out that a clerk made an error and credited the payment to the wrong account.

Assignment: Write a letter to Mr. Jones apologizing for the notice of termination of service. Blame the computer for the error. Try to assuage the angry feelings of the customer by telling him he is a valued customer, and that you personally will set the matter right. Offer your assistance for any future problems.

Writing Assignment 5
Situation: You are the office manager of a small supply firm. One of your clients, Mr. Wilbur Fox, has not paid for a shipment he received over six months ago. The terms of sale called for payment within 60 days.

Assignment: Write a letter to Mr. Fox and try to convince him to pay his account immediately. Try to be diplomatic. Avoid making any direct threats. Try to use positive wording. Tell Mr. Fox you are sure he wants to maintain a good credit rating. Say you know he wants to avoid having his delinquent account turned over to a collection agency. Encourage him to write or phone you to discuss ways of resolving the matter in a mutually satisfactory manner.

Writing Assignment 6
Situation: You have been involved in a traffic accident through no fault of your own. Your car was struck from behind by a Mr. Fred Adams while you were waiting at a red light. Your car sustained damages amounting to $900. Your insurance company will pay for the damages, except for the $150 deductible, which you must pay.

Assignment: Write a letter to Mr. Adams, of 110 Crescent Drive, San Diego, CA 94701. Tell him in a firm but courteous manner that he is responsible for your loss and must therefore pay you $150. Mention that you may suffer a further loss by having your insurance premium increased. Advise Mr. Adams that, if necessary, you will take him to court to recover your loss, but you hope that that will not be the case.

Writing Assignment 7
Situation: You rented a car from Smooth-Ride Auto Rental in Madrid, Spain, on August 1, at a weekly rate of $250 plus $50 for turning in the car in Paris, France. While en route to your destination the car began to overheat in Biarritz, France. The Smooth-Ride office in Biarritz solved the problem by giving you a substitute vehicle with which to continue your trip. Upon arrival in Paris, you duly delivered the car and paid the total charges of $300 with your credit card. Five weeks later your credit card bill arrives at your home. There is the charge from the Paris office of Smooth-Ride for $300. But in addition you see a charge of $130 from the Madrid office, for car rental from Madrid to Biarritz.

Assignment: Write a letter to the Madrid office telling them their charge is improper. Explain the circumstances. Also, write a letter to your credit card company asking them to set aside the $130 charge because it is improper. Enclose a copy of your letter to Smooth-Ride in Madrid.

Writing Memorandums

Memorandums are a vital part of everyday communication. They are used for interoffice as well as intraoffice communication. Memorandums are the principal vehicle for transmitting written messages within an organization, even in relatively small firms.

Memorandums, commonly called *memos*, tend to be less formal and more direct than business letters and reports destined for someone outside the home organization. Nevertheless, the same principles of good business writing—clarity, conciseness, and courtesy—still apply.

Clarity

Memos should be clear and concise. If one has to telephone the writer of a memo to ask for clarification of a point, this usually indicates a flaw in the communication. The purpose of a memo is most important. The writer should keep this purpose in mind when planning and composing the memo. Is the memo for informational purposes only? Is it designed as a morale booster expressing appreciation for a job well done? Or is the memo intended as a reprimand for parties known or unknown? Perhaps the object is to produce some kind of action or response. Whether it be stated explicitly or merely implied, the purpose of the memo must be clear to the reader.

Conciseness

Memos should be concise as well as clear. Conciseness is just as important in writing memos as it is for writing letters. No one wants to have to read long, laborious memos. Often the essential points may become lost or obscured if the memo is too wordy or if it contains elaborately phrased, overly formal language. Of course, the degree of formality varies according to the relationship of the memo writer to the recipient(s). But whether one is writing a very formal memo or one to a close, personal friend the principles of clarity and conciseness still pertain.

Courtesy

One should never lose sight of courtesy. Being polite and avoiding unnecessary criticisms, stated or implied, will usually pay dividends.

Since writing is a permanent record, one should find other ways to vent one's temporary feelings of anger or annoyance. One often regrets the wording of memos fired off in a moment of anger.

Memo Format

A memo may consist of just a few sentences jotted down on a piece of paper addressed to a specific person(s), as in the following example:

Sample 11

JAN. 18 1983

TO NANCY

RE Jake's AUTO DISMANTLE
MADERA, CALIFORNIA

PLEASE RUSH A QUOTE ON THIS ONE.
CALL ME WITH THE FIGURES AS SOON AS
YOU CAN. I WILL TRY TO DELIVER
FOR A 7/1 BINDING. TRY FOR
SOMETHING LESS THAN $1,000 ANNUAL
AND I THINK HE WILL MOVE. HE'S
BEEN WITH CONTINENTAL FOR 18 YEARS,
BUT HE DOESN'T LIKE THE AGENT!

THANKS,

Jerry

But most memos follow a conventional format with these headings:

MEMORANDUM   Date: October 8, 19 _____
                                              File No. A 17

TO: All concerned

FROM: Don Ashley,
           Building Coordinator

SUBJECT: Parking lot permits

It has come to my attention that ...

DA:ej

Tone and Degree of Formality

Memos written by salespersons tend to be more personal, more conversational in tone, and less concise than others, in keeping with their desire to come across as friendly and interested in their client's welfare. Here are two examples of short, informal memos:

Sample 12 (Memo concerning a prospective client)

           MEMORANDUM

TO: Jerry   November 9, 1983

FROM: Sidney

RE: Jess Taylor
        Coleman Convalescent Home

Give him a call, Jerry, and use the name of William Easton as a referral. We provide the insurance for Mr. Easton at Doby Office Furniture and he suggested that we call, since we provide insurance for the Community Care Industry and we might be able to help him.

Since the memo writer's name already appears on the memo, there is no need for a name or signature below the writing. However, the writer will usually sign his or her initials next to the name opposite FROM. Note that sometimes a simple RE is used instead of SUBJECT.

Sample 13

M E M O R A N D U M

TO: Jerry

FROM: Sidney

SUBJECT: Pay-As-You-Go Report

Here's a copy of the Pay-As-You-Go report that Ferguson Insurance uses. They use it very effectively, and they have gotten all of their customers to complete and extend, and attach a check with their worker's comp or their receipts, on a monthly basis. Why don't you show it to John and Helen? Then if they think it's a good idea, let's go over it with the sales force and get it working here.

SLJ:cll
Attachment

Note the two sets of initials in the lower left corner. The first are the initials of the writer. The second set are those of the typist.

Make an Outline

When writing long, more complicated memos in which several points must be covered, it is often advisable to make a preliminary outline to ensure coverage of all important points. Making a preliminary or rough outline also helps the writer to proceed in an orderly, logical manner. Of course, changes are usually made as the writer begins to actually compose the memo.

Use Subheadings

To catch the eye of the reader as well as to ensure unity, it is often a good idea to use subheadings. The subheadings can be gotten from one's preliminary outline. This use of subheadings will enable the reader to know at a glance what is contained in the memo—a boon for hardworking, busy employees and colleagues.

Here are more examples of memos, this time longer, more formal ones:

Sample 14 (Memo in academia)

MEMORANDUM

October 20, 1983

TO: Dr. Robert H. Nilsen
            Chairman, Academic Senate

FROM: Jan Van Esswyk, Chairman   ૨ V₳
            Academic Policy and Planning Committee

SUBJECT: College Level Examination Program (CLEP)

Background Information

On October 14, 1983, the Academic Policy and Planning Committee approved the proposal that Podunk State College grant credit for achievement outside the classroom evidenced by successful completion of CLEP examinations and that the following statement of policy appear in the catalog:

> "The College Level Examination Program (CLEP) is designed to be a means through which recognition, academic credit and advanced placement may be given for less conventional forms of educational experience. The CLEP examinations are of two types and credit will be granted as follows:

> 1. *General Examinations*
>
>   For each General Examination passed with a minimum scaled score of 500, six units of credit applied to the appropriate General Education area except for the English Composition general examination for which three units will be granted.

> 2. *Subject Examinations*
>
>   For each Subject Examination passed with a minimum scaled score of 50, three to six units of credit depending upon the course equivalency assigned by the appropriate department."

JVE/js

Sample 15 (Assessment of future profits)

M E M O R A N D U M

TO: George Markley
           Vice President for Product Development

FROM: Ben Hill
           Chief Systems Analyst

SUBJECT: Bartlett Corporation, profitability of

Background

The Bartlett Corporation, our wholly owned subsidiary, has been going downhill for the last three years. While sales have not greatly decreased, the cost of production has risen continuously over the last five years, with a concomitant decrease in net profits. In fact, this company suffered net losses the last two years.

The Problem

The prospects for future profits are not encouraging. Productivity has declined due to the age of the plant machinery and other factors. The prospects for increased sales over the next five years are none too bright for two principal reasons: First, several competitors, with more modern and efficient production facilities, have entered the market. Second, the market for the Bartlett product, according to our most recent market survey, has reached the saturation point. Consequently, unless we undertake to modernize our production plant Bartlett Corporation will continue to operate at a loss.

Recommendation

In my considered judgment, projected sales for the next five years do not justify the huge expenditure that would be necessary to modernize the plant facility. I therefore recommend that Bartlett Corporation be put up for sale in the very near future.

BH:lp

Sample 16 (More academia)

MEMORANDUM

TO: Members of the Faculty   Date: May 3, 1984

FROM: Richard H. Brown
           Dean of Student Affairs

SUBJECT: 1984 Commencement

The following instructions are to be followed with reference to the graduation ceremonies scheduled to take place on Saturday, May 19.

Standard Procedure

President Johnson will again host a "coffee" for faculty who will be participating in Commencement beginning at 7:45 a.m., Saturday, May 19, on the west side of the Press Box in Bulldog Stadium. Faculty are asked to bring their academic regalia to the "coffee" because they will assemble for the academic processional at that site. The procession will begin at 9:00 a.m.

School Groupings

The faculty will march as a single body; however, members will be grouped by school so as to provide a better visual effect when asked to stand during the ceremony. Emeriti will also march with their department/school.

In the event of rain

The chance of rain on Commencement Day is remote. Nevertheless, the following contingency plans have been developed:

Contingency Plan A

In the event of a light rain or occasional light showers, the "coffee" will be held and the ceremony will proceed as planned in the stadium.

Contingency Plan B

In the event of a heavy rain storm that is forecast to be of relatively short duration, the "coffee" will be cancelled and the ceremony postponed to 1:00 p.m. in the stadium. Faculty are asked to assemble at the Press Box at 12:30 p.m.

Contingency Plan C

In the event of a heavy rain storm that is forecast to continue throughout the day, the ceremony will be relocated and a modified program presented. Faculty are encouraged to participate and are asked to be at their respective site one-half hour prior to the times listed below:

School of Agriculture & Home Economics	North Gym	10:00 a.m.
School of Arts and Humanities	College Union	11:15 a.m.
School of . . .		

RHB: lj

Writing Memorandums: Your Turn

Writing Exercise 8 (Rising expense accounts)
Situation: You are the sales manager for an insurance brokerage firm. Your problem: The expense accounts of your salespersons have been getting out of hand. In particular your sales force has been taking clients to lunch much too often.

Assignment: Write a memo to your salespersons urging them to cut down on the number and cost of these business lunches. At the same time you do not want to discourage your top salespersons who may not be abusing their expense accounts.

Writing Exercise 9 (High cost of Xeroxing)
Situation: You are the department chair of the English department at a small private university. Your problem: There are two months remaining until the end of the semester and you are worried that you may run out of funds to buy necessary supplies. Your secretary informs you that the liberal use of the Xerox machine is fast depleting the budget for supplies and services. She tells you that for 20 copies or more it is more economical to use the ditto machine instead of the Xerox.

Assignment: Write a memo to: Members of the English Department. Ask all concerned to use the ditto instead of the Xerox machine for anything over 20 copies, whenever absolute clarity is not essential. You want to be firm without being offensive. In particular, you must be careful not to offend those instructors who already try to conserve supplies and avoid unnecessary waste.

Writing Assignment 10 (Vacation policy change)
Situation: You are the manager of a medium-sized electronics firm. Up to now the company has had a liberal policy regarding vacations with pay. Lately, recently hired employees seem to have a high rate of absenteeism; they seem to be working less and taking time off more frequently than did previous new employees. Top management has asked you to tighten up the vacation policy so as to decrease the rate of absenteeism.

Assignment: Write a memo to "all employees" telling them that effective immediately there will be a new policy regarding eligibility for paid vacations as well as unpaid leaves of absence. Tell them the new policy supersedes that which was in effect up until now, and that the former "1,000 hours of service" rule is no longer in effect. Instead, to be eligible for vacation or leave of absence, an employee must have been on the job for a minimum of 120 working days. In addition, any absences in excess of 10 per cent of the total time worked will be added to the minimum time required for vacation eligibility. Invite the employees to call you or your secretary or to come in person, should they have any questions about the new policy.

Writing Assignment 11 (Responding to a complaint memo)
Situation: You are the assistant operations manager for a large insurance company. You have received a memo from your immediate boss, Helen Parker, dated October 22, 19 ____ , complaining that it has come to her attention that some employees under your jurisdiction are taking too much time for lunch. In her memo to you, she also states that several employees are making and receiving more than a reasonable number of personal telephone calls. Not only is this practice time-consuming and distracting, writes Ms. Parker, but it lowers the efficiency of the office operation as well.

Assignment: You are to write a response memo to your boss telling her that you too had noticed that some employees were abusing certain privileges. You are to propose new procedures in regard to lunch time and personal phone calls that will help to curtail, or at least hold to a minimum, these abuses. Tell Ms. Parker you will be glad to meet with her to discuss these matters in more detail.

SECTION
C

Guidelines for Essay Organization

UNIT 7   BASIC STRUCTURE OF AN ESSAY

Principal Parts: Beginning, Middle, and End

A statement attributed to the Greek philosopher Aristotle affirms that all things can be viewed as having a beginning, a middle, and an end. Accordingly, an essay can be divided into three principal parts: an introduction, a main body, and a conclusion.

In a short essay, three or four paragraphs may be sufficient—one for the introduction, one or two for the main body, and one for the conclusion. In longer essays there may be any number of paragraphs in the main body. And in very long, involved essays a writer will sometimes use more than one paragraph for his/her introduction.

Each paragraph should be a discrete unit, treating one aspect of the general topic or theme. And each unit should be unique, that is, unlike any other. If two or more paragraphs "sound alike," excessive redundancy will result and detract from your writing. Perhaps such paragraphs are unnecessary and should be eliminated.

The Introductory Paragraph

A clear beginning is necessary to give direction to one's writing. The writer should try to catch the reader's eye and let him know, if only in general terms, what he, the reader, can expect to find in the rest of the essay. A well-written paragraph encourages the reader to proceed further with his reading—to pursue the author's message.

The introductory paragraph also serves a very important function, namely, to introduce the central idea or *thesis*. For more about *thesis*, see Unit 15. At the same time the introductory paragraph serves as a connecting link to the main body which follows.

The Main Body

The main body of an essay serves to develop, expand, and provide support for the central idea or thesis stated in the introductory paragraph. The main body should present arguments or statements which support or expand upon the main idea or thesis. In a rather short essay the main body may consist of a single paragraph; in a long research paper it will undoubtedly consist of many.

No matter whether one is writing a single paragraph or many paragraphs, one should exercise thought and care in arranging the points of argument or description. Generally speaking, one should avoid putting the minor points at the end; this makes for a weak ending. Rather, one should save the most persuasive argument or arguments for last. This is generally regarded as being more effective because a reader tends to remember best that which he read last.

Tiny, Underdeveloped Middle Paragraphs

Paragraphs representing the main body should be of appropriate length, especially in comparison with the introductory and closing paragraphs. Each paragraph of the main body not only should support the central idea or thesis of the essay as a whole but should also develop and add to the topic sentence of that paragraph.

The following essay, written by a well-meaning university student, is *not* satisfactory. It is not satisfactory because the two middle paragraphs, the main body, are too short and underdeveloped. They lack supporting detail and examples; they do not say enough to support the topic sentence. The result is two tiny, underdeveloped paragraphs. To repeat, the following essay is *not* satisfactory because the paragraphs representing the main body are too short and lacking in details.

What I Like and Dislike about Living in Santa Cruz, California

Introductory paragraph

When I was in my country, my greatest wish was to come to California. Well, I finally got my wish. For the last three months I have been living in this small California city, working towards a Master's degree in economics. And like everything else, this situation has its good side as well as its bad.

Main body

The one thing I like best about living in this city is the opportunity to have new experiences. I have gotten to know other people and other customs. This is important to me.

On the negative side, the thing I miss the most is family life. It is really nice when you can eat with your family or have tea with them in the afternoon. I also miss chatting with my family about different things.

Concluding paragraph

On balance, however, I am satisfied with my life here. I am enjoying my new experiences and have made new friends. I hope I will enjoy the rest of my stay in this small California city.

The Conclusion

A good introduction and main body merit an equally good conclusion. Some writers use the concluding paragraph to summarize the main points of the essay. Often a final comment is added to bring the essay to a close. This may be in the form of a wish on the part of the writer, a plea for greater understanding or awareness of a particular situation, or even a call for action of some kind.

In any event, a conclusion is needed to advise the reader that you have finished and that there is no more to come. One should try to leave the reader with a feeling of satisfaction—the feeling that he, the reader, has received the writer's message and knows his or her point of view.

BASIC STRUCTURE OF A TYPICAL ESSAY

_____ Introductory Paragraph
                              ↓
_____ 1st Main Point
                              ↓
_____ 2nd Main Point
                              ↓
_____ 3rd Main Point
                              ↓
_____ Concluding Paragraph

Writing Assignments

A.   Write a short essay using the following guidelines:

1.   Your title will be, "What I like and dislike about living in _____ ."

2.   Your essay will consist of four paragraphs, no more, no less, as follows:

Paragraph 1. Introductory statement

Paragraph 2. The one thing I like most about living in _____ is . . .

Paragraph 3. The one thing I dislike the most is . . .

Paragraph 4. Conclusion

B.   Write a short essay using the following guidelines:

1.   Title: "How I Evaluate My Parents"

2.   Write four paragraphs as follows:

Paragraph 1. Introductory statement

Paragraph 2. The one characteristic I like most about my parents is . . .

Paragraph 3. The one characteristic that bothers me most about my parents is . . .

Paragraph 4. Conclusion

C.   Complete the following essay. In the first line of paragraph 2 decide whether you agree or disagree and continue the paragraph accordingly. Follow the guide words for the last two paragraphs.

Many famous people were vegetarians—people who refused to eat meat of any kind—for humanitarian reasons. Many people today also believe in this philosophy and are against the killing of animals for food supply. Some even go so far as to refuse to eat eggs or dairy products since these items also come from animals.

> *I think that* . . . (agree/disagree)
>
> *I also believe* . . .
>
> *In conclusion* . . .

D.   Complete the following essay using the guide words to start your paragraphs.

The Killing of Porpoises

Porpoises are cetacean animals known to possess high intelligence. These aquatic mammals—very similar to and often confused with *dolphins*—are playful animals that grow five to six feet long. Unfortunately, hundreds of porpoises are killed daily when they get caught in the nets of tuna fishermen. Some people say that this is cruel and inhumane, and that laws should be passed to stop or minimize the slaughter of these peaceful, highly intelligent animals. But the tuna fishermen protest saying that their jobs and the tuna they catch are more important than a few porpoises.

> *There are two ways of looking at this problem. Some people feel that* . . .
>
> *On the other hand,* . . .
>
> *My own opinion is that* . . .

E.   Complete each of the following sentences to make a topic sentence. Then develop each one into a short essay of three to four paragraphs.

1.   *Anyone who would attempt to cross the Sahara Desert on foot is* . . .

2. *When they initiate sightseeing trips to the moon, I will* . . .

3. *The most important qualities to look for in a husband or wife* (as the case may be) *are* . . .

4. *Whenever I hear about the possibility of an earthquake* . . .

5. *When they begin to train monkeys to operate sophisticated computers* . . .

6. *Whoever said that living in a small town is better than living in a big city* . . .

UNIT 8   WAYS OF ORGANIZING AN ESSAY

All good writing reflects some kind of logical organization—some kind of structure. The writer's thoughts and ideas should be presented in a clear, logical sequence. It is a good idea to keep the reader in mind when organizing any piece of writing. If he or she can follow your ideas easily, you will know you have organized well.

There are any number of ways to structure your writing—to arrange your ideas in a logical manner. For example, to organize by geographical characteristics (spatial organization) would be useful in describing the physical features of a country; a chronological or temporal development can be used to recount historical events or to relate a sequence of events. One very common organizational strategy is for the writer to put forth the main points of his argument or the principal reasons for a certain belief by enumerating them. (First, . . . Second, . . . Third, . . .)

Another general classification is that of *analytical development.* The writer organizes by means of *comparison and contrast, cause and effect, definition,* and a few more ways. Many writers combine several of these techniques in a single essay or other type of writing.

It is beyond the scope of this book to go into great detail or to attempt to illustrate all of the various ways of organizing an essay. However, a few examples, some in outline form only, will serve to illustrate some of the simpler types of organization.

Organizing by Spatial Development: geographical features

The following outline illustrates an essay (or short term paper) organized spatially, that is, according to location and topography.

A. Introduction
    The State of California offers a great variety of topographical features.
B. The Western Seacoast Region
    1. The northern redwoods
    2. Sandy beaches and marvelous sunsets
    3. Seaports and natural harbors
C. The High Sierras of Eastern California
    1. The mountains
            the ski areas
    2. Lakes and rivers
            fishing and water skiing
    3. The meadows and other high plateaus
D. The Central Valleys
    1. The flat agricultural lands
    2. Water and irrigation systems
            Lakes and dams
E. The Desert Regions
    1. Recreation Areas
        a. Palm Springs area
        b. Death Valley
F. Conclusion
    From the foregoing one can appreciate the wide diversity of terrain
    which . . . .

Organizing by Time

The following, in outline form, illustrates an essay organized
chronologically.

I. Introduction
    The vowel sounds of English have undergone extensive changes in the
    last one thousand years. The purpose of this paper is to briefly trace the
    development of the vowel system from Old English to modern times.
    A. Old English: 450 A.D. to 1066 A.D.
        Beginning in about the year 450 A.D., in the period known as "Old
        English," there were . . .
    B. Middle English: 1066 to 1500
        From the end of the 11th century through the year 1500 the vowel
        system shows marked changes from the . . .
    C. Modern English: 1500 to the present
        1. Early Modern English
            The period from about 1475 A.D. through the end of the 17th
            century is designated as "early modern English." During this
            time . . .

2. Late Modern English
   In late modern English, the period from about 1700 until the
   present time, more changes took place in the . . .

D. Conclusion
    The development of the English vowel system has been traced from
    450 A.D. to the present time. I have tried to show . . .

Organizing by Enumeration

A common method of developing an essay is to organize it around
three or four main ideas, all of which are related and interrelated
with the basic theme. Many writers put their main points in
sequence by using such terms as *first, second,* etc. Such terms are
often called *sequence indicators.*

The following is an illustration of this kind of organization. It
represents a letter to the editor of a newsletter published by a
university faculty organization.

To the Editor:
In the March 1969 issue of *The California Professor* the "colored" views of
Miss Lisa Henry of the *San Francisco Examiner* were given prominent space in
your publication. Miss Henry commented on the issues of degrees, black
students, and Black Studies Department. I would like to take issue with her
comments.

First, I think she needs to recognize that admission of black students or any
other students of any ethnic or racial group does not mean that those students
will be graduating four or more years from the time of admission with a degree
in anything. She has implied that admitting all black students who wish to
attend would somehow lower the educational status of Ramona College.

Second, she implies that all of the black students will major in Black Studies.
It could conceivably happen, but the probability of that happening would be the
same probability of white students all majoring in foreign languages, history,
anthropology, biology, or any one of the other dozens of majors available at
Ramona College. She should recognize by now that all of the black students are
not the same—either in appearance, actions, or ambitions. It would be more
proper to point out that all of the black students are different—just as all of the
white students are different.

Third, she needs to recognize that some students obviously do not care about
degrees; these students will get a degree only if they meet the requirements for a
degree. What they do with it is their business. The degree is related to courses and
other requirements established by the college and is in no way connected with
the entrance requirements of the college.

Finally, I would like to take issue with the California Teachers' Association about the questionable practice of including a reprint of an article with such shallow views in a supposedly prestigious publication and giving it additional support by highlighting it. Needless to say, I was quite disappointed.

Robert Y. Fuchigami
Ramona College

Writing Assignment
Write a short essay following the outline below.
1. *There are three main reasons why I am a pacifist.* (or sportsman, nature lover, bird watcher, soccer fan, or whatever)
   First,
   Second,
   Finally, I am a _____ *because . . .*
2. *There seems to be a mistaken idea concerning . . .*
   In the first place, . . .
   Second, . . .
   In the final analysis then, . . .

Organizing by Sequence

A composition sometimes requires the writer to recount a series of events in sequence. To aid in the organization of this kind of writing, words called *sequence indicators* are usually employed. These include words like the following:

Sequence Indicators

first,	after that,	last
then	afterward	finally
next		

The following paragraph illustrates the use of sequence indicators in telling about a simple experience:

> Last weekend two friends and I ate dinner in an elegant restaurant and this is what we had. *First* they served a fresh shrimp cocktail. This was *followed by* French onion soup. *Then* we ate a delicious tossed salad. *Next* they brought in a huge broiled fish covered with small mushrooms. *After that* we indulged ourselves in a marvelous frozen dessert. And *last but not least* they served us some delicious coffee and Napoleon brandy.

The following sequence of events, as they appeared in police records, is suggestive of a plot. Tell a story by reconstructing the events, filling

in details from your imagination. Write your own conclusion. Use
sequence indicators wherever appropriate.

January 2   Received complaint regarding two men who were arguing loudly
at a local bar. The men were identified as Al Smith and Fred
Jones.

January 3   Carlotta Smith, wife of Al Smith, purchases unidentified object
from pawn shop.

January 4   Al Smith is found dead in bedroom of his apartment. Body
removed to morgue for examination.

January 5   9 AM Pathologist performs autopsy. His report: "Cause of
death—small caliber bullet entering right side of heart."
10 AM Telephoned report from a Mr. Fred Jones. "Somebody
has stolen a small handgun from my house. I noticed it was
missing at about 5 PM. That was yesterday, January 4th."

January 6   2 PM Carlotta Smith arrives at funeral home.
2:10 PM Fred Jones arrives at funeral home wearing a black
hat.
2:11 Jones nods to Mrs. Smith. Mrs. Smith looks at Jones
briefly, then looks away.
3:00 Jones leaves funeral home.
3:05 Mrs. Smith leaves funeral home and enters black Cadillac
driven by a man with a black hat.
3:06 Black Cadillac drives off.
8:00 Telephone report from funeral director. "One of my
employees has just found a small pistol in a client's casket.
The name of the client was Al Smith."

Organizing by Comparison and Contrast

It is sometimes appropriate or necessary for the writer to organize his
or her essay by means of *comparison* and *contrast*. One does this by
making points of contrast between two or more objects, persons,
theories, or opinions. In making these contrasts, however, it is assumed
that there are some basic similarities between the things or persons
being compared. Otherwise there would be no basis for making the
comparison in the first place.

One can put things in contrast by alternating paragraphs—one
paragraph to describe A, and the next one to describe B. Or, one can
state the points of contrast within a single paragraph. This latter
technique is particularly indicated if one wants to make a close, point
by point comparison. In the final analysis, then, it is the writer's choice

whether to use the technique of alternating sentences within one paragraph or alternating entire paragraphs.

Many good writers make comparisons and point out contrasts by merely placing a description of two things or two persons side by side; that is, they put them in juxtaposition in the manner described in the preceding paragraph. However, in addition to placing side by side, some writers find it useful to use certain words and expressions in making comparisons:

like

> *Like governments all over the world, the South American nations are trying to provide a higher standard of living for all its citizens.*

compared to

> *Compared to countries like Switzerland and Holland, France is considered a big nation.*

unlike

> *Unlike the Russians, who use their fishing vessels to gather strategic information, United States merchant ships are engaged solely in commercial operations.*

whereas

> *When meeting strangers for the first time, Englishmen believe in keeping their social distance, whereas Americans tend to greet first time acquaintances with a hearty handshake or even a friendly pat on the back.*

some . . . others

> *Some Englishmen are very polite, stiff and formal; others are a bit more relaxed and friendly.*

just as . . . so

> *Just as the Christian religion has its savior in Jesus Christ, so Islam has its prophet in Muhammad.*

while

> *While Japan and Taiwan are preoccupied with their industrial and economic development, mainland China is more concerned with its cultural revolution.*

in contrast to

> *In contrast to Germany, which has a large land area devoted to agriculture, Switzerland is limited by its geography to a small area for food production.*

on the other hand
> *According to the audiolingual theory, information about . . .*
> *According to the cognitive theory, on the other hand, the differences should be explained to the student.*

The following selection illustrates the use of comparison and contrast. The last paragraph is an example of comparison and contrast within a single paragraph.

The lack of a proved theory becomes particularly acute when we try to understand the process of learning a second language. Examination of the practices of foreign language teachers and the writings of several theorists suggests that there are today two major theories of foreign language learning. One may be called the audiolingual habit theory; the other, the cognitive code-learning theory.

The audiolingual habit theory, which is more or less the "official" theory of the reform movement in foreign language teaching in the United States, has the following principal ideas: (1) Since speech is primary and writing is secondary, the habits to be learned must be learned first of all as auditory-discrimination responses and speech responses. (2) Habits must be automatized as much as possible so that they can be called forth without conscious attention. (3) The automatization of habits occurs chiefly by practice, that is, by repetition. The audiolingual habit theory has given rise to a great many practices in language teaching: the language laboratory, the structural drill, the mimicry-memorization technique, and so forth.

The cognitive code-learning theory, on the other hand, may be thought of as a modified, up-to-date grammar-translation theory. According to this theory, learning a language is a process of acquiring conscious control of the phonological, grammatical, and lexical patterns of a second language, largely through study and analysis of these patterns as a body of knowledge. The theory attaches more importance to the learner's understanding of the structure of the foreign language than to his facility in using that structure, since it is believed that provided the student has a proper degree of cognitive control over the structures of the language, facility will develop automatically with use of the language in meaningful situations.

The opposition between these theories can be illustrated by the way they would deal with the findings of contrastive linguistics. According to the audiolingual habit theory, information about the differences between the learner's native language and the target language is of use to the teacher in planning drills and exercises because it would pinpoint the student's difficulties, but it would confuse the student, who needs only to imitate the foreign language sounds and patterns until by practice he masters them. According to the cognitive code-learning theory, on the other hand, the differences between the native language and the target language should be carefully explained to the student, so that he may acquire conscious control of the target language patterns.

Below, in chart form, are some facts about two rival pizza chains in the United States. One company calls itself Pizza Hut;[1] the other is called Straw Hat.

Economic Factors	Pizza Hut	Straw Hat
Number of pizzas sold yearly	70 million	30 million
Gross sales in dollars	$224 million	$114 million
Number of pizzas sold per "hut"[1]	38,462	60,000
Gross sales per one pizza sold[2]	$3.20	$3.80
Number of "huts" in operation	1,820 in 47 states	500 in 45 states
Growth expectations	3,000 huts by 1980	to catch up with rival by 1982

Social/ Psychological Factors	Pizza Hut	Straw Hat
Decor and atmosphere	Sedate and cozy. Table service (waiters/waitresses). Tablecloths, comfortable chairs.	Gay Nineties[3] spirit. Informal and noisy. Plain, bare tables, low wooden benches.
Entertainment	None	Old films, mostly comedies. Free balloons for kids.
Employee uniforms	Standard	Gay Nineties' costumes: Colorful clothes and straw hats.

Writing Assignments
1. You are a newspaper reporter doing research on the pizza business in the U.S. Write a short essay based on the fact sheets, above.

---

[1]hut—a small, humble dwelling, usually with a thatched roof. The word *hut* often has a romantic, south sea island connotation. Here it means store or restaurant.

[2]Both chains sell beer, wine, and soft drinks in addition to pizzas and other dishes.

[3]Gay Nineties: the years of the 1890s when the mood of the U.S. was characterized as being happy and carefree.

The Great Pizza War

SPAGHETTI

Spaghetti
Spaghetti & Meat Balls
Child's Plate

SALADS

Individual
Family Bowl
CHOICE OF DRESSING
Italian · Bleu Cheese
French · Thousand Island

STRAW HAT
Pizza Palace

© STRAW HAT PIZZA PALACE 1970

People Pleasin' PIZZA

DELUXE CHEESE Made with 6 Tasty Cheeses
ITALIAN SAUSAGE Mildly Seasoned
LEAN BEEF & ONION
PEPPERONI Sliced Hot & Spicy
SALAMI Italian Dry
BLACK OLIVE
IMPORTED ANCHOVY Mediterranean
GREEN BELL PEPPER Fresh
HAM
LINGUICIA
   Portuguese Sausage, Mildly Spiced
CANADIAN BACON

WHITE MUSHROOMS
LINGUICIA & OLIVE
ITALIAN SAUSAGE & LINGUICIA
ITALIAN SAUSAGE & PEPPERONI
ITALIAN SAUSAGE & BELL PEPPER
BEEF & BELL PEPPER
CANADIAN BACON & Fresh Ripe Tomatoes
MUSHROOMS & SAUSAGE
MUSHROOMS & PEPPERONI
PALACE SPECIAL Mushroom, Bell Peppers,
   Olives, Anchovies on Request
STRAW HAT SPECIAL Everything—
   Anchovies on Request

CHARLIE HORSE RIDES

SANDWICHES

PALACE DELIGHT
Knockwurst
Cheese &
Pickles

OLD TIME MOVIES

HAM

HAM & SWISS CHEESE

HOT HAM DIP

SALAMI & CHEESE

HOT PASTRAMI DIP

PASTRAMI & SLAW

MEATBALL
with Melted
Cheese

Submarine

OLD CHICAGO
Hot Ham
Pastrami
& Slaw

CANADIAN BACON, LETTUCE & TOMATOE

SWISS CHEESE

HOT ITALIAN SAUSAGE

Hot Beef Dip
on
French
Roll

ROAST BEEF SANDWICH

2111 NORTH BLACKSTONE, OPPOSITE RATCLIFF STADIUM, FRESNO, CA 93703 (209) 224-6770
1414 E. SHAW AVE., SHAW & 6TH STREET, FRESNO, CA 93710 (209) 222-7476
4134 N. WEST AVE., WESTLAN SHOPPING CENTER, FRESNO, CA 93704 (209) 222-2491   5153

2.   You are a business executive employed by a firm interested in
     buying a pizza business as an investment. Write a report to the
     president of the company advising him as to which pizza chain to
     buy, Pizza Hut or Straw Hat.
         In making your report analyze the facts given in the fact sheets,
     and make recommendations accordingly. Be sure to state the
     reasons for your choice of one pizza company over the other.

Organizing by Cause and Effect

Another way of organizing which is fairly common is by *cause and
effect*. For any event or condition (effect) there may be multiple causes;
and a single cause may bring about numerous effects. A writer may
present these basic elements in any order. He or she may state a single
cause and then enumerate its various effects, as in *example 1* below; or
the writer may begin instead by describing a certain condition (effect)
and then write down the varied causes, as in *example 2*. Of course, the
organization of an essay or other piece of writing does not often occur in
a pure form; rather this method is used in combination with one or more
others.

Example 1
     Every schoolboy knows that vitamin D—the sunshine vitamin—is essential for
good health. Up until the twentieth century, those who lived in temperate
climates tended to suffer every winter from the lack of this particular vitamin.
And although knowledge of vitamin D has been with us for more than fifty years,
many people still suffer the effects of not having enough of it.
     A lack of vitamin D in infants and children can cause a disease called *rickets*.
Rickets affects bone growth in the very young. It throws their bone-growth
metabolism off, resulting in gruesome malformation. Manifestations of rickets
include fragile and easily broken bones and soft teeth, extremely susceptible to
decay. The outward signs of rickets include bowed legs and bent backs.
     In adults, vitamin D deficiency can bring on osteomalacia, or adult rickets, a
condition marked by the softening of the bones along with accompanying pain,
tenderness, muscular weakness, lack of appetite, and loss of weight. This too
comes from a vitamin D deficiency.
     The elderly also suffer from a lack of vitamin D. In their case, the disease is
called osteoporosis, a condition marked by a mineral depletion of the bones,
leaving their normally solid structure pitted with holes like a sponge. Consequently the bones become weak and brittle. The elderly, as a result of this problem,
live in constant fear of simple falls which could—and often do—lay them up for

months unless their systems have an adequate supply of vitamin D. Then, they avoid osteoporosis.

A little over fifty years ago, scientists discovered the cause of as well as the cure for rickets. But even today, with full knowledge of how to prevent and cure rickets, deaths are still being attributed to the disease.

Example 2

Today, the ocean is sick—very sick. To my best estimate, in the past twenty-five years overall productivity of sizeable creatures (shrimps to whales) has decreased by 30 to 40 percent. Such a tragic situation is substantiated not only by undersea observation and photography but also by the analysis of the world fish catch. The whale population is today less than 10 percent of what it was at the turn of the century. Coral reefs are dying rapidly all around the world. On a number of popular beaches, a swimmer may be exposed to skin diseases or even to hepatitis.

The sickness of the ocean has its origins in our heredity: ignorance, superstition, thirst for individual power. The diagnosis points to uncontrolled proliferation and growth, a disease of the cancer family. The cancer that plagues the ocean is *our* cancer. At this stage of emergency, the "drugs" used recently (such hallucinogens as "better living by owning more") have proved to be inoperative; major surgery is needed, although we have not yet decided to turn to surgery. The cancer operation will be painful; it will not include the use of nuclear weapons, but it will result in spectacular transfers of wealth and in radical changes in our living habits and our moral standards.

Writing Assignment

1. Write a short essay of three or four paragraphs. In the first paragraph state the cause for something. In the succeeding ones state what you think are some of the effects of that cause.
2. Begin an essay by describing an event that has occurred recently or a condition that now exists. Decide upon several possible causes. Then develop each cause into a short paragraph. End your essay with a brief conclusion.

SECTION
D

Adding Variety to Writing

UNIT 9   STYLISTIC VARIATION

Negative Interrogatives

Students of writing should be aware of the stylistic differences illustrated by the following sentences.

A. *Relatively Informal*	B. *Formal*
Shouldn't we be more aware?	Should we not be more aware?
Don't you have a goal in life?	Do you not have a goal in life?
Wouldn't that be wonderful!	Would that not be wonderful!

Comments: 1) The meaning is the same in A and B.
2) The more informal style is characterized by the use of the contracted form, *n't.*
3) In the very formal style, the full form *not* follows the subject noun or pronoun.

Exercise 1   Rewrite these questions in formal style.

Example: Didn't he advise you in advance?
Did he not advise you in advance?

1.   Aren't you capable of assuming the responsibility?
2.   Isn't she worthy of the trust?
3.   Don't you believe in equality for all human beings?
4.   Shouldn't she be advised of her rights?
5.   Haven't they the responsibility to search after truth?
6.   Wasn't he the injured party in the affair?
7.   Wouldn't you do the same if you had to do your duty?
8.   Didn't they warn you of the possibility of failure?
9.   Couldn't he be encouraged to change his ways?
10. Hadn't they announced the plane's departure before it left the loading gate?
11. Doesn't he support you in the manner to which you are accustomed?
12. Hadn't he warned you of the possibility of failure before you signed up for the examination?
13. Can't we count on your assistance in this matter?
14. Mustn't we be more sure of the facts before proceeding further?
15. Wouldn't it be wise for you to reconsider?
16. Wouldn't that be too expensive for the average student?
17. Aren't you satisfied with the way things are?
18. Can't we help each other in these difficult times?

Relative Pronouns Plus Prepositions

Observe the stylistic variation effected by position of preposition.

1a.   The man **whom** I spoke **to** is Tom's uncle.
1b.   The man **to whom** I spoke is Tom's uncle.

2a.   The book **which** he took his examples **from** is by H. Sled.
2b.   The book **from which** he took his examples is by H. Sled.

Comment: The nonseparated pattern—*to whom I spoke*—is more characteristic of formal expression (written as well as spoken) than of colloquial language.

Note: The less formal (separated) pattern permits the substitution of *that* for *who/m* and *which*, whereas the other pattern does not. This is illustrated in the following:

Pattern A

The man **whom** I spoke **to** is Tom's uncle.
The man **that** I spoke **to** is Tom's uncle.

The book **which** he took his examples **from** is by H. Sled.
The book **that** he took his examples **from** is by H. Sled.

Pattern B
(substitution not permitted)

The man **to whom** I spoke is Tom's uncle.
The book **from which** he took his examples is by H. Sled.

In other words: English does not permit such sentences as:

#*the man to that I spoke*
or
#*the book from that he took his examples*

Exercise 2　　Combine into a single sentence using the appropriate relative. First write in the colloquial form; then write the more formal pattern, as in the example.

Example:　　(A woman is my wife. You are speaking about that woman.)
　　　　　　a.　*The woman **whom** you are speaking **about** is my wife.*
　　　　　　b.　*The woman **about whom** you are speaking is my wife.*

1.　(An old man lives in my neighborhood. There was an article about that old man in the newspaper.)
2.　(Mr. Smith is a nice man. I borrowed the money from Mr. Smith.)
3.　(I spoke to some impatient students. We had ordered those textbooks for those students.)
4.　(Someone contaminated the salt solution. The sample was drawn from that solution.)
5.　(I bought some of those bright blue flowers. The island is noted for those flowers.)
6.　(Allen West is a philosopher. I got my inspiration from Mr. West.)

7. (That is Tom Blonsky, the famous sociologist. I went to school with Mr. Blonsky.)
8. (The police interviewed the frightened jeweler. The diamonds had been stolen from the jeweler.)
9. (You have to send in an application. You must attach your check to the application.)
10. (Sam gave us the answers to some math problems. We are now working on those math problems.)
11. (The lack of funds caused many problems. I was not prepared for these problems.)
12. (Mr. Johnson is the man who developed the new program. We have heard so much about that new program.)
13. (Please indicate below the names of the committees. You are willing to serve on these committees.)
14. (Much of the territory in North America had been previously owned by the French. The British acquired large tracts of land from the French.)

Preposition Plus *Which*: Nonseparation

In ordinary relative clauses (as previously noted), a stylistic variation is effected by the separation or nonseparation of a preposition and *which,* as illustrated in the following example:

> Separated: The book **which** he took his examples **from** is by H. Wilson.
> Nonseparated: The book **from which** he took his examples is by H. Wilson.

In certain clauses, however, the separated pattern does not ordinarily occur. Note the following:

A. This position, **for which** a master's degree is required, pays a high salary.
B. The fifth chapter, **in which** the author discusses psychology, is rather hard to understand.

> for which = for this position
> in which = in the fifth chapter

In sentences A and B above, the use of the separated pattern (e.g.: **Which** *a master's degree is required for*) would be stylistically awkward and inappropriate for *any kind* of writing.

Exercise 3   Combine into one sentence using a preposition plus *which.* Follow the example.

Example: Julius Black wrote a great novel. In the novel the hero becomes a famous movie star.
Julius Black wrote a great novel, in which the hero becomes a famous movie star.

1.   My friend told me about an ugly incident. A nervous wife shot her husband in the incident.
2.   For me, the best part of the book was the introduction. The author describes the tropical island in the introduction.
3.   A conference on International Education will be held the last week of March. The faculty is requested not to give exams during this time.
4.   We now face a very serious problem. A solution must be found to this problem.
5.   The study consists of an analysis of Hawthorne's creative processes. The writings of this American novelist came into being by these creative processes.
6.   Every student is required to obtain an I.D. card. No student will be permitted to use the library without this I.D. card.
7.   The peasants lack an adequate education. It is difficult to advance themselves economically without an adequate education.
8.   All recently graduated teachers will be sent to one of these four schools. New curriculum changes have already been implemented at these four schools.
9.   The peacock has a brightly colored tail. This beautiful bird can be easily recognized by its tail.
10.   I will attempt to describe these basic processes. The economy of the country can be expanded by these processes.
11.   That is the present level of income. One is considered to be poor below this level.
12.   There are certain limits of decency. We should not go beyond these limits.
13.   That is the new school plan. We all gave our approval to the new school plan.

14. The dean of the School of Social Sciences cancelled two geography classes for lack of enrollment. The Geography Department is a vital part of the School of Social Sciences.
15. We are now going to discuss the various routes. Many new words came into the English language by these various routes.

Some Problems with Word Order

Despite the fact that word order in English is fairly flexible, there is a normal sequence, as follows:

> *The man I told you about   usually   goes to work   downtown*
> (noun)   (relative clause) (frequency)   (verb +   (place)
>   complement)

> *at ten o'clock   in the morning.*
> (time)   (time)

Deviation from this normal word order will sometimes make a sentence sound non-English, if not ungrammatical. Here are a few examples:

a. #*The population of Stockholm, Sweden, was in 1978 1.4 million.*
b. #*There are many workers from other countries, all of whom came after the discovery of oil to work.*

The proper word order for these two sentences is:

c. *The population of Stockholm, Sweden, was 1.4 million in 1978.*
d. *... countries, all of whom came to work after the discovery of oil.*

Analysis:
Sentence a: The *time* expression should follow *place.*
Sentence b: The verb form "came to work" should not be separated.

Exercise 4   The word order of the italicized phrases is faulty. Change the word order to a more acceptable sequence.

1. #There has been, *since Aristotle,* and will continue to be, much progress in this area.
2. #There are several industries *located in the suburbs* such as light manufacturing and food processing.

3. #*Those places* I have dreamed of visiting for a long time.
4. #They have moved the factories out of the city to keep the *fresh air*.
5. #Our ultimate happiness is to have a child of our own to *make complete* our family.
6. #There are a lot of nice places *there* to visit.
7. #I have to see *yet* a more beautiful beach.
8. #I stayed for two days *there*.
9. #The winner has been *already* decided.
10. #Not only did she steal away Susie's boyfriend, but she took *also* her job away.
11. #Some people want to move to the city because they look on the *only* bright side of urban life.

Normal vs. Emphatic Word Order

While it is true that expressions of time, especially frequency adverbs (always, never . . .), may occur in initial as well as in final position, the more usual and normal position is somewhere in the middle. Time expressions in initial or final position give emphasis to these time words. Compare the following:

> Normal, nonemphatic:
> Tom *always* eats breakfast at 7:00 a.m.
> Emphatic positions:
> *Always*, Tom eats breakfast at 7:00 a.m.
> Tom eats breakfast at 7:00 a.m. *always*.

The problem is that beginning writers often place expressions of time in an emphatic position when such emphasis is not intended.

Exercise 5   Rewrite the following sentences, putting the time expression in parentheses in its normal, nonemphatic position. The first one is done for you.

1. Mr. Brown is willing to listen. (always)
   Mr. Brown is always willing to listen.
2. Carl was late for his appointments. (often)
3. I am a student at Michigan State University (presently).
4. I am interested in your offer of a part-time job. (very much)
5. The winner has been decided. (already)
6. I have earned a total of 13 units. (now)

7. Nancy comes to school late. (never)
8. My little sister walks to school. (frequently)
9. If I were to become rich I would buy a nice farm. (suddenly)
10. I have been fond of those fattening desserts. (never)
11. I am attending Ball State University in Indiana. (now)
12. Bill has studied very hard. (usually)
13. Maria has been homesick. (hardly ever)
14. Albert must have studied hard. (always)
15. One can find those books in the library. (seldom)
16. Automobile exhaust fumes are blamed for air pollution. (especially)

SECTION
E

Cultural Perspectives

UNIT 10   READING SELECTIONS
            AND ESSAY ASSIGNMENTS

It goes without saying that people from different countries view many
aspects of everyday life according to the context (or framework) of
their own individual culture or social tradition.

Of course, many aspects of modern life may be universal, at least in
their underlying form, so that some cultural differences may be only
superficial. I have in mind such things as music, art, literature, and
other aspects of culture. But whether or not cultural differences are
seen as basically different or only superficially so, people from
different cultures and with different traditions often look at things
with different perspectives—with different attitudes and points of view.

There follow a few short reading selections, most of which were taken
or adapted from newspaper and magazine articles. These articles reflect
some of the attitudes and beliefs current in the United States today. You
will be asked to comment on these topics, both orally and in writing.

Concern for pets

The word *pet* can be defined as "an animal kept as a companion and
treated with affection." In the United States, the most common
household pets are dogs and cats; tropical fish and parakeets are
also popular.

In most medium- and large-sized cities in the U.S., dog grooming is a good business.

That dog and cat owners show great concern for their pets is evidenced by the many services offered to the pet-owning public. There are boarding facilities and hospitals especially for dogs and cats. There are emergency telephone numbers to call a veterinarian in case Fido gets sick or is injured after working hours or during weekends.

There are dog grooming salons where dogs, especially poodles, can get a shampoo, have their hair trimmed and combed, and also have their toenails clipped. There is even a pet-sitting service for people who do not wish to leave their animals alone while they are away from home.

The processing of cat and dog food is big business. Food comes in all shapes, varieties, and flavors. There is special food for big cats and little kittens; for young puppies and old dogs. They also sell artificial bones and special biscuits for the pets to chew on so as to maintain good teeth. Special vitamins for dogs and cats are also sold.

Since people in the cities have no place to bury their pets when these animals die, pet cemeteries have come into existence. The National Association of Pet Cemeteries recently held its fifth annual convention in San Francisco, attended by about 135 pet cemetery owners from all over the nation. And it is not unknown for pet owners to leave money in their wills for their beloved animal companions to assure their good care, after the owners die. There seems little doubt that for some pet owners in the United States, "animals are almost like people."

The importance of a pet

Injury, Death

Editor of The Bee—Sir: This letter is a difficult one to write. Sometime around 9 PM on Sunday evening, March 2, my husband and I were driving back from a weekend at Yosemite when we pulled into a self-service gas station on Blackstone Avenue. At that moment, we noticed a small brown dog lying at the side of the street while two men stood by, obviously wondering what to do with the injured animal. We asked about it and learned that the car that had hit him a short time earlier had not even slowed. The men had been unable to wave down a policeman, knew of no veterinarian in the area and—certainly, none that would be open or available late on a Sunday night.

We wrapped him warmly in our dog's soft quilt and carried him to the car and drove to the nearest phone to call the SPCA.[1] They responded, undoubtedly as quickly as they could, but the dog died just before their arrival about forty-five minutes after our call. It was a long, long forty-five minutes—watching the poor little dog gasp for breath, while we tried to sooth and calm him.

My reason for writing is this: The dog did have a flea collar on, but no other identification of any kind. Though he appeared to be fed adequately, his fur was matted and one got the impression of little care. I realize that this could be incorrect and that some owner, somewhere, is missing this little brown poodle and should know what occurred. Also, when passing through your city, I will drive and walk with extra care. Other than the concern of two men on motorcycles and a young woman in a blue car who stopped to help this injured creature, the rest of your citizens chose to look the other way.

R.A. SMITH

Los Angeles

---

[1]SPCA—Society for the Prevention of Cruelty to Animals.

The above letter illustrates the concern that many people in the United States have for animals, especially for house pets such as dogs and cats.

Writing Assignment
After a careful reading of the preceding letter "Injury, Death," write a short essay covering the following points:

1. What do you think is the attitude of the author, R.A. Smith, toward dogs? Give evidence for your conclusion.
2. What is your personal feeling about house pets, especially dogs and cats?
3. Assuming that R.A. Smith's attitude is representative of most Americans, compare this attitude with that of your own culture.

The following true incident, involving a very sensitive 16-year-old girl, gives some idea of how many people in the United States feel about their pets.

CLARICE, MY LOVE

Jennifer arrived home from school to find one of her three parakeets lying dead on the bottom of the cage. The birds were a present for her sixteenth birthday which she had celebrated a few months before. The dead parakeet was the only female, whom Jennifer had named "Clarice." I say "whom" advisedly, because Jennifer treated her birds as if they were people. When Jennifer's fourteen-year-old sister tried to comfort her saying that it was "only an animal," Jennifer replied, "animals are people too, you know."

With tears in her eyes Jennifer began constructing a coffin out of a small wooden box and some green cloth from her mother's sewing box. When the coffin was finished, Jennifer's mother brought the dead bird, which had been lying on her daughter's bed, wrapped in a piece of newspaper.

Jennifer burst into tears as her mother, following her daughter's instructions, tenderly wrapped Clarice in a bit of cloth and gently placed her in the coffin. Then Jennifer, hardly able to control herself, replaced the top of the box and set the coffin down in a prominent place in the family room.

The next day Jennifer announced she was not going to school. She mentioned the word "funeral," and said she planned to bury the parakeet in the backyard in the afternoon. Respecting the feelings of my daughter, I managed to get off from work early that day in order to assist at the burial.

Jennifer chose a central location in the backyard—a mound with flowers and a small palm tree—as the final resting place for her lost pet. The site selected, I measured with my eye the size of the coffin and carefully began to excavate sufficient dirt to accommodate the parakeet. In the meantime Jennifer had dispatched her youngest sister—twelve-year-old Stephanie—to collect some flowers from the front yard.

When all was in readiness, with Jennifer's mother and youngest sister in attendance, Clarice was gently laid to rest. "I hope there is a heaven for parakeets," someone said. "I'm sure there is," responded the mother. As I gently covered the coffin with fresh earth and patted it to make it firm, Jennifer began to cry. She placed the flowers on the freshly dug grave, and, still sobbing, tapped a wooden grave marker into the moist ground. On the marker was inscribed: "Clarice my love, R.I.P. Died March 10, 1975."

Writing Assignment
After reading the above, write a short essay covering some or all of the following points:

1. How do you personally react to this true story?
2. Is Jennifer's reaction to her parakeet's death culturally determined by her having grown up in the United States, or is it a universal characteristic of sensitive young girls in all cultures?

3. Would you say Jennifer's attitude toward pets is typical or atypical of young people in the United States?

Youthful Grandmothers

The following advice column illustrates the spirit of youth and independence possessed by many elderly grandparents of both sexes. Being young seems to be a psychological state of mind, as evidenced by this articulate grandmother who is seventy-two years young.

Tell It to Mary!
By Mary Simpson

Dear Mary:

My grown-up children are trying to protect me too much. I'm seventy-two years old and live alone in my own house; and I like it that way. But my children held a conference and decided I was too old to live by myself. They want to portion me out among themselves as if I were a piece of furniture.

They want me to sell my house and live with each of them for two months of the year. Nonsense! I resent being babied as if I were a ten-year old. I'm healthy and have all my faculties—plus a gentleman friend.

Why is it that everyone's attitude changes toward you when the calendar says you're over seventy? People don't really listen to you anymore; they start pampering you; and some even raise their voice a little when they speak to you, as if to say, "Well since you're old you must be hard of hearing."

I'm quite sure I never worried about my children when they were small the way they worry about me now. Why do people try to push you into senility? I'm not quite ready for the rocking chair yet. As I said, I'm healthy and enjoy the company of a gentleman friend. How can I get my well-meaning children "off my back"?

Helen Anderson

Writing Assignment

After you have read the above advice column, write a short essay on the subject treated. Among other things try to cover the following points:

1. How do you, as a young person, react to this article?
2. Contrast the attitude of this 72-year-old woman to that of any grandparents in their seventies that you may be acquainted with.
3. How would people in your own culture react to this grandmother's attitude as reflected in her letter?

A Look at Divorce in the United States

Whereas marriage, a very basic social institution, has served man down through the ages, divorce—the dissolution of marriage—is a relatively new development in man's cultural history. But divorce is beginning to make its mark on the social structure; more and more people, all over the world, are using this legal means of ending their marriages.

But perhaps nowhere is divorce more prevalent today than it is in the United States. In 1975 the number of divorces passed the one-million mark for the first time in history, according to the National Center for Health Statistics. This is more than double the 479,000 divorces recorded ten years earlier, in 1965.

In a medium-sized city in California the County Clerk issued 3,863 marriage licenses and granted almost as many divorces— 3,374 to be exact—in the year 1975. This does *not* mean the divorce rate for that year was over 87 percent, because people do not usually get divorced the same year they get married. The figures have to be adjusted to produce a reliable percentage. Nationwide, it is estimated that one-third of all marriages now end in divorce.

The majority of American divorces, about 10 percent, come in the second year of marriage. The next prime period is during the third year, about 8.6 percent, and it diminishes from there. The number of divorces is increasing in all age categories, but the proportion is greater in the younger age groups. As for people who try a second marriage, about half end up in a second divorce.

It is generally much easier to get a divorce today than it was, say ten years ago. There is much less stigma attached to divorce than previously. More people are willing to accept divorce as a fact of life. And there is not as much social pressure today to stay in a marriage as in years past. However, many people are of the opinion that it is just too easy for man and wife to dissolve their marriage.

THE HIGH DIVORCE RATE IN THE U.S.

Attitudes toward divorce may vary from country to country. And even within each country there are probably differences as to how people feel toward this question. Read the following newspaper article by G.A. Fitzgerald.

A LOOK AT DIVORCE

Year	Number	Rate per 1,000 Population
1974*	970,000	4.6
1973*	913,000	4.4
1972*	839,000	4.0
1971	773,000	3.7
1970	708,000	3.5
1969	639,000	3.2
1968	584,000	2.9
1967	523,000	2.6
1966	499,000	2.5
1965	479,000	2.5
1964	450,000	2.4
1963	428,000	2.3
1962	413,000	2.2
1961	414,000	2.3
1960	393,000	2.2

*Provisional
Source:
AP National Center for Health Statistics

Divorce Barriers Crumble Before Changes In Laws

By G.A. Fitzgerald
Associated Press Writer

Changing state laws and the availability of free legal services on a large scale are toppling divorce barriers and increasing the rate at which marriages are legally ended.

The United States set a record last year both in the number and rate of marriages dissolved. It was part of a 12-year upward trend in divorce which the new laws and legal aid are helping fire.

A committee of the American Bar Association's family law section says 27 states have replaced or amended divorce laws since mid-1972. New York State's divorce rate, for years the lowest in the nation, has increased more than 6½ times in the eight years since it changed its law.

From an annual average of fewer than 4,000 divorces granted for adultery, the only permitted ground before 1967, state courts in 1974 processed nearly 55,000. Five additional grounds have been added: cruelty, desertion, imprisonment for three or more years and two types of legal separation for a minimum one-year period.

Other states have gone even further. Thirteen of them and the Virgin Islands have eliminated traditional divorce grounds altogether.

In Vermont, a free legal services program opened the same year the state reduced waiting periods for uncontested divorces from two years to six months. A state court official says these are the main reasons Vermont's divorce rate went up 155 per cent between 1969 and 1973.

The new laws and legal aid are not the only reasons for the rate increases. Divorce is becoming a more acceptable, if unpleasant, alternative for unhappy couples. Such attitudinal changes are difficult to measure, but there is no question that American society views divorce differently than it did even a decade ago. Thus even in some states where laws have not been changed, divorce rates are up. Rhode Island—about 65 per cent Roman Catholic—has not greatly loosened its strict divorce laws recently. Yet while the U.S. divorce rate went up 38 per cent between 1969 and 1973, Rhode Island's rose 86 per cent.

During the same period, divorce was up 53 per cent in Mississippi, 96 per cent in Arkansas and 58 per cent in West Virginia. The ABA's divorce law committee has not identified relaxation of divorce laws in those states either.

The recent wave of national reform began with the passage in 1969 of a pioneering California divorce law that rejected the concept of a "guilty" party and replaced it with the idea that the marriage, not the parties to it, should be placed on trial.

Divorces granted in California rose quickly in the first year of the new law, from 81,546 in 1969 to 112,942 in 1970, a 40 per cent increase. The 1970 California rate of 5.7 per 1,000 population dropped to 5.4 in 1971 and 1972 but rose again in 1973 to 5.7.

Divorce rate experts now say the sudden upsurge in 1970 was due not to the more liberal philosophy of the new law. It came from a reduction in waiting times from one year to six months, and from fewer Californians seeking divorces in neighboring Nevada and Mexico.

They say that Nevada's divorce rate dropped from 24 per 1,000 in 1969 to 15.6 in 1973, a 35 per cent decline. Mexico closed its doors to foreigners seeking quick divorces in 1971.

The philosophy of the California reform is not yet officially reflected in the divorce laws of states like New York and Rhode Island. Yet its acceptance elsewhere apparently influences judges.

"At one time we took the position that the state was part of the institution of marriage and we tried very hard to keep them together," said Brooklyn's Justice Heller. "We don't do that any more. Today we ask: Is this a dead marriage? If it is, we try to put it at rest, give it a decent burial."

Writing Assignment

After reading the preceding articles on divorce, write a short essay covering the following points:

1. How do you personally react to the article?
2. What do you think is the explanation for the relatively high divorce rate in the United States?
3. Compare the attitude toward divorce in your country with that of the United States.

The Question of Alimony

The word *alimony* comes from the Latin word *alimonia* meaning *sustenance,* which in turn is derived from the Latin verb *alere, to nourish.* Webster's *Third New International Dictionary* defines *alimony* as "an allowance made to a woman for her support out of the estate or income of her husband (or to a husband from the property of the wife). . . . "

Essentially, alimony is money paid under a court order by one former spouse to the support of the other. Child support is a similar outlay for the children. For tax purposes, alimony is counted as income for the recipient and a deduction for the payer.

It isn't hard to understand why divorced husbands complain about alimony. The money alone would be reason enough, but there's more to it than that. Rightly or wrongly, a man may feel that the payment of alimony is his wife's way of getting back at him, and that she wants it to hurt. It is an emotional punch that carries all the resentment and anger pent up during the months or years when the marriage was turning sour.

Now, women may have the tables turned on them. A relatively new idea about alimony that is gaining ground is that it should be available, at least in theory, to men as well as women, depending on which partner has the greater earning power and which the greater need. In more than thirty of the fifty states, this is now the case. In others, including New York State, where it is against the law for a man to receive alimony, laws to take the sex bias out of alimony have been introduced.

Apropos of the possibility of alimony for men, the following article tells of a bill before the Nevada State Legislature which would allow alimony for men as well as women. This bill, no doubt, is a consequence of the campaign for equal rights for women.

MEN MAY RECEIVE
ALIMONY

CARSON CITY, Nev. (AP)—A bill to allow alimony for men as well as women passed the state Senate Judiciary Committee Monday despite objections that it could be an undeserved break for "shiftless" males.

The motion to allow alimony payments for both men and women passed on a 5-2 vote. The measure was then sent to the

Senate floor for final action in the upper house.

Under the bill, factors such as a man's income, his wife's ability to support herself and other elements would be considered before a male could receive alimony.

Sen. Carl Dodge led opposition to the bill, pushing unsuccessfully for an amendment to grant alimony to men only if they're clearly unable to provide for their own support. "I can buy that, but take the shiftless guy," said Dodge, R-Fallon. "I don't want him in court trying to get alimony off his wife. I don't particularly care to make our law fully reciprocal."

Sen. Norman Hilbrecht, D-Las Vegas, countered that Dodge's proposed amendment could create an unconstitutional "dual standard."

Sen. Thomas Wilson, D-Reno, agreed that Dodge's proposal might not survive a court test under equal protection provisions of the Constitution.

Glossary

Apropos: concerning; with regard to
(AP): Associated Press
Nev.: Nevada (State of)
Shiftless: lazy, unwilling to work
Sen.: Senator
R-Fallon: Republican from Fallon County
D-Las Vegas: Democrat from Las Vegas County
D-Reno: Democrat from Reno County
"I can buy that": "I can accept that."

Writing Assignments

1. What is the status of alimony in your home country? How would your parents and friends react to a news item like the one above if it were to appear in their local newspaper? Write a short essay based on these questions.

2. Write a short essay stating whether you are *for* or *against* the proposed bill. Give reasons for your position.

Superstitions

If you have any of the following objects,

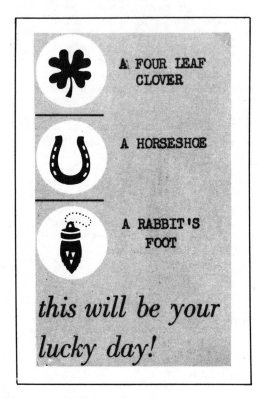

SUPERSTITIONS

Every culture has its own fundamental beliefs, and some of these can be classified as *superstitions*. A superstition is a belief founded on irrational feelings, especially of fear—also, any rite or practice inspired by such belief. Here are some superstitions about having good luck or bad luck that are fairly common in the United States:

1. It is lucky for a person to find a four-leaf clover. (Most have only three leaves.)
2. A horseshoe hung over a door brings good luck.
3. A rabbit's foot brings good luck to the bearers. Some people carry their "lucky rabbit's foot" around with them.
4. A black cat crossing your path will bring you bad luck.

5. He who breaks a mirror will have seven years of hard luck.
6. The number thirteen is very unlucky. Friday the thirteenth is a particularly unlucky day. Many hotels of more than twelve stories skip number thirteen when they number the floors in the building.
7. Knock-on-wood. This expression (and physical action) is used to avoid bad luck. The belief is that if one does not knock or rap on something made of wood his good fortune may not last. For example: "I haven't been sick since I was ten years old. Knock on wood." The person then knocks on a wooden object.
8. If you accidentally spill some salt you throw a bit of the salt over your left shoulder with your right hand. This will avoid your having bad luck in the near future.

Glossary
superstition (noun): a belief founded on irrational feelings, especially of fear; also, any rite or practice inspired by such belief
superstitious (adjective): disposed to believe in or be influenced by superstitions
bearer: the person carrying something
hard luck: bad luck

Questions for Discussion
1. Do you have any superstitions? If so, what are they?
2. Do you have friends or acquaintances who are superstitious? If so, what are they superstitious about?
3. Do you consider yourself to be a superstitious person? What is your reason for saying yes or no?

Writing Assignment
1. Describe a few superstitions that you or someone else may have.
2. How do you feel about superstitions and people who are superstitious?

The Loch Ness Monster—Fact or Fiction

Monsters have always held a peculiar fascination for humans. Through the years legends have developed about mysterious creatures being sighted in various parts of the world. Monster enthusiasts have searched the mountains of the Pacific Northwest in the United States looking for Sasquatch, or Bigfoot, a giant, manlike creature who supposedly lives there. Others have tried, with a similar lack of success, to track down the yeti, or Abominable Snowman said to reside somewhere in the higher elevations of the Himalayas, a mountain chain in northern India, Tibet, and Nepal. But perhaps the most sought after creature of them all is the famous Loch Ness monster.

Loch is a Scottish word meaning *lake.* One of the most well-known lakes in Scotland is called Loch Ness, Britain's largest, deepest and most mysterious body of fresh water, measuring 24 miles long and 700 feet deep over much of its length. Unlike Loch Lomond, known for its bonny[1] shores and bright sunshine, Loch Ness is famous for a prehistoric monster said to reside in its dark, chilly waters.

The Loch Ness monster, or Nessie as it is familiarly called, was first reported in 565 by St. Columba, who witnessed the funeral of a man who had been killed by a water beast out of Loch Ness. Ever since then, people have been keeping an eye on the waters, hoping to catch sight of the resident monster.

In 1972, an American research group began taking photographs in Loch Ness with a specially developed high-speed camera. More recently, photographs were taken forty feet below the Loch's surface with the help of a strobe-flash light. These photographs were unveiled at Edinburgh, Scotland in December 1975. One picture showed a large mass with what some experts identified as a flipper-like[2] appendage. Some scientists seem to be convinced of the existence of a large creature in the lake. They believe the Loch Ness monster—estimated to be thirty to forty feet long—may be a prehistoric reptile, dating back seventy million years. The monster may be an example of what is known as a living fossil. Sharks as fossils go back even prior to the time of dinosaurs.

But scientists from the British Museum found the pictures too fuzzy[3] for accurate interpretation, and others questioned the controls under which the photographs were made.

Today, as every day, tourists and others still keep a watch on the lake, hoping to catch a glimpse of that which inspired this durable

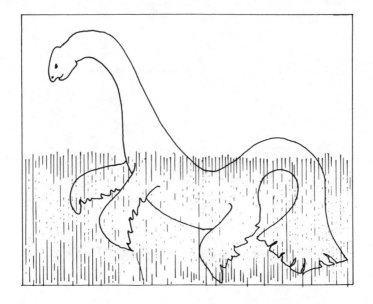

Is this the Loch Ness monster?

legend of a sea monster. The Loch Ness Investigation Bureau says there have been more than four thousand claimed sightings of horned sea serpents and all the other grotesque[4] forms the mind can imagine.

Glossary

[1]bonny: nice looking; cheerful

[2]flipper-like: like a flipper (Seals and dolphins have flippers.)

[3]fuzzy: blurred, unclear

[4]grotesque: odd or unnatural in appearance; fantastically ugly

Writing Assignment

Some people claim that legends and myths contain a kernel of truth, and that they express certain universal characteristics of human beings—characteristics common to all cultures.

1. What is your opinion as to the existence of a Loch Ness monster? Give reasons for your opinion.
2. Is there a story or legend in your country that is in any way similar to that of the Loch Ness monster? If so, write about it.
3. Tell a story or legend from your country or region that borders on the supernatural.

SECTION
F

Complex Sentences and Concise Writing

UNIT 11   UNDERSTANDING COMPLEX SENTENCES

Principal and Subordinate Clauses

Mature writing is often characterized by complex sentences. A complex
sentence is nothing but several simple sentences combined in various
ways. One part of the complex sentence functions as a nucleus to
which are attached other structures called *clauses.* Take the following
sentence, for example:

> *My parents, who happened to like flowers very much, named me
> Hui-Lan, which means "beautiful orchid" in Chinese, in hopes
> that I, too, would grow up appreciating the beauty of nature.*

The above sentence consists of a *principal clause* (the nucleus) which
is really an independent sentence that can be extracted from the whole
without any changes at all, as follows:

> *My parents named me Hui-Lan in hopes that I, too, would grow
> up appreciating the beauty of nature.*

The remaining parts of our complex sentence are known as *subordinate
clauses.* Subordinate clauses are made from sentences which have been

shortened or modified in some way and joined to (or embedded in) the principal clause. Subordinate clauses cannot usually stand alone as grammatical sentences because they begin with words like *who, which,* etc., or have had essential parts deleted. If we extract the subordinate clauses exactly as they appear in our complex sentence above, they would look as follows:

> Subordinate clauses:
> *who happened to like flowers very much*
> *which means "beautiful orchid" in Chinese*

Although they do have subject and predicate forms, subordinate clauses can be generally recognized by the fact that they cannot stand alone as a complete sentence.

Before we begin combining subordinate clauses with a principal clause, it may be instructive for us to proceed in reverse order; that is, to practice breaking down long sentences into their component parts.

Exercise 1   Sentence Breakdown. Break down each of the following complex sentences into their simple components. List the principal clause first. Then convert each subordinate clause into the simple sentence it is derived from. Be sure to write complete, grammatical sentences.

Example: In 307 B.C., the son of the great Indian emperor Ashoka came to Ceylon (now called Sri Lanka) as a Buddhist missionary to preach a new religion so exacting that not even an image of the Buddha was permitted in its places of worship.

The son of the great Indian emperor Ashoka came to Ceylon in 307 B.C. to preach a new religion.
Ceylon is now called Sri Lanka.
The son of the emperor came as a Buddhist missionary.
The new religion was very exacting.
Not even an image of the Buddha was permitted in its places of worship.

1.   Mr. Nelson, whose daughter Jack is in love with, does not trust young men, whom he considers to be foolish and unreliable, perhaps influenced by memories of his own youth.

2. Mr. Morgan, who teaches English Literature here in California, married Susie Brown, whose father owns that new restaurant on Broadway which opened just recently.

3. The Statue of Liberty, whose torch has symbolized freedom and economic opportunity for millions of immigrants, most of whom viewed America as the land of plenty, was a gift from the people of France to the United States.

4. America's language, like America itself, has undergone a vigorous growth and development, which has tended to widen the differences between the English of England—from whence America's language came—and that of America.

5. The organization's members, who had received orders to launch a strike against the railroad company, were quickly and quietly arrested by the FBI, tipped off by an informer who had infiltrated the leftist organization.

6. The Apollo XI astronauts, two of whom were the first men to set foot on the surface of the moon, were enthusiastically welcomed aboard the aircraft carrier which had been assigned to the recovery operation to pick up the returning space heroes.

7. In refusing to grant an immediate stay against the controversial underground blast scheduled to go off within a week, the Appeals Court said it was dealing only with the legal question of disclosure of information.

A Word About Principal Clauses

Before going on to practice sentence combining something more has to be said about principal or main clauses. It is true, of course, that any clause can function as the main one; however, the writer must be certain that what appears as the principal clause—as judged by the reader—is actually the one intended. In other words, the writer must be careful not to mislead the reader; he must be sure the clause he gives most prominence to is the one he wishes to stress or focus upon—the one that, from the viewpoint of the writer, is the most important point of the sentence.

Let us take note of the principal clause of the following sentence written by a student from Taiwan:

> *The island of Taiwan, which exemplifies all the best of old and modern China, has an area of 35,000 square km. and a population of about fifteen million.*

From the way this sentence is written one would assume the principal clause to be that which refers to area and population. However, it was obvious from the rest of the essay that the student did not intend to focus upon those points. What he really intended was the following:

> *The island of Taiwan, with an area of 35,000 square km. and a population of about fifteen million, exemplifies all the best of old and modern China.*

Let us look at another example of faulty subordination in which the writer unintentionally fails to focus upon the most important point.

(not good)
> *I finished the compulsory education sequence, which is required of all youngsters under the age of sixteen, and it took me nine years.*

(better)
> *It took me nine years to finish the compulsory education sequence, which is required of all youngsters under the age of sixteen.*

It is for the writer to decide what the main point of the complex sentence will be. Suppose one has two facts, as follows:

1. The San Joaquin Valley is one of the richest agricultural regions in the U.S.
2. The San Joaquin Valley is conveniently located in central California, midway between Los Angeles and San Francisco.

Either of these facts could serve as the main clause. If one wishes to emphasize the importance of the San Joaquin Valley itself, he might write:

> *Conveniently located in central California, midway between Los Angeles and San Francisco, the San Joaquin Valley is one of the richest agricultural regions in the U.S.*

But should the writer wish to consider location to be most important, he or she would write:

> *The San Joaquin Valley, one of the richest agricultural regions in the U.S., is conveniently located in central California, midway between Los Angeles and San Francisco.*

In final analysis, then, it is the writer who decides which clause(s) to subordinate and which to treat as the principal one.

Sentence Combining

We have just said that a complex sentence consists of several simple ones combined in various ways. The simple sentences may be combined using relatives (*who, which,* etc.), words of comparison and contrast (*but, like, in contrast to,* etc.) and other words used to link clauses, rather than stringing them together with several *ands.* As an example, let us take a sentence you were asked to break down previously. The breakdown would probably be as follows:

> *America's language has undergone a vigorous growth and development.*
> *America itself has undergone a vigorous growth and development.*
> *This growth and development has tended to widen the differences between the English of England and the English of America.*
> *America's language came from England.*

With the exception of the first sentence (the main clause) the above can be converted into subordinate clauses as follows:

> like
> ∧ *America itself ~~has undergone a vigorous growth and~~*
>   which
> *~~development. This growth and development~~ has tended to widen*
>   ∧
>   that
> *the differences between the English of England and ~~the English~~*
>   where   ∧
> *of America. America's language came from ~~England.~~*
>   ∧

With the above changes our modified sentences can now be combined as follows:

> *America's language, like America itself, has undergone a vigorous growth and development, which has tended to widen the differences between the English of England—where America's language came from—and that of America.*

Exercise 2   Combine each set of simple sentences so as to make one complex sentence. Use relatives and make other reductions as

appropriate. The principal clause is listed first, in boldface (dark)
letters.

Example: **Hawaii was discovered in 1778 by Captain Cook.**
              Hawaii consists of eight principal islands.
              Cook was the first westerner to visit these Pacific islands.
              Hawaii, which consists of eight principal islands, was
                discovered in 1778 by Captain Cook, (who was) the
                first westerner to visit these Pacific islands.

1. **Mary Wilson won the annual teaching award.**
    Mary Wilson teaches sixth grade at Kratt Elementary School.
    The award is given for outstanding service to students.
2. **Hawaii was settled by Polynesian people from Tahiti.**
    Hawaii is often called the "island paradise."
    The Polynesians sailed across the Pacific in large canoes.
3. **A hormone has been synthesized for the first time.**
    This hormone is responsible for growth in the human body.
    It was synthesized by research scientists at the Medical Center.
4. **William Faulkner's *Two Soldiers* is one of the finest short stories**
        ever written in America.
    The story is about an 8-year-old farm boy.
    The boy's older brother goes off to enlist in the army.
5. **Larry Francis has won the award for community service.**
    Mr. Francis is a customer service manager in Chicago.
    Mr. Francis coaches a little league baseball team in Chicago.
    Mr. Francis has won the award two years in a row.
6. **The new governor of Texas has proposed new legislation to solve**
        the current financial crisis.
    The new governor was confronted with a deficit budget.
    The previous governor was (also) confronted with a deficit budget.
7. **The award for the best short story was won by James Robinson.**
    Robinson is a young author.
    Robinson really knows how to write a suspenseful tale.
    This is according to the editor of *Literary Review.*
8. **Captain Kane will be asked to testify in the court martial trial next**
        week.
    Captain Kane is the company commander.
    Captain Kane claims he gave no unlawful order to Lt. Smith.

Exercise 3   Combine each set of simple sentences to form one complex sentence. Use connectives (conjunctions) and substitute words (pronouns) as appropriate. The principal clause is listed first, in bold-face (dark) type.

Example: **Professor Chomsky attempts to describe the deep structure of sentences.**
Earlier students of language did not attempt to do this.
Earlier students were content to merely describe usage.
Professor Chomsky, unlike earlier students of language who were content to merely describe usage, attempts to describe the deep structure of sentences.

1. **Nathaniel Hawthorne wrote several novels which deal with the gloomy spirit of Puritanism.**
    Hawthorne was an American novelist and short-story writer.
    Many of Hawthorne's short stories deal with the gloomy spirit of Puritanism.

2. **The state of emergency affects the capital city and the provincial area around it.**
    The state of emergency was declared after new disorders broke out late this morning.
    About a third of the country's nine million people live in the capital city and the provincial area around it.

3. **Successful candidates for the job will be chosen by a special committee.**
    The committee will consist of seven employees of the company.
    At least three of the committee members must be under thirty years of age.

4. **The Suez Canal is important because it represents a short route between the Far East and western Europe.**
    The Suez Canal is important for both Egypt and other maritime nations.
    The Suez Canal has always been a vital region in peace as in war.

5. **American submarines are assigned to keep open shipping lanes and to escort convoys.**
    Soviet subs are not assigned to do this.
    Soviet subs are used to keep track of fishing vessels and to gather strategic information.

6. **The university will definitely be affected by the new ruling.**
    The university has no fixed policy regarding part-time instructors.
    The community colleges (also) have no fixed policy regarding
        part-time instructors.
7. **In Spain, many people in the small towns are escaping to the cities.**
    In some parts of the U.S. many people in small towns are (also)
        escaping to the cities.
    These people hope to find better economic opportunity in the
        cities.
8. **The racing cars were now thundering down the track at speeds in
    excess of 200 miles per hour.**
    The racing cars had been slowed just minutes before by the yellow
        caution flag.
    This rate of speed (200 miles per hour) was not thought possible just
        a few years ago.

UNIT 12   TOWARD CONCISE WRITING

Deletion of Relative Pronouns

We have already stated that conciseness is characteristic of much good writing. Conciseness is partially achieved by combining simple sentences into complex ones through the use of relative clauses. In doing so, however, the beginning writer sometimes ends up with too many *wh-* words. This tends to produce awkward sounding sentences and works against conciseness. Note the effect of having three *wh-* forms in the following sentences:

> *Isaac Newton,* **who was** *born on Christmas day, 1642,* **which was** *the year of Galileo's death, came from a family of farmers* **who were** *small but independent.*

But with a few deletions and one other change the above sentence can be made more concise, as follows:

> *Isaac Newton, born on Christmas day, 1642, the year of Galileo's death, came from a family of small but independent farmers.*

Deletion of *wh-* words plus *be* in restrictive clauses

In restrictive relative clauses containing a form of *be,* both the *wh-* form and *be* are often deleted. This deletion, where permitted, is a useful device for shortening clauses, thus making the sentence as a whole more concise. The following illustrate deletion in restrictive clauses: (The part that may be deleted is enclosed in parentheses.)

a.   *The white hunter (who is) shooting the tiger is Dick Brown.*
b.   *The five men (that were) accused of the crime were innocent.*
c.   *The problem (which is) being investigated now is very complex.*
d.   *The man (who is) bored with his job never smiles.*
e.   *The guest (who is) in room 227 wants a taxi.*
f.   *The new law (which was) put in effect just recently is a good one.*

Exercise 1   Reconstruct each sentence by filling in the relative pronoun and the form of *be* that has been deleted.

Example: *The man* _____*who was*_____ *chasing the bear is Tom Brown.*

1. The plane _____ now landing on runway two is TWA flight 117.

2. The package _____ from Aunt Harriet _____ marked "fragile" contains strawberry jam.

3. The man _____ talking to you just now is my uncle Charlie.

4. The boy _____ desperately trying to catch the bus stumbled and fell.

5. The car _____ traveling at high speed crashed into a tree.

6. The man _____ seen jumping from a window turned out to be the owner of the house.

7. A man _____ happy in his job is at peace with the world.

8. Sociologists _____ studying the problem agree that land _____ available for living space is a critical factor.

9. The new cigarette lighters _____ made of plastic will not rust.

10. All students _____ waiting to register must fill out the forms _____ distributed earlier.

11. The experiment _____ being performed now is very dangerous.

12. This is the crisp center _____ lavished in the milk chocolate _____ smothered in almonds.

13. The new bridge _____ being built by the Thompson Company will cost two million dollars.

Deletion in nonrestrictive clauses[1]

We have just noted the process of deletion in restrictive clauses. This deletion also occurs in nonrestrictive clauses and is especially common in noun phrases in apposition—*Bob Brown, (who is) the vice-president, wants. . . .* This kind of deletion also occurs frequently in other kinds of constructions, as illustrated by the following sentences:

a.   *John Hunt, (who is) the oldest resident of the town, says he remembers the incident well.*

b.   *A huge fish, (which was) either a shark or barracuda, glided silently toward the swimmers.*

c.   *Mr. Jones, (who was) tormented by the memory of his dead wife, became very melancholy.*

d.   *The young soldiers, (who were) tired from the long hike, dropped to the ground for a welcome rest.*

e.   *State Highway 168, (which is) now being repaired, will be back in service in a few days.*

Exercise 2   Put parentheses around the words that can be deleted. Underline those *wh-* words which cannot be omitted.

Example: *James Nails, (who is) the new vice-president, is a tough administrator.*

1.   The Empire State Building, which is still one of the world's tallest office structures, attracts thousands of tourists every year.

2.   Botswana, which is another African republic that has undergone a name change, is located just north of the Union of South Africa.

3.   The recently dismissed employees, who were denied their constitutional rights, are now appealing to the courts.

4.   The testimony of the witness, which was described as being vulgar and highly offensive, was stricken from the record.

5.   Miss Cha-Cha Lamour, whom the beauty contest judges are looking over right now, is sure to be declared the winner.

6.   The two youths, who were near exhaustion from many hours in the water, swam wearily toward the island which loomed above them.

---

[1]For the difference between restrictive and nonrestrictive clauses see *Preparation for Writing,* Section E.

7. Richard likes knitting, which is a skill he learned during the war when youngsters knitted sweaters for the troops overseas.

8. We sincerely hope that this alternative, which is for all students who desire to use it, will be approved by the principal.

9. The K and B Construction Company, which is now experiencing labor trouble, showed a loss in earnings for the last quarter.

10. Those two students, whom the teacher was talking to just now, received the highest grades in the class.

11. New disorders broke out this morning when students, who were barred from staging a planned rally, poured into downtown streets shouting slogans.

12. The Taj Mahal, which is a marble mausoleum which was built for the emperor's favorite wife, is considered one of the world's most beautiful buildings.

Exercise 3 (more of the same) The deletion of the *wh-* word plus *be* is particularly indicated in sentences containing two or more clauses to avoid a bulky, awkward style. Make the following sentences more concise by placing parentheses around those words which can be omitted. (Not all of the *wh-* words can be deleted.)

> *Example*:   *Smith said the mortgage on his New York house, (which he) bought in 1970, was paid off in 1975, while his Florida home, (which he) purchased in 1971, has not yet been paid off.*

1. William Faulkner's *Two Soldiers,* which is a novel that is about an 8-year-old farm boy who lives in Mississippi, is one of the finest short stories ever written in America.

2. *Soviet Life* magazine, which is a slick publication in English which is distributed in this country by the Russians, is part of a cultural exchange program which was worked out between the U.S. and Russia.

3. The Republic of Yerba Buena, which produces some of the best coffee in the world, is faced with an over-supply of coffee beans, which are its only natural resource.

4. Carol White, who is the dead man's widow, was seen entering a black Cadillac, which was driven by a man who was wearing a black cap of the type which is usually worn by chauffeurs.

The purpose of the following exercise is to gain practice in writing complex sentences, making them concise by omitting unnecessary words wherever possible, without changing the meaning or emphasis intended.

Exercise 4   Combine each set into one complex sentence, using relative clauses in their full form. Then make deletions and other changes to make the sentence more concise. The principal clause appears in boldface (dark) letters.

Example: **Chia-Yi is a friendly little town.**
I grew up in Chia-Yi.
The town is located in the southern part of Taiwan.
Taiwan is the island which was formerly known as Formosa.

Chia-Yi, where I grew up, is a friendly little town, ~~which is~~ located in the southern part of Taiwan, ~~which is~~ the island ~~which was~~ formerly known as Formosa.

1. **Yesterday, Jack Bishop approved the new regulations.**
    Jack Bishop is Administrator of social services.
    The new regulations were scheduled to go into effect May 1.

2. **World-famed Yosemite National Park will be the site of this year's meeting of the Audubon Society.**
    The national park's scenery has inspired poets and nature lovers over the years.
    The Audubon Society is an organization which is dedicated to bird watching and conservation.

3. **I was pleased to receive your letter dated April 15.**
    The letter was forwarded to me by Mr. Johnson.
    Mr. Johnson is our sales manager.
    In your letter you expressed interest in our products.

4. **The FBI quietly arrested the club members as they arrived for the meeting.**
    The FBI had been tipped off by an informer.
    The meeting had been called by the executive committee.
    The informer had infiltrated the leftist organization.

5. **Bill Jones has written a new novel.**
    Bill Jones is a promising young author.
    The new novel is said to be his best effort so far.

Deletion and Front Shift

We have just seen how long sentences can be made more concise through deletion and other changes. A further stylistic variation can be effected through deletion and front shift. Note that the following sentence

> *The San Joaquin Valley, which is located in central California, midway between Los Angeles and San Francisco, is one of the richest agricultural areas in the country.*

can be profitably changed to:

> *Located in central California, midway between Los Angeles and San Francisco, the San Joaquin Valley is one of the richest agricultural areas in the country.*

This deletion plus front shift is a useful device to keep intact one's main clause, thus avoiding fragmentation caused by the insertion of one or more relative clauses. This technique of front shifting is one alternative to keep in mind when sentences begin to become long-winded and awkward.

Exercise 5   This exercise, like the sentence below, contains only *nonrestrictive* relative clauses. Whenever possible, delete the relative plus *be* and shift the remaining clause to front position. Where deletion is not permitted, rewrite the sentence as is. (For help in deciding whether deletion is permitted see page 154.)

Example: Mary Brown, who was terribly embarrassed, excused herself and left the room.
   a.   *Mary Brown, **terribly embarrassed**, excused herself and left the room.*
   b.   ***Terribly embarrassed**, Mary Brown excused herself and left the room.*

1. Ted Smith, who is now at home in Vermont, is able to continue writing novels.
2. The history professor, who was offended by the student's remark, walked out of the room.
3. Dolores Simpson, whom the FBI is now investigating, has been accused of being a spy.

4. Joe Sampson, who had been denied membership in the Sports Club, made a claim of racial discrimination.
5. John Hunter, who had been sworn in as a deputy sheriff, easily captured the escaped convict.
6. Mr. Snodgrass, who was educated in London, speaks with a British accent.
7. Mrs. Bluegrass, who was angered by the remark, got red in the face.
8. The night nurse, who was alarmed by the great loss of blood, ran quickly for the doctor.
9. The huge trees, which had been uprooted by the fierce storm, lay on the ground like fallen giants.

Exercise 6   (more of the same) Rewrite each sentence twice. First, delete the relative and *be*. Then rewrite a second time and shift the shortened clause to front position.

Example: The Palmer Hotel, which was built eighty years ago by R. Palmer, is a good example of early American architecture.

    a. *The Palmer Hotel, **built eighty years ago** by R. Palmer, is a good example of early American architecture.*

    b. ***Built eighty years ago** by R. Palmer, the Palmer Hotel is a good example of early American architecture.*

1. Richard H. Wilson, who is now an ex-president and private citizen, is busy writing his memoirs.
2. The old man, who was soon forgotten by his old friends and neighbors, continued to lead a lonely life.
3. The new American ambassador to England, who was speaking with his newly acquired British accent, gave his first public speech since his arrival in London.
4. John Coleman, who is a 1946 graduate of Harvard Law School, was at one time a law clerk to the late Supreme Court Justice Felix Frankfurter.
5. The Greek government, which is furious over the Turkish invasion of Cyprus, plans to expel the 4,000 U.S. troops based in Greece.
6. The government of Greece, which was powerless to intervene militarily against the Turks, took its case to the United Nations.

7. Mr. A. Bishop, who is now retired from his position as editor-in-chief of *Harper's Magazine*, is a contributing editor to the newly created monthly *Wednesday Review*.
8. The champion, who was wrapped in a heavy blue bathrobe, climbed into the ring with the agility of a mountain goat.
9. Timothy Brown, who was rescued from a man who was trying to drown him, had a joyous reunion with his mother at the New London Police Station.

More on front shifting

How can the following be combined into one sentence?

> *The appeals court said it was dealing only with the legal question of disclosure of information.*
> *The appeals court refused to grant an immediate stay against the controversial underground blast.*

One way is to use a relative clause, as follows:

> *The appeals court, which refused to grant an immediate stay against the controversial underground blast, said it was dealing only with the legal question of disclosure of information.*

Another way is to use *front shift* plus the preposition *in* as follows:

> ***In refusing to grant an immediate stay*** *against the controversial underground blast, the appeals court said it was dealing only with the legal question of disclosure of information.*

Front shifting is a very useful technique in that it avoids the splitting up of the noun phrase (*the appeals court*) and the verb (*said*), thus allowing the predicate to occur directly after the subject.

Exercise 7
Shorten and combine into a single sentence by front shifting the second sentence of each pair. Use the prepositions "in" or "by" as appropriate. Follow the example.

Example: **Mr. Harris has contradicted the testimony given by Mr. Johnson.** Mr. Harris denied he ever accepted a money bribe.
In denying he ever accepted a money bribe, Mr. Harris has contradicted the testimony given by Mr. Johnson.

1. *The President affirmed his support of the concept of government aid to the small farmer.* The President approved the new law just passed by Congress.
2. *The U.S. government has demonstrated support for the principle of arms reduction.* The U.S. government decided to reduce its military budget.
3. *Jones has made himself liable for perjury.* Jones admitted that he lied on the witness stand.
4. *The accused man has finally admitted he stole the jewelry because he was in need of money.* The accused man threw himself on the mercy of the court.
5. *The tobacco industry has tried to calm smokers' anxiety about lung cancer.* The tobacco industry proclaimed the wonders of its new micronite filters.
6. *The U.S. War Department had hoped to educate and thus "civilize" the American Indians on the reservation.* The U.S. War Department granted $10 a month to each participant for room and board in 1895.

Exercise 8
Restructure each sentence by front shifting. Follow the example.

Example: I had to wait in the airport for over four hours until they finally announced my flight. I was hungry and chilly from the too-strong air-conditioning.
Hungry and chilly from the too-strong air-conditioning, I had to wait in the airport for over four hours until they finally announced my flight.

1. *Hannibal and his African armies conquered major portions of Spain and Italy.* Hannibal is regarded by many as one of the greatest generals of all time.
2. *Hannibal won a great victory over the Romans in northern Italy.* Hannibal marched his army with African war elephants through the Alps to surprise the enemy.
3. *The music library has a large collection of recordings ranging from classical to pop and rock music.* The music library contains more than 35,000 record albums.
4. *Please send us your application request for the extension courses, both credit and noncredit, you wish to take next semester.* Please

send us this request at your earliest convenience, but no later than March of next year.

5. *Please send us a complete transcript of your high school studies properly translated into English.* Please do this in order not to waste time and create unnecessary confusion.

6. *A divorced husband in West Germany has sued his former wife for alimony to support him and their four children in his care.* This was West Germany's first such case.

7. *The disgruntled student drove his red sports car onto the grass lawn and parked it next to a large maple tree.* He was angry and upset because he had been denied permission to park in the reserved parking spaces.

Note: Caution must be exercised in using the technique of front shifting because not all relative clauses can be front shifted. The following is an example of a clause which *cannot* be front shifted:

> *That old camera, which Tom bought at an auction sale, takes big, beautiful pictures.*

Front shifting the above would result in an ungrammatical sentence:

> *#In buying [it] at an auction sale, that old camera takes big, beautiful pictures.*

Front shifting would be possible if the clause were in passive form (*which was bought by Tom at an auction sale*), but the result, though grammatical, would be awkward and unacceptable:

> *Bought by Tom at an auction sale, that old camera takes big, ...*

SECTION
G

Technical Writing and Term Paper Skills

UNIT 13   TECHNICAL WRITING

The Passive in Technical Writing

In technical writing the passive construction enjoys high frequency of occurrence, especially when the identity of the subject (actor or agent) is unknown or unimportant. Note the frequent use of the passive in the following example of technical writing:

On completion of test trial 1, the groups were subdivided into male study and control groups, and female study and control groups. The male study group received an initial estrogen implant at the age of 120 days. The estrogen pellets were implanted subcutaneously on the neck dorsally, by means of a pellet implanter. A second estrogen implant was given 14 days after the first implant. The female study group received testosterone pellets. As there were a number of deaths in the female study group resulting from the testosterone, the use of this group was discontinued after test trial 2.

Test trial 2 was commenced 15 days after the initial implants into the study groups; test trial 3 was carried out 15 days after test trial 2, when the rats were 150 days old. The day after the final test trial, two control males and two estrogenized male rats were randomly selected for purposes of physiological examination.

Writers sometimes avoid use of the passive by using impersonal or unspecified subjects such as *someone* or *people,* as in the following examples:

Someone announced that . . .

Active: One can argue that . . .

People recognize that . . .

An alternative to this use of unspecified subjects is to use the passive with *it* as the grammatical subject. Compare the following with the preceding examples:

It was announced that . . .

Passive: It can be argued that . . .

It is recognized that . . .

As a matter of fact, there are times when this construction effects a stylistic improvement over the active form. Compare:

Active: *Someone brought to the attention of the Committee **the fact that** the regulations controlling the disposal of State property do not apply to fraternities.*

Passive: *It was brought to the attention of the Committee **that** the regulations controlling the disposal of State property do not apply to fraternities.*

Exercise 1   Change each phrase to its equivalent passive form and complete the sentence in a logical way.

Examples: a.   Someone announced that . . .
It was announced that the tickets will cost $5.00.
b.   People believe that . . .
It is believed that Bill Smith is innocent.

1.   Everyone assumes that . . .
2.   Everyone recognizes that . . .
3.   One cannot deny that . . .
4.   One cannot say that . . .
5.   People often claim that . . .

6. One can argue that . . .
7. All of us well know that . . .
8. People have suggested that . . .
9. Everyone often takes for granted that . . .
10. Everyone understands that . . .
11. Some people think that . . .
12. Someone can show that . . .
13. Someone has reported that . . .
14. Someone has pointed out that . . .
15. Someone has rumored that . . .
16. Someone has demonstrated that . . .

More on the passive

There is a small class of verbs which can be changed into the passive construction in two ways, as follows:

> *We feel that education is the only answer to the problem.*
> a. *It is felt that education is the only answer to the problem.*
> b. *Education is felt to be the only answer to the problem.*

Exercise 2   Change each of the following sentences in the two ways shown in the example above:

1. Everyone assumes that William is innocent.
2. Someone has said that money is the root of all evil.
3. People have always known that the practice of medicine is an art and not a science.
4. Some people believe that passive resistance is the only alternative to violence.
5. They claim that the manuscript is over six hundred years old.
6. Some people say that women generally are not mechanically inclined.
7. Some people hold that crime prevention costs less than law enforcement.
8. Many people feel that passing stricter laws is the only solution to the problem.
9. Medical researchers have revealed that cholesterol is injurious to the blood vessels.
10. Nutrition experts have found that good eating habits contribute greatly to good health.

11. One expects that good citizens will report crimes to the police.
12. The law requires all citizens owning guns to register with the police.
13. Sociologists contend that economic frustration is at the root of all crime.
14. Some students say that writing exercises like this is a waste of time.

Writing Assignment
Write up an imaginary scientific experiment using the passive form wherever appropriate. State your hypothesis, describe the experiment, state the results, and make a conclusion.

Plagiarism

One of the cardinal sins in writing term papers and research reports is that of *plagiarism*—the passing off of someone else's work as your own. One kind of plagiarism is the use of someone else's facts or ideas without acknowledging the source. Sometimes students do this inadvertently, without realizing they are doing wrong. Of course, ideas or facts that are considered to be common knowledge do not have to be documented or acknowledged as to source. For example, that man first landed on the moon in 1969 is common knowledge.

A more flagrant violation of professional ethics, however, is the misappropriation of another man's exact phraseology; that is, the borrowing of someone's exact words without acknowledging the original author through use of the appropriate conventions for direct quotations.

Paraphrase: Introduction

In writing a term paper or research report one often depends on the writing of others as a source of facts and ideas. And since one should avoid the overuse of direct quotations the use of *paraphrasing* is heavily relied upon. Paraphrasing is the reporting of information composed and written by someone else. In essence, to paraphrase is to restate in one's own words what someone has said or written, retaining the basic meaning of the original. Paraphrasing usually involves simplification, with some of the details being omitted.

Of course, one should always acknowledge the source of his facts and ideas (except for facts and ideas which are common knowledge) in order to avoid the "sin" of plagiarism.

Some examples of paraphrasing

Of course a sentence can usually be paraphrased in a variety of ways while still preserving the basic meaning. Observe the following sentence and some of the ways it can be paraphrased:

Example 1

Original Version

Imposition of a requirement that, before a child can effectively participate in the educational program, he must already have acquired basic language skills is to make a mockery of public education.

Paraphrase 1

> *If we say that before a child can effectively participate in the educational program he must already possess basic language skills, we will only be mocking public education.*

Paraphrase 2

> *To require a child to already have basic language skills before he can effectively participate in the educational program is to ridicule public education.*

Paraphrase 3

> *If we impose a requirement which says that before a child can take part in the educational program he must already know the basics of language, we will be making a mockery of public education.*

Paraphrase 4

> *To make a regulation stating that a child has to acquire basic language skills before he can effectively participate in the educational program only serves to hold public education up to ridicule.*

Paraphrase 5

> *It would be a mockery of public education to insist that a child must already possess basic language skills in order to effectively participate in the educational program.*

It seems clear that learned, overly formal academic writing cries out for paraphrasing, which can usually be done without too much difficulty. But even ordinary passages containing simple language and written in a straightforward manner can be paraphrased, as illustrated in the next two examples:

Example 2

Original Version

The Weather in Hawaii

Hawaii has mild, tropical weather year round. There is almost never a time when it is too cold to swim or wander around enjoying the outdoors.

However, there are some variations. In summer it may be hot, with occasional afternoon rains. In winter and spring, you just might catch a Kona storm, but the rain is so gently warm that it is kind of fun to wander around in it, wearing as few clothes as the law allows.

Fall is the driest time of year.

From *Sunshine Magazine,* March 1976, p. 23.

Paraphrased Version

According to *Sunshine Magazine,*[1] Hawaii's tropical weather is so mild that one can go swimming and enjoy the outdoors all year round.

But the weather does vary somewhat according to the season. In summer, it sometimes gets hot, with an occasional shower in the afternoon. In winter and spring, there are a few rainstorms, which are known as "Kona" storms. However, the rain is so "gently warm" that most people enjoy walking around wearing just a minimum of clothes.

The article also reports that it hardly ever rains in the fall.

Note: The phrase, "gently warm" is quoted exactly. One is justified in using direct quotation when phrases or sentences are uniquely

---

[1] *Sunshine Magazine*, March 1976, p. 23.

worded. There are other reasons for using the exact words of an author. The beginning writer, however, is advised to use direct quotations sparingly.

Example 3

Original Version

Enlarging the National Council

When the National Council of Churches was founded in 1950, it was unthinkable that the Roman Catholic Church would join. Not only were the doctrines and attitudes of the Catholics different from those of the Protestant founders of the NCC, but the Catholic Church had the potential to dominate the organization by sheer force of numbers; there are 48 million Catholics in the U.S., and only 42 million members in the 33 Protestant and Orthodox denominations that make up the council.

But attitudes and doctrines have a way of changing and suddenly it appears likely that the American Catholic Church will become part of the NCC before the end of next year.

From *Religion Today*, November 6, 1976.

Paraphrased Version

Enlarging the National Council of Churches

No one thought the Roman Catholic Church would ever join the National Council of Churches when it was first founded back in 1950. Aside from differences of doctrine and attitudes between the two groups, another reason, according to *Religion Today*,[2] was the fact that the Catholic Church, with its large membership, had the potential to dominate any organization it might join. The Catholics in the U.S. number 48 million as against only 42 million in the Protestant and Orthodox denominations of the council.[3]

The article also states that attitudes and doctrines sometimes do change, and suggests that the American Catholic Church will probably become a member of the National Council by December of next year.

Example 4

And now for something a bit more challenging. Here is a paragraph from a statistics textbook and its corresponding paraphrase:

---

[2]*Religion Today*, November 6, 1976, p. 23.

[3]*Ibid.*

Descriptive Statistics

Frequently in social research a person will find himself in the position of having so much data that he cannot adequately absorb all of his information. He may have collected 200 questionnaires and be in the embarrassing position of having to ask, "What do I do with it all?" With so much information it would be exceedingly difficult for any but the most photographic minds to grasp intuitively what is in the data. The information must somehow or other be boiled down to a point at which the researcher can see what is in it; it must be summarized. By computing measures such as percentages, means, and standard deviations, it may be possible to reduce the data to manageable proportions. However, in summarizing data by substituting a very few measures for many numbers, certain information is inevitably lost, and, more serious, it is possible to obtain results which are misleading unless cautiously interpreted. Therefore the limitations of each summarizing measure must be clearly indicated.[4]

Paraphrased Version

Descriptive Statistics

The author of this text[4] says that when doing social research a person will often find himself with so much data that he cannot assimilate all of the information. He might have hundreds of questionnaires and, to his embarrassment, still wonder what to do with all that data. With such a large amount of information it would be very difficult, except for people with photographic minds, to easily understand what is in the data. According to Blalock, one must somehow condense and summarize the information so that the researcher can clearly see what it contains. One can reduce the data to manageable proportions by calculating percentages, means, and standard deviations.

However, when replacing many numbers with a very few measures, the author warns us, the loss of certain information is unavoidable; and, more importantly, one may get misleading results if the data are not interpreted with caution. For these reasons, one should clearly indicate the limitations of each summarizing measure.

The Art of Paraphrasing

It seems clear that paraphrasing is more of an art than a science. However, we would like to suggest some basic steps one might use in attempting to paraphrase a sentence or paragraph, namely:

---

[4]Taken from Hubert M. Blalock, Jr. *Social Statistics*, p. 4.

Step I.   Analyze for Basic Meaning
Step II.   Substitute and Simplify
Step III. Break Down Complex Sentences into Smaller Units
Step IV.   Put It All Together

I.   Analyze for Basic Meaning

Before one can paraphrase one must be certain one clearly understands what is written. After reading a sentence or paragraph one should go back and analyze for basic meaning. One should ask oneself the question, "Do I really understand what is being said?" One should go back and focus on unfamiliar words, structure markers, and the use of key words and expressions. Let us examine each step in detail.

A.   Unfamiliar words and expressions

Try to determine the meaning of unfamiliar words and phrases. Consult a good dictionary to find out the meaning of the unknown item in the context in which it appears. If still "in the dark," ask a knowledgeable friend for some sentences which illustrate the meaning in that context. For example, let us try to discover the meaning of the following word and verbal phrase:

1. *striking* (adjective)
    Definition: Noticeable; attracting attention.
    Defining sentences:
    > *With her long, black hair and sparkling eyes, Mrs. Walters is a **striking** woman.*
    > *There is a **striking** contradiction between what politicians say and what they do.*

2. *to make a mockery of* (verbal phrase)
    Definition: To ridicule; to treat with scorn.
    Defining sentence:
    > *To allow crime to go unpunished is to **make a mockery of** our system of justice.*

B.   Structure markers

One should be on the lookout for "structure markers"—words and phrases such as **like, unlike, in contrast, just as, despite,** and others. These words give the structural relationship of phrases

and clauses, and are esssential for the correct interpretation of a
sentence.

Examples: a.   *We think their culture is strange, **just** as they think ours
is peculiar.*
b.   ***Unlike** the Americans, the British are hesitant to
introduce themselves to strangers.*

C.   Key words

One should take note of key words and expressions and be sure
one understands their meaning. Because of the importance of key
words and expressions one should not rush to use a substitute. If
one cannot find a good synonym it is better to repeat the key word
of the original. Note the repetition of the terms "attitudes and
doctrines" in the sample paraphrase of Example 3 (page 168). In
paraphrasing one should not feel that one must change every.
important word or expression used in the original. In fact, one
sometimes finds there are a number of words and expressions for
which it is difficult to find satisfactory substitutes. Examples of
this are such terms as *impact, criteria, potential, reluctance, to
afford to do something*, and *to stigmatize*. It is also difficult to find
satisfactory substitutes for many technical terms. In such cases one
is justified in repeating the words and phrases of the original
rather than using a misleading substitute.

II.   Substitute and Simplify

A.   Lexical changes

1. *Common vs. Formal*
In paraphrasing one tries to substitute simple, commonly used
words and phrases for more formal, bookish, or less familiar
ones. Sometimes, of course, common words and expressions are
used in writing that is so straightforward and simple that
paraphrasing is hardly necessary. But should one come across
an unfamiliar expression, one usually feels more comfortable
substituting a more familiar one. For example, one might
substitute the verb *to ridicule* for the less familiar *to make a*

mockery of, as was done in Example 1 on page 166. Or one can write "Mr. Smith's *death,*" instead of the bookish "the *demise* of Mr. Smith."

2. *Alternate Constructions: Lexical Equivalents*
Another technique used in paraphrasing is to substitute a different construction having the same meaning. Here are two examples:

to succeed: *Lexical equivalents*
  a. *to be successful*
  b. *to have success*
  c. *to make a success of*

to be patient: *Lexical equivalents*
  a. *to have patience*
  b. *to (wait) patiently*

3. *Eliminating Redundancy*
Some expressions contain unnecessary words which can be eliminated. Some examples are:

a. *The fire **caused an explosion to occur.***
   *The fire **caused an explosion.***
b. *Thanks for your letter **informing me of the information about** the position.*
   *Thanks for your letter **informing me of** the position.*
c. *You will be responsible for **initiating the formulation of** new policy.*
   *You will be responsible for **formulating new policy.***

4. *Negative/Positive Restatement*
   a. *It is **not uncommon** to . . .*   →   *It is **common** to . . .*
   b. *It is **hardly fair** to give Bill an advantage.*   →   *It is **unfair** to give Bill an advantage.*
   c. *High medical costs are **not inappropriate** for wealthy countries.*   →   *High medical costs **are appropriate** for wealthy countries.*

B.   Grammatical changes

Various kinds of grammatical changes can be made without changing the basic meaning of a sentence. These changes include, but are not limited to, the following:

1. *Sentence Expansion*

   We can put back parts of a sentence the writer has omitted— words and phrases that are implicit but not stated. These or similar words have probably been omitted by a process called "reduction." Some examples are:

   a.   *Not knowing* *what else to do, the man called the police.*
   Because the man did not know *what else to do, he . . .*

   b.   *This procedure was effective in detecting foreign sub-stances, **thus eliminating** the need for further tests.*
   *This procedure . . . foreign substances, **and this (procedure) has eliminated** the need for further tests.*

2. *Alternate Construction*

   Use an alternate grammatical construction to express the same basic meaning. Some examples are:

   a.   ***Had** the government **not** dragged its feet, the problem would not exist today.*
   ***If** the government **had not** dragged its feet, . . .*

   b.   ***Imposition of** a requirement that, before a child . . .*
   ***If we impose** a requirement that, . . .*
   ***To impose** a requirement that, . . .*
   ***Imposing** a requirement that, . . .*

3. *Nominalization[5] and Reverse Paraphrasing*

   The process of changing a clause or sentence into the form of a noun phrase is called "nominalization." This and its reverse process are useful techniques for paraphrasing. Some examples are:

   a.   *No one wants to do this job, **which consumes time**.*
   *No one wants to do this **time-consuming** job.*

---

[5]For work on nominalization see Section F in *Preparation for Writing: Grammar*, a companion text to this volume.

b.   *The **unanticipated** price increases caused more unemployment.*
*The price increases, **which were not anticipated**, caused more unemployment.*

c.   *Mr. Jones denied any **corporate wrongdoing**.*
*Mr. Jones denied **that the corporation had done** any **wrong**.*

4. *Word Order Change*
The English language permits a great deal of flexibility in word order, and this kind of change is often utilized in paraphrasing. However, one should not change the word order just for the sake of change, or merely to disguise the form of a sentence in order to avoid plagiarism. Changes should be made with a view toward simplifying the structure or to accommodate alternate constructions. The judicious use of word order changes can often make a sentence easier for the reader to understand. Such changes include the following:

a.   Changes in the position of adverbial phrases (front shifting)
*The development of the embryo during nine months of pregnancy can now be observed **with this new technology**.*
***With this new technology**, the development of the embryo during nine months of pregnancy can now be observed.*

b.   Rearrangement of principal and subordinate clauses
*These results may be viewed as "positive" if the contaminating substance **can be detected by the Mersene process**.*
***If the Mersene process can detect** the contaminating substance, we may view these results as "positive."*

c.   Changes from active to passive, and vice versa
*We can now **reveal** the prenatal existence of man clearly and in sharp detail.*
*The prenatal existence of man can now **be revealed** with clarity and sharpness of detail.*

III. Break Down Complex Sentences into Smaller Units

A.   Smaller units

Long, complex sentences can usually be more easily understood if they are broken down into smaller units. To do this, the following procedure is recommended:

1. Locate the principal clause[6] and write it down.
2. Find the subordinate (dependent) clauses and write them down as independent sentences, each with a subject and predicate.
3. Arrange the sentences in logical order.

Breaking down a complex sentence in this manner should make it easier to get at the meaning of the sentence.

B. Sample breakdown

Unanticipated price increases have, in certain South American countries as well as in the United States, generated increased temporary employment, just as unanticipated declines in the rate of price increase caused temporary rises in unemployment in the past.

Principal clause:

Unanticipated price increases have generated increased temporary employment.

Subordinate clauses:

These price increases occurred in certain South American countries and in the United States.
Unanticipated declines in the rate of price increase occurred in the past.
These declines caused temporary rises in unemployment.

IV. Putting It All Together

The final step is to recombine and reorganize the sentences, incorporating all the changes and making last-minute adjustments as necessary. Of course, sources have to be acknowledged with such phrases as "the author states," "according to . . . ," and others. For example, the sentence above, which was broken down into smaller units, can now be recombined as follows:

The author states that unanticipated price increases occurred both in the United States and in certain South American

---

[6]For work on principal and subordinate clauses, see Unit 11.

countries. These price increases have caused increased temporary employment. Likewise, unanticipated declines in the rate of price increase in the past caused temporary rises in unemployment.

Paraphrasing overly formal language

Some writers, college professors and administrators among others, are often guilty of using learned, overly formal words and phrases in place of simple, common ones. They often use overly formal, complex sentence patterns where more informal, simpler constructions would give the same message. For example, a bank manager might write:

Dear Sir:

We wish to inform you that the amount of funds remaining in your checking account was not sufficient to cover the total amount of the checks written by you during the month of April.

Admittedly this kind of overly formal language may be appropriate for some kinds of writing—that used by diplomats, for example. But the above sentence can be paraphrased and simplified as follows:

Dear Sir:

Please be advised that your checking account was overdrawn in the month of April.

Practice exercises

The proof of the pudding is always in the eating. Try to put to use some of the preceding suggestions in doing the series of exercises that follow.

Overly formal language

Exercise 3   Paraphrase each of the following sentences using simpler, more common words and phrases together with simpler, less formal sentence constructions. The first one is done for you.

1. We are all cognizant of the fact that the optimum manner of causing offense to Mary is to respond negatively to her invitation. *We all know the best way to offend Mary is to refuse her invitation.*

2. It is of the utmost importance that one agitate the bottle before initiating use of same.
3. You are requested to remove yourself from these premises prior to the arrival of the new owner.
4. We request the chairman to take cognizance of the extreme hardship this assignment would entail.
5. It is, of course, hazardous in the extreme to predict the impact of these policies on the economy.
6. It is my estimation that the number of units you have thus far acquired is insufficient to enable you to achieve graduation in the spring.
7. It is my considered opinion that the amount of money we spent on that project was in excess of the amount that was really required.
8. It is my firm conviction that the goals set forth by Mr. Johnson are beyond the domain of reality.
9. We request that you maximize your efforts in effecting completion of this job in the least amount of time possible.
10. I shall endeavor to the utmost of my ability to effect termination of this project within the prescribed time limit.
11. We are most desirous of having your participation in this attempt to resolve the problem.
12. I believe, with a high degree of certainty, that I have a great many things to communicate, but I do not possess a vocabulary which is sufficient in size to express these things accurately.

Stylized reporting

Certain occupations use specialized terminology and writing style. Here is an actual quotation from a letter by a police officer praising the action of a 10-year-old boy who had helped apprehend[7] a purse snatcher.

> *It is apparent the absence of the youth's assistance would have prolonged the search and the suspect possibly could have escaped.*

Exercise 4   Paraphrase the police officer's sentence above using more ordinary language.

---

[7]Apprehend: to arrest; take into custody.

Practice sentences

Exercise 5   It should not be too difficult to write several different paraphrases of the following sentence. One version is given below. See if you can write two or three additional paraphrases of the same sentence.

Original Version

> *It is difficult to refrain from conjecturing as to the course of action that would be taken if the same fate—loss of one's job— were to befall some of those middle-aged administrators.*

Paraphrase 1

> *It is hard not to try to guess what some of those middle-aged administrators would do if they lost **their** jobs.*

Paraphrase 2

_____

_____

Paraphrase 3

_____

_____

Paraphrase 4

_____

_____

Paraphrase 5

_____

_____

Exercise 6   Here are some additional sentences to challenge your ability to paraphrase. Some words are glossed below.

1. Homework assignments should be somewhat challenging, for a goal too readily reached offers no thrill of accomplishment.

2. The principal object of science is to ameliorate[8] the condition of man by adding to the advantages which he naturally possesses.
3. A plan was implemented[9] by the school board to devise a program in which remedial instruction in reading would be effected.
4. It has been recognized for some time that courses in English for foreign students at the university level frequently fall short of[10] meeting graduates' needs.
5. A thin line separates what is done to promote a product or service in the name of public relations and what is done in the name of marketing.
6. When one looks at any nation's life expectancy statistics and finds significant changes in them, the question of these changes becomes very important.
7. People are manifesting[11] their will for peace, and governments are obliged to implement this will to prevent the world from sliding into a hopeless nuclear conflict.
8. Administrative policy concerning our new sports program has never been sufficiently well defined.
9. The necessity of compliance[12] with new federal and state laws precludes[13] further delay in the formulation of our policies affecting the administration of this program.
10. With regard to the research activities of Chi Min Ling, it is suggested that he be restricted from any access to unpublished or classified government-funded work.
11. Few people would deny that these instructions are not beyond the comprehension of the average student.
12. By use of these major parameters,[14] time interval and shock intensity, avoidance conditioning of laboratory animals should be amenable[15] to further genetic analysis.
13. We cannot afford not to pay attention to present-day society's unfair and irrational treatment of women.

---

[8]Ameliorate: to improve; make better.

[9]To implement: to put into effect; fulfill; carry out.

[10]To fall short of: to fail to (do something); not to reach (something).

[11]To manifest: to show clearly; display; make evident.

[12]Compliance: the act of complying or conforming.
To comply: to do as required; satisfy a requirement.

[13]To preclude: to not allow; prevent; exclude the possibility of.

[14]Parameters: independent variables; unit, qualities, or characteristics used to limit, define, or describe conditions or events.

[15]Amenable: capable of being tested or judged; willing or able to respond.

Paraphrasing short paragraphs

Paraphrase the following short paragraphs. Be sure to indicate that these are someone else's ideas, not your own. Do *not* use direct quotations.

Exercise 7

Women in the Work Force

Measured in the number of women working, the changes in the economic position of women add up to a feminist success. Twenty-four million working women cannot be ignored. But weighed in the scales of quality instead of quantity, the change in women's economic status is not so striking. It is true that women now work in virtually every job listed by the Bureau of the Census. Moreover, the popular press repeatedly tells of the inroads[16] women are making into what used to be thought of as men's jobs. Two years ago, for example, a woman won a prize as the mutual fund salesman of the year. Women are widely represented in advertising and in real estate, and even women taxicab drivers are no longer rarities.

Exercise 8

Scientific Warfare

The problem which most preoccupies the public mind at the present moment is that of scientific warfare. It has become evident that if scientific skill is allowed free scope, the human race will be exterminated, if not in the next war, then in the one after that. To this problem there are two possible reactions: there are those who say, "let us create social institutions which will make large-scale war impossible"; there are others who say, "let us not allow war to become *too* scientific. We cannot perhaps go back to bows and arrows, but let us at any rate agree with our enemies that if we fight them, both sides will fight inefficiently."

For my part, I favor the former answer, since I cannot see that either side could be expected to observe an agreement not to use modern weapons if war had broken out. It is on this ground that I do not think that there will long continue to be human beings unless methods are found of permanently preventing large-scale wars.

Paraphrase with short quotations

In paraphrasing it is often helpful to include short quotations to capture the tone and preserve some of the "flavor" of the original.

---

[16]To make inroads into: to invade; penetrate; make advances.
Inroads: advances; penetration.

Especially when parts of a piece of writing are uniquely worded, the use of direct quotations is indicated so as not to lose the effectiveness of the source material. The following was adapted from the editorial page of a newspaper.

Should Everyone Go to College?

One constructive approach to the problems of higher education would be to reevaluate the prevailing notion that every young person must attain a college diploma if he is to succeed in life. This notion has been aptly termed "sheepskin psychosis" by Professor Emeritus Emil H. Smith.

Smith contends that many students go to college because "it's the thing to do." He suggests that some students might very well rather be in a school for arts and crafts, in a trade school, or in some sort of technical school.

What has long been needed, at the high school level, is a system of counseling which more specifically measures the aptitudes and long-range goals of youngsters and provides them with a wider range of choices as to their futures.

In the opinion of the retired professor, information given by high school counselors has emphasized the need for a college degree in order to make "a decent living." If the student does not know of the alternatives, how can he make an honest judgment?

The professor put it well when he said: "What we need most is the public realization that not every youngster wants to go to college; a college degree is not a guarantee of the good life." Smith adds that a person with a skill or trade can be as financially successful as a Ph.D., and that society needs skilled persons as well as intellectuals.

Exercise 9　Paraphrase a short article from a magazine or newspaper. Use phrases like "the article states" . . . to remind the reader you are paraphrasing someone else's ideas. You may use short quotations if you think it advisable to preserve some of the original wording.

Exercise 10　Paraphrase the following short essay. You may use short quotations where you think it necessary to preserve the exact wording of the original.

In 1798, the English economist Thomas Malthus published an essay, the explicit purpose of which was to account for much of the poverty and misery observable among the lower classes in all nations around the globe. Malthus' thesis states that "the population of a nation tends to outrun its capacity to produce the food and fiber needed to sustain itself." Malthus contends that population tends to increase at a constant geometric rate, whereas the output of food grows only arithmetically. And because of these different rates of growth the ever-increasing world population will inevitably press upon the food supply, resulting in subsistence living levels, misery, and perhaps even starvation.

All of us are well aware that mankind has been undergoing an extraordinary expansion of numbers, such that the term "population explosion" has become commonplace. Indeed, the growth of the world's population in just the last two centuries has been three times larger than the accumulated expansion of mankind since the dawn of history.

Given this incredible population growth and its projected continuance, and given the hard fact that only a finite amount of land exists on this planet, is it not highly relevant at this time to inquire as to the extent to which Malthus' gloomy forecast has come to pass or will come to pass in the near future? Perhaps we should ask ourselves the following question: "Will a limited food supply in the future mandate bare subsistence living for the world's inhabitants in the twenty-first century?"

Paraphrasing Difficult Passages

Admittedly one is sometimes faced with a long, complex sentence or paragraph that is difficult to understand and even more difficult to paraphrase. Take, for example, the following complex sentence which talks about making a syllabus to teach English as a second language.

> *By adding to the existing criteria for **structuring the grammatical content of learning** a new criterion, which could be called the criterion of **semantic value**, and by giving it high priority in relation, say, to the criterion of **simplicity**, we can keep within the basic philosophy of **the notional approach**, while making the task of **controlling the grammatical content** rather easier.*

Our first difficulty is probably caused by terminology. We may not be familiar with some of the key words. To simplify our task let us first substitute some more commonly used words while keeping the same sentence structure, as follows:

1   *By adding to the existing criteria for **evaluating a healthy***   1
2   ***meal** a new criterion, which could be called the criterion of*   2
3   ***good taste**, and by giving it high priority in relation, say,*   3
4   *to the criterion of **simplicity**, we can keep within the basic*   4
5   *philosophy of **good nutrition**, while making the task of*   5
6   ***preparing a healthy meal** rather easier.*   6

Even though we have simplified the vocabulary, the paraphrasing of the modified sentence still presents a problem. The solution lies in a complete restructuring of the sentence.

Restructuring

In restructuring, the focus will be on the main idea. Our task will be to write down the essence of the sentence in simple, understandable language. Of necessity a few details are sometimes omitted to facilitate the restructuring and to avoid getting "bogged down" in a forest of detail.

What Is the Sentence About?

A good way to begin the restructuring is to state the general topic in broad terms. In the case of our modified sentence the author talks about "criteria for evaluating a healthy meal." At this point we may need further clarification of vocabulary items. *Criterion* is the singular form of *criteria*; and a *criterion* is "a standard of judgment."

Our next step will be to break the sentence down into smaller units, using simple language as much as possible. It is often advisable to start off with an introductory statement, such as a sentence which provides background information. This information is usually *implicit*. Implicit information is that which is implied by the author but not explicitly stated. Such a sentence should be used whenever the information provided helps make the passage easier to understand. We then search out and write down the main idea or ideas. And finally, we write down any subordinate ideas not yet stated.

We are now in a position to restructure the sentence as follows:

We are told that:

1. there are existing criteria for evaluating a healthy meal; (lines 1–2)
                                and
2. we can keep within the basic philosophy of good nutrition if we do two things: (lines 4–5)
    a. we must add a new criterion. We can call it *the good taste criterion*; (lines 2–3)
    b. we must give this new criterion high priority in relation to the criterion of simplicity. (lines 3–4)

3. And by doing this we can, at the same time, make it easier to prepare a healthy meal. (line 6)

The above can be improved and made more concise by combining some of the sentences, eliminating some repetition, and rearranging the units as follows:

> *The author tells us we can keep within the basic philosophy of good nutrition and at the same time make the job of preparing a healthy meal easier if we do two things: First, to the existing criteria for evaluating a healthy meal we must add a new criterion, which we will call* **good taste**. *And second, we must give this new criterion high priority in relation to the criterion of* **simplicity**.

Analysis of the original sentence

The writer of the original sentence complicates the message by starting with an adverbial clause, followed by a relative clause, and then introducing a second adverbial clause; and all of this occurs before he states the main or result clause, which is, in turn, modified by still another adverbial clause. All of this contributes to making our task of paraphrasing a rather difficult one. Thankfully, few writers use so complicated a style.

Longer is better

You have probably noticed that the final paraphrased version is longer than the original. We must remember, however, that the main purpose of paraphrasing is not to shorten the original or to make it more concise. We should not confuse paraphrase with summary. A good paraphrase will often be longer than the original; and this is justified if it results in making the passage clearer and easier to understand, which is one of the purposes of paraphrasing in the first place.

Passages for paraphrase

Exercises
Paraphrase the following sentences and paragraphs. Restructure and simplify as appropriate.

Exercise 11
   Hit by the recession and by competition from smaller companies, the giant corporations no longer inspire the fear they once did.

Exercise 12
Not only is the quality of submitted material high, but, as can be seen from the table of contents and details of forthcoming articles on the back of this leaflet, the papers do vary in nature, as we originally hoped they would.

Exercise 13
A passionate call to uphold peace, avert a nuclear conflagration and curb the senseless but extremely dangerous arms race has again resounded from the speaker's platform at the 16th Congress of the White Dove Peace Association.

Exercise 14
As the world's largest reservoir of fresh water, representing 20 per cent of the global reserves, the value of beautiful Lake Baikal increases as the problem of fresh water grows more complex and as the area around the lake, situated as it is in one of the industrial centers of Eastern Siberia, becomes increasingly affected by human economic activity.

Exercise 15
In the case of giant corporations operating overseas, some developing countries prohibit the repatriation of any of the firms' profits; consequently, when a company's business is thriving and its profits are rising, the host government may require that it develop employment-generating facilities by recycling those profits earned in the country, thus wielding yet another weapon against the multinationals.

Exercise 16
Just as the business monopolist is not interested in selling the greatest possible number of products, so the union members are not interested in providing the greatest number of jobs in their line of work. Like the businessman, the union members are interested in maximizing their own income. While a union is not likely to force its wage up to the point at which many of its own membership cannot find work, if the industry itself faces an increasing demand for its product, the workers who lose jobs in the industry may be those who never have worked in the industry but would have if the high wage rate had not reduced the quantity of labor demanded. We should not be surprised if the union does not give much consideration to this vague group of workers.

Exercise 17
History has long made a point of the fact that the magnificent flowering of ancient civilization rested upon the institution of slavery, which released opportunity at the top for the art and literature which became the glory of antiquity. In a way, the mechanization of the present-day world produces the condition of the ancient in that the enormous development of labor-saving devices which amplify the capacities of mankind afford the base for the leisure necessary for widespread cultural pursuits. Mechanization is the present-day slave owner, with the difference that in the mechanized society there is no group of the community which does not share in the benefits of its inventions.

UNIT 14   WRITING SUMMARIES

One is often called upon to make summaries of things one has heard or read. To summarize is to report information using a lot fewer words than were used in the original communication. The thing to do is to look for essentials—the main points and ideas of the piece of writing. Of necessity one must omit some details, or at least state them more concisely. But none of the basic information should be lost. No main point or idea can be omitted, nor should one change the emphasis of the original. The summary should be a true reflection of the original, with some of the details and examples left out.

Incidentally, an excellent way to study and learn school materials is to make summaries of what one reads.

The following short news article appeared in a weekly newspaper:

Patients Sometimes Die Because of
Unqualified, Untrained Technicians
by A. Gribben

A 23-year-old college student was playing touch football with some school chums. While running for the ball he fell and whacked his head, hard. Hours later he complained of a "bad" headache. The young man was taken to a major West Coast hospital where doctors examined him and diagnosed brain hemorrhaging. A team of surgeons operated on the injured man at once. A short while later the surgery was declared a complete success.

But unfortunately the young man died. An uncertified, poorly trained respiratory technician tending the patient bumbled during an emergency in the recovery room.

The National Observer, April 21, 1973

Summarized Version

Here is a summarized version of the above article:

According to *The National Observer,*[1] a 23-year-old college student sustained a severe head injury while playing touch football. Later, the young man was taken to a

---

[1]*The National Observer,* April 21, 1973.

hospital where doctors diagnosed brain hemorrhaging and performed a successful operation. But the patient later died in the recovery room at the hands of an unqualified respiratory technician.

Now try your hand at writing summaries.

Exercise 1   Write a summary of the following article, stating the main points in your own words as briefly as you can. Avoid using direct quotation.

Can Vegetarians Get Complete Protein Nourishment?

What did people like Henry Thoreau, Benjamin Franklin, Voltaire, Leonardo da Vinci, Milton, Pope, Gandhi and George Bernard Shaw have in common besides their fame? Each was a vegetarian, avoiding the meat of any and all animals.

Although vegetarianism has existed throughout history, the late 1960s and early 1970s have seen a gigantic rebirth in the movement as a way of life—kind of a by-product of the "back to nature" or "greening of America" movements. With almost religious fervor, young and old alike are turning to the humanitarian philosophy which refuses to slaughter animals for feed.

Every time the question of vegetarianism arises, a companion question comes up too: Can vegetarians be well nourished, especially when it comes to getting enough protein? The question of protein is all important because in some cases, the modern vegetarians, with their new-found respect for all living creatures, refuse to eat eggs or dairy products, the only nonmeat foods that are rich in high-grade protein.

Some authorities have always recommended the inclusion of animal products in diets because, unlike plant foods, they furnish protein that is biologically complete. We do not, however, dispute that it is possible (with a little effort) to maintain health and vigor on a purely vegetarian diet. And recent research indicates that some mixtures of special flours may just provide the proper amounts of protein to equal that of meat, so that a vegetarian can accomplish a good protein intake merely by eating the right kind of bread or cereal.

Exercise 2   Summarize the following article in your own words. Use direct quotations sparingly.

Table Talk: How to Enjoy Vegetables
by Shelagh Jones

The United States is not a nation of vegetable eaters. In fact, people tend to avoid them—and, not so incidentally, the myriad vitamins and minerals they contain—because they seem so dull. But the reason vegetables bore Americans has nothing to do with their inherent qualities. It is their own fault—Americans really do not know how to cook them.

America's culinary vocabulary is curiously lacking in ways to make vegetables elegant. And no matter how popular carrots, for instance, may be with some families, serving them the same way all the time is sure to make their popularity pale, if not disappear. Another, more basic, cause for the lack of enthusiasm greeting platters of vegetables all over America is the lack of restraint in cooking them. That is, Americans simply do not know when to stop. The longer they stay on the stove or in the oven, the shorter they are on taste, texture, color, and nutritional content.

Americans are not alone in the tendency to make pablum out of perfectly good beans, turnips, asparagus, etc. The British have made mushy brussels sprouts a national institution as unavoidable as fog. The French are more subtle—they conceal their vegetable casualties under exquisitely seasoned sauces. This does make it possible to enjoy them, but not exactly for themselves alone.

The only place in the world where vegetables are traditionally venerated, where their individual personalities are extolled, rather than concealed or destroyed, is in the Far East. The Chinese are champions at this particular art (among many others) and there is much to learn from what goes on in their woks—as well as what goes into them.

The Chinese have gentle methods for sautéeing and boiling vegetables. They are adept at throwing together seemingly incompatible kinds of food in a way that makes the combination seem predestined. And they season things lightly, bringing out the flavor of each ingredient rather than creating a pungent, but amorphous, whole. Their emphasis is on simplicity and harmony.

Glossary

Pablum: a soft, tasteless baby food which used to be popular in the
      U.S. some years ago.
Mushy: soft and moist; pulpy, like "mush" (mush: in the U.S., *mush*
      is corn meal boiled in water).
Wok: a round, deep cooking utensil.
Pungent: producing a sharp sensation of taste or smell.
Amorphous: shapeless.

Exercise 3   Have a member of the class give a talk (in English) on some topic of interest. Take notes, and then write a summary of the talk. You might want to use phrases like "the speaker stated . . . ," "he thinks . . . ," "he is of the opinion that . . . ," and other appropriate phrases.

Exercise 4   Summarize an article from a newspaper or magazine. State whether or not you found the article interesting, and why. Give full bibliographical data such as the name and date of periodical, and the author's name if given.

UNIT 15   DEVELOPING A THESIS SENTENCE

Finding a Topic

In choosing a subject to write about one should limit the topic and narrow it down to a workable size. For example, a topic like "Agriculture in the United States" is too large to handle adequately in the usual college essay. A title like "Agriculture in the Imperial Valley" is a bit better, but perhaps still too broad. This topic can be narrowed further by selecting a single crop, perhaps resulting in a title such as "Cotton Production in the Imperial Valley."

Definition of a Thesis Sentence

We have already stated that it is desirable to have a clear beginning to writing. Most of the essays and reports you will be likely to write should begin with a sentence that presents your point of view, that gives your main idea, or states in a general way what you want to report on. Such a sentence is called the *thesis sentence.* Using the technique of a thesis sentence should help to give direction and clarity to your writing.

The *thesis sentence* should not be confused with a *topic sentence* which gives the main point of a single paragraph. The *thesis sentence* states the main idea of the entire essay. It is broader in scope than the topic sentence because it relates to the writing as a whole. In effect, then, the thesis sentence states the writer's main idea or purpose and lets the reader know what to expect in succeeding paragraphs.

To return to the previous example, one could write, "Cotton production in the Imperial Valley is on the decline," and have an adequate thesis sentence. But such a sentence is not particularly exciting, nor does it state a particular point of view. All one can expect from this thesis statement are perhaps some dull facts and figures. But if the writer has an opinion as to the cause, he might write, "Cotton production in the Imperial Valley is on the decline because of ecological abuses." He now has a more exciting thesis.

Of course the writer must be sincere; he should not distort the truth just to attract attention. Certainly, it helps to choose a thesis that one is interested in or even excited about—one that may well be interesting to the reader as well.

Thesis Sentences in Essay Writing and News Reporting

Different kinds of writing demand different styles. In essay and news reporting, for example, the writer may want to be very direct; he or she may want to shock his readers to make them "sit up and take notice." In such cases the writer makes a very strong, perhaps controversial statement, often in the very first sentence, as in the following examples:

Example A
> *The trouble with Americans is that they attempt to accumulate too many material things in too great a hurry, without giving thought to the cost of such acquisitions in terms of philosophical values.*

Example B
> *By raising the standard of living of the peasants and urban workers and providing educational opportunities for the poor, Fidel Castro has given the world a lesson in democracy.*

Glossary
Controversial: subject to or characterized by controversy; debatable
Controversy: a dispute or debate

In contrast, a writer who does not wish to shock his readers with such strong, direct statements may choose not to state the thesis immediately. Instead, he may lead up to it gradually with readily accepted, noncontroversial statements. The writer narrows the topic and states the thesis at or near the end of the opening paragraph. He or she may even delay it until the second paragraph, thus adding an element of suspense, as in the following example:

> Robert Alex Baron is a man with a quiet obsession. For eight years he has fought odds-on, trying to conquer a problem that most people consider

inseparable from everyday living. For eight years he has tried to convince
industry, government, and the public that they are sitting on a time bomb that
every year ticks faster and faster, louder and louder.

Baron is obsessed by noise.

He has been so ever since 1964, when clangorous subway construction
outside his. . . .

> From *The National Observer,* November 11, 1972. "For Whom
> the Decibel Tolls," by Barbara J. Katz.

Thesis Sentences in Term Papers and Research Reports

We have just said it is desirable to start one's essay with an exciting,
perhaps controversial, thesis sentence. However, it is not always
possible, nor always appropriate, to have such a lively, attention-
getting statement. Rather, much writing employs a straightforward
style in which the purpose of the essay or report is stated in a clear,
direct, matter-of-fact way. This is particularly true of the kind of
writing usually found in college textbooks, term papers, and the like.
Here are some examples of thesis sentences of this kind:

Example C

> *One of the most important problems the world will have to face
> in the near future is the rapid growth of its human population.
> The number of inhabitants has. . . .*

Example D

> *The purpose of this paper will be to illustrate some social
> problems related to the struggle for equal rights of African
> women. In African society, women have not. . . .*

Example E

> *The major concern of this paper will be to study the social
> consequences and impact of the political dominance of the high
> middle and upper class as it affects the working class struggle for
> economic security. It has been said. . . .*

Example F

> *Recently the concept of planning commissions in city government
> has come under attack. Whether or not these planning organiza-
> tions are needed in today's society will be the main concern of
> this paper.*

Writing about Controversial Issues

The focal point of an essay is often a controversial issue. A thesis
sentence will usually emerge by coming out in favor of or against the
issue; that is, by taking one side or the other.

There follow some controversial issues which you will be asked to
write about. Try not to be neutral. Commit yourself to defend one
side or the other. Here is an incomplete example of this kind of
argumentative writing:

*Issue: that the president of
_____ should be impeached*

I do not agree that the president of our country should be impeached, merely
because he made an honest mistake. Many honorable men in the past made
honest mistakes for which they were never punished. Furthermore, . . .

Writing Assignment
Read the following paragraph. Then continue the composition by
giving your opinion on the topic. State the reasons for your belief.

Issue No. 1   that boxing is a cruel sport which should be abolished
Prize fighting or "boxing" as it is more commonly called is a popular sport in
many countries around the world. But some people are of the opinion that boxing, like bull fighting, is a cruel and dangerous sport which should be abolished.
Others, however, feel that boxing is a good sport requiring skill and endurance,
and that it is no more cruel or dangerous than other contact sports.
In my opinion, . . .

Issue No. 2   that the killing of whales is cruel and should be banned
Whales are Earth's largest animals. These cetaceous mammals of fishlike form
represent one of the largest living forms on earth, second in size only to the giant
Redwood trees of California and elsewhere.
Whaling has always been an important industry in some parts of the world. A
few countries use specially constructed ships to locate, kill, and process whales.
Many men earn their livelihood by hunting down and killing these majestic
creatures of the deep.
But conservationists are very much disturbed by the whaling industry. They
firmly believe it is cruel and inhumane to hunt and kill these aquatic mammals—
the largest animals in nature.

Writing Assignment
Write a short essay on Issue No. 2. State whether you agree or disagree,
and then defend your point of view.

Issue No. 3   that women are taking away men's jobs

For some years now the Women's Liberation Movement in the United States has encouraged women to pursue different roles in society. Women have been told they are not necessarily destined to be only a mother and housewife. They are being told they have the same right to work at a job outside the home as any man. In addition, the movement has urged women to seek jobs formerly thought to be only for men.

Some men resent the idea of women working at jobs previously reserved for males only. They feel that women may be taking away their jobs—men's jobs—and that the man, traditionally, is supposed to be the breadwinner—the one who supports the family. This attitude is reflected in the following letter to the editor of a local newspaper.

TAKING JOBS

Editor of the Bee—Sir: Men who want to work to support and feed their families are drawing unemployment compensation or are on welfare because the women are taking over the jobs. The offenders are women whose husbands have excellent jobs, and yet they go out and insist upon taking over the male's job—a job he needs to support his family. This is the reason for the high unemployment among the male population.

This is one big reason for the large teenage problem we have today; there is no home life or parental supervision, and the teenagers are on their own. How about the unemployed men forming a men's liberation movement to get the jobs back that are rightfully theirs to support their families and help the taxpayers?

John Morris

Fresno, California

Writing Assignment

Write a short essay based on the above. In your essay try to reply to the following questions:

1. Do you have any sympathy for the writer of the letter?
2. Which point of view do you agree with—that of the man who wrote the letter, or that of the women's liberation movement? State your reasons.

Issue No. 4   *that the Bermuda Triangle is just a hoax*

The Bermuda Triangle is an imaginary line connecting Bermuda, Florida, and Puerto Rico. Sometimes the triangle is extended into a square shape to enclose Cuba and the Azores. Altogether the area contains more than 400,000 square miles of the Atlantic.

Since this section of the ocean is an important commercial and tourist route, many ships and planes pass through it. Yet it is considered one of the most dangerous areas on earth.

According to the Bermuda Triangle legend, more than 1,000 people and 100 ships and planes have disappeared in this area. But what is most unusual is the fact that they—people, ships, and planes—have vanished into thin air without leaving a trace. There were no bodies, no wreckage, not even an oil slick—nothing.

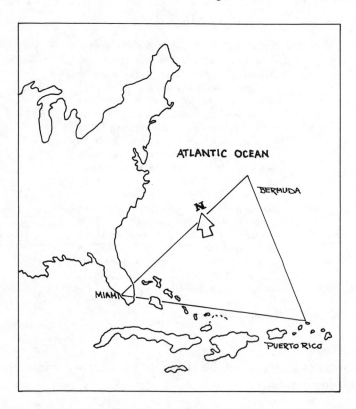

The Bermuda Triangle—Is there anything unusual about this stretch of Atlantic Ocean?

Not only that, but many ships' captains and pilots have reported strange occurrences after returning from the Bermuda Triangle. Some said their compasses spun wildly and refused to provide accurate directions; or sometimes a ship's electrical system suddenly went dead.

Several pilots have told of weird lights flashing on their planes' instrument panels. Others commented about glowing, greenish clouds appearing in a clear sky.

The Bermuda Triangle legend probably started with Columbus' first voyage to America. Columbus recorded in his log that his crew was scared by a column of fire that blasted down from the sky and by the odd movements of their ship's compass.

There have been many other strange occurrences since Columbus sailed through the Bermuda Triangle. Consider the schooner *Carrol A. Deering.* It floated calmly into a North Carolina port in January 1921. When seamen boarded the vessel, they found nothing unusual. Nothing except that the ship's crew was missing. And a full meal was still warm on the galley stove.

Still another puzzling incident is the story of flight 19, the Navy code name for five bombers that vanished in December 1945. The bombers took off from Fort Lauderdale, Florida, on a routine patrol. Within an hour the flight leader reported that they were lost. Confused, garbled messages followed the announcement. Then silence.

A huge flying boat with 13 men on board left to rescue Flight 19. Twenty minutes later the plane reported it was in the vicinity of Flight 19's estimated position. That was the last message the rescue plane ever sent. It was never heard from again. Altogether, six planes and 22 men vanished.

Theories

Several theories have been offered to explain these unusual occurrences in the Bermuda Triangle.

According to the Atlantis theory, thousands of years ago there were more continents on earth than now exist. A highly intelligent civilization supposedly lived on the continent of Atlantis. But then Atlantis mysteriously sank into the ocean.

Along with the continent went the civilization's source of power that was used to run machines and to generate light for the cities. But even under the ocean, believers say, the power source continues to work. And every once in a while the power source turns on and sends a ray of energy surging to the surface. When this ray erupts out of the ocean, it seizes anything in its path and drags it into the sea. Or it simply blasts ships and planes to atoms.

Another popular theory is known as the UFO Conspiracy. Some people claim that UFO's (Unidentified Flying Objects) are the culprits in the Bermuda Triangle. For a long time UFO's have been reported flashing back and forth over the Atlantic. Perhaps UFO's have snatched planes and ships right off the earth. According to one expert, UFO's are large enough to pick up a vessel and then shuttle it off to another galaxy.

Several people have offered what they believe are rational explanations for the seemingly strange incidents that have occurred in the area. Adi-Kent Jeffrey, author of a paperback best-seller entitled *The Bermuda Triangle,* disputes both the UFO and the Atlantis theories. Mrs. Jeffrey claims the disappearances in the Bermuda Triangle are caused by electromagnetic disturbances.

According to Mrs. Jeffrey, when explosions on the sun (called "sunspots") occur, they bombard the earth with cosmic particles that cause all kinds of problems. These solar disturbances affect people's minds. They lose track of time, and they don't know where they are. Their minds just don't operate in the usual way—their thoughts go out of control.

By way of explanation Mrs. Jeffrey states that every solid object is made up of atoms which are bound together with electrical energy. This applies to brain waves as well. And when brain waves are broken apart by solar disturbances they in turn destroy the electrical force that holds the atoms of physical objects in place. The atoms just break up and scatter.

One might well ask, "Don't these solar disturbances occur in other parts of the globe and cause other strange incidents to happen?" The answer is that they probably do, but the connection between those events and solar disturbances is not made. According to Mrs. Jeffrey, there are more of these disturbances in the Bermuda Triangle than in other areas because of strange magnetic conditions there. And that, she feels, is the real solution to the Bermuda Triangle mystery.

A common sense explanation

Lawrence D. Kusche stands almost alone against the Bermuda Triangle believers. Kusche says that almost all the supposedly "mysterious" events in the Triangle have reasonable explanations. Among these are human error, malfunctioning equipment, and inexperienced mariners and pilots. Also, he reminds us that "natural phenomena have caused many disasters at sea. The weather changes quickly in that area and storms may come up too fast for the captain to get off a distress signal. Seaquakes, waterspouts, and hurricanes happen all the time."[1]

Kusche feels the legend grew out of careless research in which writers simply repeated misconceptions, added false details, or covered up some possible explanations. The legend was repeated over and over again until it began to look like the truth. "My conclusion, then," states Kusche, "is that the Bermuda Triangle legend is a manufactured mystery."[2]

Suggested Assignments

1. Class discussion. What is your reaction to the above article? Do you think there is any truth to the "mysteries" of the triangle?
2. Write a short composition on the Bermuda Triangle. Take a position on the matter. Where do you think the truth lies? Give reasons for your opinion.

---

[1] Lawrence D. Kusche, *The Bermuda Triangle Mystery—Solved.*
[2] *Ibid.*

*Issue No. 5   that we should **not** make a special effort to feed the millions of starving people all over the world*

Let 'em Starve

A new approach to world hunger

Does it not seem cruel and heartless to entertain the idea that we ought not to try to prevent the starvation of millions of people? Certainly the humane thing to do would be to make every effort to feed the starving, even if it means great sacrifice on our part.

The lifeboat hypothesis

Not so, says scientist Garrett Hardin. If one looks at the problem objectively, dispassionately and realistically, one could come to the conclusion that more people will die of disease and starvation if you feed them. Writing in the journal *BioScience,* Hardin makes an analogy to people set adrift in lifeboats. He writes as follows:

> Each rich nation amounts to a lifeboat full of comparatively rich people. The poor of the world are in other, much more crowded lifeboats. Continuously, so to speak, the poor fall out of their lifeboats and swim for a while in the water outside, hoping to be admitted to a rich lifeboat, or in some other way to benefit from the "goodies" on board. What should the passengers on a rich lifeboat do?
>
> If people in the rich lifeboat give their substance to the doomed persons who are continuously falling out of the others, they reduce the chances of their own survival. But they do not improve things on the other lifeboats, where food and fuel are quickly translated into more babies, who in turn push more passengers over the side to struggle in the water of starvation.

In his article, Hardin contends that "every life saved this year in a poor country diminishes the quality of life for subsequent generations." He asks the question, "Are good intentions ever an excuse for bad consequences?"

William Paddock, agronomist and expert on tropical agriculture, puts it this way:

> It's true we can support a great many more people than we are supporting today. If the United States turns completely vegetarian, our agriculture can support 800 million people instead of 200 million. But the world is increasing at 90 million people a year, so that only gives us nine years. What do you do for an encore after those nine years?

In effect then, these scientists are suggesting that to let people starve may be both moral and ethical, and, in the long run, the more humane solution; they are suggesting that we should turn away from famine victims for their own good as well as ours. Adds Hardin:

> We should refuse to do it [send food to desperately needy countries] because the lives that we save today are going to be paid for by worse loss

of life and worse misery in the generations that will follow. Although world food production apparently has grown a little faster than world population over the last generation, a decisive share of the extra food has been raised and eaten in the richer countries. That's the main reason why the gigantic American food surplus was all sold off, and why bigger-than-ever American food harvests produce aid only a fraction as large as a decade ago.

At a recent conference of scientists in Philadelphia, a professor from The Massachusetts Institute of Technology (M.I.T.) was quoted as saying: "We are at a point now where we must give up the idea that good is good in the ideal sense and realize that what is good now may be bad in the future."

Writing Assignment
Incorporate Issue No. 5 into a thesis sentence which will express your own opinion about the issue. Then continue writing and develop your thesis sentence into a short essay.

SECTION
H

Punctuation Marks and Their Use

UNIT 16   A GUIDE TO PUNCTUATION

In general, marks of punctuation serve to guide the reader. Although punctuation marks sometimes correspond to pauses that occur in speech, this is certainly not always the case. At times punctuation is necessary to avoid ambiguity, to prevent misreading, or to make the meaning clear. At other times it is just a matter of convention—a set of agreed upon rules. The following "rules" or comments may be useful to the beginning writer:

I. Punctuation Marks Used to End a Sentence

A.   *The period* (.) is used in ordinary declarative and imperative (command) sentences.
> *My sister called yesterday.*
> *Please answer as soon as possible.*

A period, *not* a question mark, is used with the following:
1. courtesy questions.
> *Would you please advise us of your new address.*
2. indirect questions (sentences which are not interrogative).
> *I asked him what he wanted.* vs. *What do you want?*
> *We would like to know when you are coming.* vs. *When are you coming?*

B.   *The exclamation point* (!) is used for emphasis or to express
     strong feeling or emotion.
> *Get out of here!*
> *What a beautiful view!*
C.   *The question mark* (?) is used:
     1. in direct questions.
> *When is your birthday?*
> *Are you happy?*
     2. in tag questions.
> *You're a student, aren't you?*
> *You can come, can't you?*
     3. to indicate rising intonation to signal a question.
> *You're from France?*
> *You call that good?*

II. Punctuation Marks Used to Join Phrases and Clauses[1]

Comma

A.   *The comma* (,) has many and varied uses. Here are some of the
     principal ones:
     1. Clauses joined by the conjunctions *and, or, but, nor, for.*

     (clause 1), *and* (clause 2)

> *This is a very disturbing situation, **and** I see only one
>   solution.*
> *We sent the two girls to bed early that night, **but** they
>   were so excited they couldn't sleep.*
> *Please don't ever do that again, **or** I shall be forced to fire
>   you.*
> *I do not believe in easy solutions, **nor** do I attempt to
>   ignore the real tough problems.*

     a. There is a tendency in current usage to use the comma
        sparingly; that is, only when necessary. This is especially
        true in rather short sentences, as in *He can go **and** so can I.*
     b. Commas are *not* used when the conjunction is used to form
        a compound predicate rather than to join two clauses.
        Compare the following:

---

[1] A clause is defined as a portion of a complex sentence containing a subject and
predicate.

Let the children run and jump.
Let the boys run around, and let the girls practice
sewing.

Tom likes nothing but music.
Tom not only likes music, but he goes to concerts all
the time.

John likes to play football and go swimming.
John likes to play football, and he also loves to go
swimming.

2. Words or phrases forming a coordinate series.

He speaks French, German, and English.
She got up, walked across the room, and ran out the door.
The president, vice-president, and six senators were
present.

Note: In current usage some writers omit the last comma. For
example: *He speaks French, German and English.*

a. Two or more coordinates (that is, forms which are semantic-
ally parallel) are separated by commas, as follows:

He was a tall, dark, handsome man.
(or)
He was tall, dark and handsome.

Coordinate forms may also be joined by the conjunction
and, as follows:

He was a tall and dark and handsome man.
(or)
He was tall and dark and handsome.

While the resulting sentence may be considered awkward or
stylistically poor, it is nevertheless grammatical and serves
as evidence that such forms are indeed coordinate.

b. If the items in a series are not coordinate, then neither *and's*
nor commas should be used:

They lowered the big steel hook.
They have a new electron microscope.
Look for a red brick bungalow.

(Note that one cannot say #*the hook was big and steel.*)

c. Further examples of coordinate items are:

We need bread, milk, and cheese.
The figures are for the years 1969, 1970, and 1971.
A frown darkened his round, brown eyes.
He bought a huge, red tractor.

      d. Further examples of noncoordinate items are:

> *She has a red IBM electric typewriter.*
> *He bought a large steel desk.*
> *He lives in a white stucco ranch home.*
> *It is a lovely single family house.*

      e. It must be noted that certain set phrases are often used rhetorically rather than in a literal sense. Such phrases do not contain commas. Some common examples are:

a little old lady	*a big baseball fan*
a real good movie	*a nice old gentleman*

3. Parenthetical words and phrases (interruptors).

> *Education, he insists, must be in tune with the times.*
> *What this country needs, in my opinion, is cheaper medical service.*
> *We are, unfortunately, unable to grant your request at this time.*

4. To avoid ambiguity or misreading.

      a. Without punctuation the following sentences could be misread or cause misunderstanding:

> *We cannot blame the president for what he did was absolutely necessary.*
> *Later on Jim Wilson's recommendation Charles was given the job.*

      b. But when sentences are punctuated properly, the misreading or possible misunderstanding is avoided:

> *We cannot blame the president, for what he did was . . .*
> *Later, on Jim's recommendation, Charles was . . .*

5. Transposed adverbial phrases.

> *John managed to save up the necessary money **by working hard for two whole summers.***
> ***By working hard for two whole summers,** John managed to . . .*

> *Participants will pay for their own meals **in addition to the registration fee.***
> ***In addition to the registration fee,** participants will pay . . .*

6. Appositives and nonrestrictive clauses.

> *Helen Pons, the well-known opera star, will give a concert tonight.*
> *Gordon Taylor, the British science writer, presented a talk on ecology.*

My sister Nancy, who married a man from Detroit, is now living in Ann Arbor, Michigan.

Exercise 1   Insert commas where necessary.

1. The capital city has a huge modern airport.
2. Mr. Hill our chemistry teacher was at the party last night.
3. In the first course we study essays poems and plays.
4. As the story indicates a man should respect his wife's judgment.
5. I wrote to Mr. Smith several times but he never answered my brilliant letters.
6. The committee appreciates suggestions of this type and we hope that more people will contribute their ideas.
7. Before exporting the goods have to be inspected.
8. A college teacher for example has to fill out dozens of forms each semester.
9. Some of the diseases now under control are measles diphtheria and smallpox.
10. The courses I take are the ones which you recommend.
11. My doctor is a kind patient understanding man.
12. You can send the money to the bank or you can send it directly to me.
13. Such as it is this poem was written after days of profound meditation.
14. We have to use the big steel hook.
15. She is a tall thin middle-aged woman.
16. My Aunt Susie whom we all love very much is coming for a visit.
17. You are I think the best man for the job.
18. The shortage of water from our point of view is one of the more serious problems.
19. Mary enrolled in a college for women and her brother went to Harvard.
20. Mr. Brown arrived in town and when he heard the news about his son he became furious.
21. He was a sad dejected suicidal patient.
22. As these statistics indicate a man is safer in the air than on the highway.

Exercise 2   Punctuate the following. Capitalize the first word of every new sentence following a period (full stop).

Rawalpindi in northeastern Pakistan has recently developed into a modern city its old buildings have been replaced by modern ones ten to fifteen stories high its bridges have been widened and its old system of transport by horse and wagon has been replaced by cars buses and trains Rawalpindi a name which hardly appeared on Pakistani maps of some years ago is now one of the most important cities of the country.

Exercise 3   Write in commas where necessary.

On a cold windy November morning Harold caught a large catfish with a small steel hook and a white nylon line as he was fishing from an old deserted boat dock. Margie the little old woman who kept house for him cleaned floured and fried the fish for his usual mid-morning snack.

Exercise 4   Punctuate the following paragraph. Capitalize the first word of very sentence following a full stop.

At the time of his death in 1976 Robert Johnson's literary estate consisting of some four thousand pages of manuscript notebook sheets and dozens of letters lay scattered and almost lost

however through the efforts of Helen Johnson the author's widow virtually all of this material was recovered from such places as a Colombian bank vault and the back room of a New York bar and stored in safe deposit boxes in Newark New Jersey it is this complete and irreplaceable collection that Professor King has now systematic-ally sorted and cataloged for publication in his new book the result of six months spent in detailed analysis poring over every sheet or scrap of paper that might be of literary value.

Semicolon

B.   The *semicolon* (;) indicates a longer pause, a more distinct break in the grammatical structure than that suggested by the comma. It indicates a closer semantic relationship between clauses than that suggested by a full stop. The principal uses of the semicolon are as follows:

1. To link independent clauses in the absence of a coordinating conjunction.

   It was not only the loss of money; my ego was damaged as well.

> *The population of San Francisco in 1840 was 40,000; in 1960 it was approximately 740,000.*
>
> *You cannot buy enthusiasm; you cannot buy loyalty; you cannot buy the devotion of hearts and minds. You have to earn these things.*

2. Before connectives like *however* which relate back to the preceding sentence.[2]

> *Many art students like myself went to New York in hopes of finding gainful employment; however, jobs were hard to find at that time.*
>
> *The harassed commuter left his home twenty minutes late; consequently, he missed his train.*
>
> *Harold speaks Japanese amazingly well; moreover, he has an excellent knowledge of the culture.*

3. To separate items of a long series complicated by internal punctuation.

> *Participating in the beauty contest were Mary Snow, of Fresno, California; Helen Bloom, of Rochester, New York; and Susie Jones, of Austin, Texas.*
>
> *The main cities of Lebanon are: Beirut, the capital, with an estimated population of 800,000; Tripoli, a Mediterranean oil pipeline terminal; Zahle, which is near the desert; and Saida, a resort town in the south.*
>
> *One can drive to the countryside and buy fresh corn, Chinese cabbage, and organically grown tomatoes; but the prices are higher than they are in the supermarket.*

C. In punctuation as in speech, usage divided between the *semicolon* and *comma* is often the rule rather than the exception. The following examples illustrate (in this author's opinion) equally valid and equally acceptable alternatives:

1. Two common ways of punctuating the enumerative expressions *namely* and *for example* (in clause and final position[3]) are:

---

[2]A period (.) is often used instead of the semicolon. For example, this sentence may be punctuated as follows: *Many art students like myself went to New York in hopes of finding gainful employment. However, jobs were hard to find at that time.*

[3]Not to be confused with parenthetical interruptors like the following: *A college teacher, for example, is required to fill out dozens of. . . .*

a. *Namely*

> *According to Mendenhall, there are three categories of language learners;* **namely**, *young children, adults, and adolescents at the junior high level.*
>
> *According to Mendenhall, there are three categories of language learners,* **namely**, *young children, adults, and adolescents at the junior high level.*

b. *For example*

> *There are many well-paid occupations today which do not require a college education,* **for example**, *carpenters, electricians, plumbers and steamfitters.*
>
> *There are many well-paid occupations which do not require a college education;* **for example**, *carpenters, plumbers, electricians and steamfitters.*

2. With certain sentences either a *comma plus conjunction* or a *semicolon* may be used. The choice of one or the other is a stylistic one. (In sentences with semicolon some kind of conjunction is usually implied.) Observe the following:

> *The boys went ice skating, and the girls went to the movies.*
>
> *The boys went ice skating; the girls went to the movies.*

> *Jones has stated some implications for the improvement of reading, and herewith are some of his ideas:*
>
> *Jones has stated some implications for the improvement of reading; herewith are some of his ideas:*

Of the two styles the use of the semicolon is probably the more dramatic; that is, its more succinct form implies greater contrast or suspense.

Exercise 5   Punctuate the following sentences. Add commas or semicolons wherever appropriate.

1. It is evident our system of justice works for some but not for all in this case it has not worked at all.
2. I recommend that we move toward in effect a policy of "direct consultation."
3. Becoming a heart surgeon is like learning to do magic tricks one has to practice in order to gain proficiency.
4. Two hundred students took the examination only twenty-two passed.

5. He asked me what I was now studying at school.
6. These men are I think the best people presently available for the job.
7. Don't tease that little monkey he might bite you.
8. The young lady who broke her leg is in the hospital.
9. Mr. Snodgrass our chemistry teacher was at the party last night.
10. The child learns to base relationships with others on criteria fixed by the state other boys and girls can be rated on an objective scale.
11. Acceptance of this report without modification would be I fear an invitation to future frustration.
12. A report of this kind must come to grips successfully with the boundaries of consultation the Blue Ribbon Committee report in my opinion does not do this effectively.
13. My girlfriend's brother is a tall good looking man.
14. We Chinese are different from Americans. We are hesitant to blurt out the truth for fear of offending others they are not.
15. John's oldest brother died at the age of eighty-two his youngest brother died at seventy.
16. This morning Mrs. Johnson got up early made breakfast for herself and her husband and washed the dishes then she got into the car and drove downtown.
17. The Supreme Court's role is to review law it is not a fact-finding court.
18. This classification is extremely important to a person in our society it determines almost everything else about his future life.

Exercise 6   As previously noted, a semicolon (;) may replace a comma plus conjunction. Punctuate each of the following sentences by replacing the comma plus conjunction with a semicolon.

Example: My friend Sam, who went to high school with me, now
             attends Harvard University, and his sister goes to a
             college for women.
             *My friend Sam, who went to high school with me, now
             attends Harvard University; his sister goes to a college
             for women.*

1. It is easy for politicians to talk about fighting for one's country, but they are not the ones who have to go to war.

2.   One would think that a man with all that money was extremely happy, but as a matter of fact he is miserable.

3.   Many people call Mr. Reed a communist, and others call him the poor man's hero.

4.   Everyone should take only one piece of chicken, but if you are still hungry you can come back for seconds.

5.   In the olden days the man of the house made all the decisions, and the wife never dared to disagree.

6.   Mr. Young was a respected member of the community, and he was also the town's sheriff and dog catcher.

7.   Of course I told the sheriff about that crazy woman driver, for how was I to know she was his wife.

8.   We all agree that every institution of higher education needs such plans, for without them our day-to-day operation lacks adequate direction.

9.   This was the case with my brother, and I have found it to be true with other students as well.

10.   A man can stay alive without food for about thirty days, but a man without water will die within one to four days.

11.   The hungry student looked in the refrigerator for something to eat, and all he could find was a tiny chicken leg.

Dash

D.   The *dash* (–) represents a break in the grammatical pattern and—sometimes—an interruption in thought. It allows one to insert an afterthought as well as to illustrate or enumerate specific examples or details. In modern usage the pair of dashes tends to replace parentheses to set off interesting and informative details. Observe the following examples:

> *If you fail to do that, you have what you have here—a city under the gun, a city ready to explode.*
>
> *Later Henry earned a bachelor's degree from Reed College in Portland—graduating Phi Beta Kappa—and a Ph.D. from Columbia University.*
>
> *Of these, only two compounds—sodium nitrate and alum oxide—are known to cause oxidation.*
>
> *Engineers, architects, sociologists—these are the kinds of professional men we need to build better cities.*

1. The dash is often used with repeated words or phrases to provide emphasis or dramatic effect. Note the following:

> *But in a larger sense, we cannot dedicate—we cannot*
> *consecrate—we cannot hallow—this ground.* (Abraham
> Lincoln)
> *The same revolutionary beliefs are still at issue around*
> *the globe—the belief that the rights of man come from*
> *the hand of God.*

2. A dash is frequently used where a relative pronoun plus *be* has
   been deleted. Observe the following:

> *This awareness has produced a great deal of genuine*
> *concern, which is a necessary first step toward the*
> *solution of our problems.*
> *This awareness has produced a great deal of genuine*
> *concern—a necessary first step toward the solution of*
> *our problems.*

Exercise 7   Punctuate the following sentences by inserting a dash
(—) wherever appropriate.

1. You may call me anytime you please at 12 midnight if you wish.
2. At last I became what I had always wanted to be a trial lawyer.
3. In the north, a tourist would be well advised to visit the Atacama
   desert the driest spot on earth as well as the lovely beaches
   nearby.
4. The desire to have a good job, a decent home, and a proper
   education for our children these are the goals most people seek
   in life.
5. All these factors unity, coherence and organization are extremely important in writing good expository prose.
6. Only five other countries Peru, Ecuador, Bolivia, Chile and
   Paraguay had a relatively large homogeneous population.
7. We are asking for an enlarged budget for only one reason to
   upgrade the quality of higher education.
8. Many of the services we plan especially in health, recreation,
   and care for the aged are not yet funded.
9. We are doing this in a manner consistent with that philosophy
   nonviolently, with black and white together.
10. It is not necessary to conduct dozens of experiments to demon-
    strate the obvious that human beings are subject to error.
11. It is like experiencing two seasons in a single day winter in the
    morning and summer in the afternoon.
12. The dismissal of the dean an unexpected move by the new
    president caused many faculty members to protest vigorously.

13. Many of us read this magazine for information that cannot be obtained elsewhere for its serious research on important political developments.

14. With psychological help, the drug addict can gain security and develop strength of character achievements which can help him get rid of his addiction.

Colon

E. The *colon* (:) is used to list or enumerate. Observe the following examples:

> *This region produces most of our important crops: rice, wheat, corn, and sugar cane.*
>
> *But many things have happened since then: strikes, riots, unemployment, and an unpopular war.*
>
> *Two or more coordinate forms are separated by commas, as follows: "He was a tall, dark, handsome man."*
>
> *I urge you to vote "no" in the upcoming referendum for the following reasons: First, there is no . . .*

Exercise 8   Summary: Punctuate using a colon, semicolon, and/or comma as necessary.

1. Hoover High School was represented by the following beauty queens Rose White sophomore Helen Blue senior and Marie Gold senior.

2. Here are some steps to take before going abroad apply for a passport get the necessary shots from your doctor and ask him for a stomach remedy just in case.

3. The goals of education are these to learn about the past to study the present and to realize one's full potential in the future.

4. There are three causes for these unfortunate conditions lack of education constant poverty and few job opportunities.

5. The point I want to make is this Let's not be too quick to criticize the *other* guy.

6. Who can forget the words of Neil Armstrong as he set foot on the moon "One small step for a man one giant leap for mankind."

7. The Grand Jury outrage amounts to this It has whitewashed a highly culpable National Guard Unit it has made a severe attack on the academic community and it has tried to discredit our students.

8. The future seems reserved for fast efficient electronic communication networks.
9. Approaching the end of the decade our membership had almost tripled losing some and gaining others.

Capitalization

F. The following rules will serve as a guide to current *capitalization* practices:

1. Distinguish clearly between upper and lower case letters in script by adequate differential in size of letters.

A a J t V v W w M m

2. Capitalize the first word of a sentence. This is the basic rule, but notice the following exceptions:

a. A sentence in parentheses within another sentence normally is not capitalized.

> *He was a passenger on the same plane that brought the Vietnamese students (that was on June 29th), but he was not a student.*

b. A sentence after a colon is not usually capitalized when it explains or is closely related to the preceding sentence.

> *Her next problem was the most confusing: how could she keep her romance a secret?*

3. Capitalize the first word of a direct quotation, unless only a part of a sentence is being quoted.

> *I said, "He is a Kiowa Indian who grew up on an Indian reservation in New Mexico."*
>
> *His writing is praised for its "fearlessness and provocative" content.*
>
> *He warned them, "You're treading on dangerous ground."*
>
> *The speaker explained that the program "states unequivocally that federal relief programs have failed."*

Note: When a quotation is interrupted and resumed, do not capitalize the first word unless it begins a new sentence or the first word of the resumed quotation itself should be capitalized:

> *"I will," he declared, "defend your right to disagree, but I will not defend your principles."*
>
> *"You should have ordered the shrimp salad," she said. "It is quite delicious."*

4. Capitalize the first word of each entry in an outline.
   a. *Causes of the problem*
      (1) *Direct causes*
      (2) *Contributing factors*
5. Capitalize proper nouns in accordance with the following rules and examples thereof:
   a. People's names:
      Mrs. Robert Smith
      Aunt Helen
      Uncle Richard
      Michael Simples, Jr.
   b. Titles used with proper names
      Professor Wilson   *Dr. Smith*
      Father George Turner   *Governor Brown*
      Senator Murphy   *King George III*
      Judge Bernard   *ex-President Truman*
   c. Titles, terms of kinship or affection used in place of a name without an article
      There's Mother.
      (But: *There is my mother.*)

      I think Sister has something to say.
      (But: *My sister wishes to go now.*)
   Or when used in direct address.
      I didn't hear you, Professor.
      Yes, Doctor, I understand.
      Listen to this, Honey.
      I love you, Darling.
      Thank you, Judge.
   Note: A title used with an article is considered a common noun.
      The senator is in Washington now.
      The doctor will see you now.
      The professor has a class now.
   d. An honorary form of address associated with certain positions.
      Thank you, your Majesty.
      Yes, your Honor.
      Will you clarify that, Mr. President?

e. Salutation and complementary close of a letter.

Dear Sir: *Yours truly,*
Dear Madam: *Sincerely yours,*
Gentlemen: *Affectionately,*

6. Ships, planes, trains.
the *Queen Mary*   the *S.S. Fresno*
the *Sacred Cow*   the *Santa Fe Chief*
the *Spirit of St. Louis*

7. Trade names which have been copyrighted.
Kleenex
Ford, Chevrolet, Oldsmobile
Coca-Cola
Ivory Snow

8. Names of the Deity and pronouns referring to Him, religious writings, names of religions and concepts, temples.
"God's in His heaven; all's right with the world."
"The Lord is my salvation."
*"In the name of the Father, the Son, and the Holy
    Ghost."*
Jehovah
Islam
the Koran
the Bible
Confucianism
Christianity

Note: Do not capitalize in case of reference to multiple gods, as in *"The gods smiled on him."*

9. Names of places, including the following:
a. Continents: *North America, Africa*
b. Countries: *Russia, Japan, England*
c. States: *California, New York, New Mexico*
d. Counties: *Fresno County, Santa Barbara County*
e. Cities and towns: *San Francisco, Tokyo, Moscow, Paris*
f. Rivers and canals: *the Mississippi River, the Suez Canal*
   Note: The article *the* is not capitalized in the above two examples.
g. Oceans, lakes, and other bodies of water.
h. Mountains. If reference is to a mountain chain the name is

preceded by the article *the,* not capitalized. An article is not used in reference to a single mountain.

Mt. Rushmore   *Mt. Everest*
The Rocky Mountains   *The Andes*

i. Streets, roads, as in addresses.

942 Tenth Avenue
10 North Frederick Street
on West Clinton Avenue
Highway 99

j. Buildings, bridges

The Empire State Building
St. Paul's Cathedral
Golden Gate Bridge

k. Specific geographical areas

the Near East
the Far East
the Middle West
the deep south
The American Civil War was fought between the North and the South.

Note: Articles are used with the names of regions. The points of the compass referred to as directions are not capitalized.

"Go west, young man, go west."
We traveled south.
That's the northeast corner

But: *In the West you will find men who are men and women who are glad of it.*

10. Adjectives derived from proper names of places or of people.

A Fresnan is a person from Fresno.
Dr. Jameson is a professor of Greek literature.
Her uncle owns a Chinese restaurant.
Shakespeare was the leading author of Elizabethan drama.
That was a good example of an Australian definition.

11. Capitalize exact names of courses but not academic areas of study.

He was enrolled in Biology 290 last semester.

But: *I passed my history course.*
My favorite subjects are English and algebra.

12. Capitalize academic degrees.
>   *John Cathcart, M.D.*
>   *Richard Drilling, D.D.S.*
>   *William Willing, A.B., M.A., Ph.D.*

13. Names of languages.
>   *He speaks French, Japanese, and German.*
>   *Jacob failed English last semester.*

14. Capitalize proper names of organizations, groups, institutions.
   a. Companies
>   *IBM (or I.B.M. or International Business Machines)*
>   *Bank of America*
>   *The Prudential Insurance Company*
>   *the Ford Motor Company*

Note: The article *the* is capitalized when it is part of the corporate name.

   b. Schools, colleges, universities, academic departments.
>   *The University of Minnesota*
>   *Bullard High School*
>   *the Anthropology Department*

But: *I graduated from high school, but I did not attend a university.*

   c. Clubs, fraternal organizations, service organizations.
>   *Kappa Alpha Theta*
>   *Knights of Columbus*
>   *the Rotary Club*
>   *the American Red Cross*

   d. Political and governmental institutions, parties.
>   *the Republican Party*
>   *the Democratic Party*
>   *the Peace Corps*
>   *the Eighty-eighth Congress*
>   *the Ways and Means Committee*
>   *the State Department*
>   *the Senate*
>   *the United Nations*

But: *He is a republican; she is a democrat.*

   e. Religious bodies
>   *the Roman Church*
>   *the Greek Orthodox Church*
>   *the Salvation Army*

Note: When *catholic* is used to mean *universal* or *orthodox* to mean *traditional*, the words are not capitalized.

15. Capitalize names of historic events, periods, doctrines, and documents.

> *War of the Roses, Spanish-American War, World War I, WW II, the Reformation, the Middle Ages, the Depression, the Treaty of Trent, the Bill of Rights*

16. Capitalize names of races and nationalities.

> *Eskimo*   *Mediterranean*
> *Anglo-Saxon*   *Negro* or *Black*
> *Armenian*   *Indian*
> *Semitic*   *Caucasian* or *White*

Note: He is *black* (meaning color).
He is a *Black* (meaning race).
There is a demand for *Black Power* (meaning racial).

17. Capitalize the names of the months, days of the week, and holidays (but not the seasons).

> *April, May, June*
> *Monday, Wednesday, Friday*
> *Christmas, Easter*
> *the Fourth of July*
> *the spring months are March, April, and May*

18. Capitalize the first and all words in titles of books, magazines, movies, poems, songs, works of art or literature, except articles, prepositions and conjunctions of fewer than five letters.

> *Silent Spring* (book)
> *Time; Harper's* (magazines)
> *The Graduate* (movie)
> *"Ode to a Nightingale"* (poem)
> *"Home Sweet Home"* (song)
> *The Last Supper* (painting)

Exercise 9   Capitalize as necessary in the paragraphs below.

The professor was delighted to see the reverend thomas white again just last spring while on a walking trip in the alps. They had met first in the far east; the second time at the university of minnesota during the fall semester of 1965; their third meeting was in the dining car of the twentieth century limited.

After the professor had retired, he began an extensive tour of the usa and returned to his legal residence at 293 ocean avenue, san luis obispo, california, infrequently and for brief periods only.

After his retirement and the death of his wife, the reverend thomas discovered that mountain climbing and walking tours were economical ways to travel as well as to indulge his love of nature. he had met congressmen, senators, and judges during his trips; he had been thrilled by the grandeur of the rocky mountains and the mississippi river, by the beauty of yosemite national park, and by the autumn colors of new england.

During their most recent meeting, professor jones and the reverend white planned a camping tour. they purchased a ford station wagon, into which they loaded their camping equipment, a stock of food which included coca cola, c. and h. sugar, powdered milk, condensed milk, canned hams and bacon, and a variety of campbell soups.

Both men enjoyed reading; therefore they had a supply of books which included the bible, the complete works of shakespeare, the history of the war of the roses, world war II in retrospect, the siege of leningrad, and most of the books from the best seller lists.

Apostrophe

G.   Whether viewed as a component of spelling or as a mark of
     punctuation, the *Apostrophe* has three distinct uses.
     1. The apostrophe is used to indicate that something has been
        omitted.
        a. The omission of letters is called *contraction* and is
           demonstrated in the following examples:
           (1)   Idiomatic contractions:
                     ma'am (madam)
                     o'clock (of the clock)
           (2)   Shortened words (not the same as abbreviations, which
                 are followed by a period):
                     Nat'l (national)
                     sec'y (secretary)
           (3)   Combinations of pronouns (and sometimes nouns)
                 with forms of *be, have,* and auxiliaries *will* and *would*:
                     I'm here   he's gone
                     we'll go   she'd see
                     John's here   they'd play
                 (Context alone indicates whether *he's* is *he has* or *he is.*)
           (4)   Combinations of *be* or auxiliaries with *not*:
                     He can't   We won't
                     You mustn't   They shouldn't
                 (The form *am* does not contract with *not*; therefore
                 the form is *I'm lucky, am I not?*)

b. In certain expressions, years are shortened. When this is done in writing, the apostrophe indicates the omission.
   The class of '60 had a tenth reunion.
   Her first child was born in '42.

c. Sounds are sometimes omitted by speakers of certain dialects. In writing, omissions of sounds are indicated by apostrophes.

Yes'm	*How'm I doin'*
Where's 'e goin'	*Nice ev'nin'*

d. Syllables are sometimes omitted from words. In writing, omissions of syllables are indicated by apostrophes. As the shortened forms come into general use, the apostrophe is frequently omitted. Thus we have
   cello from *violincello*
   bus from *omnibus*
   auto from *automobile*
   phone from *telephone*
   chutist from *parachutist*
   However, some writers use the apostrophe still in
   'phone and *'chutist*

2. The apostrophe is used to indicate possession. Rules for use of the apostrophe in possessive forms may be summarized as follows:

   a. Add apostrophe + *s* to either singular or plural nouns not ending in *s*:
      a child's toy
      the children's games
      woman's one desire
      women's apparel
      an attorney's office
      a baby's world
      a week's vacation
      a dollar's worth
   Note: Usage is somewhat divided on single syllable proper nouns ending in *s*.
      Keats' poems or *Keats's poems*
      Charles' hat or *Charles's hat*
   Consistency in usage is recommended.

b. Add only an apostrophe to a plural noun ending in *s*:
> *the boys' dog* (more than one boy owns the dog)
> *the attorneys' offices*
> *the alligators' pond*
> *the camels' humps*
> *the horses' saddles*
> *the bees' wings*

c. Add only an apostrophe to a singular noun of more than one syllable and ending in *s*:
> *Hermes' wings*
> *Jesus' teachings*
> *Ulysses' travels*

d. Add apostrophe + *s* after names so as to indicate individual or joint ownership.
> *Mary and John's home* (they are co-owners)
> *Bob's and Tom's homes* (each owns a home)

e. Add apostrophe + *s* to the end of noun phrases of these types:
> *a mother-in-law's privilege*
> *a brother-in-law's home*
> *her sister-in-law's dress*
> *anyone else's theory*

Note: The possessive form of the *in-law* plurals follows the same rule:
> *my brothers-in-law's cars*
> *her sisters-in-law's ideas*

f. Add apostrophe + *s* to indefinite pronouns:
> *somebody's good luck*
> *anyone's guess*
> *someone's fault*
> *everybody's privilege*

Note: Because *his, hers, their, our, your, its,* are possessive forms, the apostrophe is not required.
> *The dress is hers. It is hers.*
> *Her opinion is known. The opinion is hers.*
> *Our house is for sale. The house is ours.*
> *His seat is vacant. The vacant seat is his.*
> *Their car is green. The green car is theirs.*

Its is the possessive neuter pronoun:
> *What is its price?*

It's is the contraction of *it is*:
> *It's not for sale.*

g. Instead of the apostrophe, use *of* to form the possessive of inanimate objects:
> *the legs of the table*
> *the roof of the house*
> *the corner of the room*
> *the point of the pencil*
> *the roots of the tree*

Exceptions in popular use:
> *city's water supply*
> *ship's mast*
> *nation's capital*

3. The apostrophe + *s* is used to form plurals which might otherwise be confusing or ambiguous.
> How many *i*'s are in *Mississippi*?
> Dot your *i*'s and cross your *t*'s.
> Her size *20*'s are too small this year.
> He got three *A*'s and two *B*'s and two *O.K.*'s.
> One of those *that*'s should be deleted.
> Her conversation is full of *and*'s.

Notice that only the letter, figure, or word is italicized/underlined, not the apostrophe + *s*.

Note: Some publications are beginning to omit the apostrophe if no confusion results: *8s, 20s, 1890s.*

Exercise 10   Write the singular possessive form and, where possible, the plural possessive form of the following words:

	Singular Possessive	*Plural Possessive*
who		
baby		
attorney		
man		
lady		
woman		
someone		
she		
it		
person		
mother-in-law		
child		
you		

Exercise 11   Add the apostrophe or apostrophe + *s* to form possessive phrases:

Charles hat	Roberts friend
Keats poems	a friend of Robert
babies tears	anyones problem

Italics

H.   In print, *italics* (a distinguishing slanting type) indicates special emphasis or distinction. In typewriting or handwriting, under-lining is used to indicate italics. The following are examples of current usage of italics/underlining.

1. Titles of books, magazines, newspapers
   Reader's Digest is published monthly.
   Time is a weekly news magazine.
   Gore Vidal wrote *Myra Breckenridge.*
   The pastor took a *Bible* with him whenever he traveled.
   I subscribe to the *San Francisco Chronicle.*
   Do you have *The World Almanac* on your desk?
   Political candidates are especially interested in the
      editorials of the *New York Times* and the *Washington Post.*

Have you read *Women: A Minority Group*?

"A Horseman in the Sky" and "An Occurrence at Owl
Creek Bridge" are included in *The Collected Writings
of Ambrose Bierce.*

Note: Chapter titles, essays, short stories, poems, television
shows, and parts of complete volumes are not italicized or
underlined, but are set in quotation marks.

2. Names of plays, movies, works of art

Richard Chamberlain starred in *Hamlet.*

Leonardo da Vinci painted the *Mona Lisa.*

The first solo album of George Harrison, a former Beatle, is
All Things Must Pass.

3. Names of ships, trains, aircraft

The *United States* has sailed her last voyage.

Valley residents hope the *Sante Fe Chief* will not be
discontinued.

The first pilot to fly solo across the Atlantic Ocean was
Charles Lindbergh in the *Spirit of St. Louis.*

4. Foreign words or expressions and scientific terms

She graduated *summa cum laude.*

A popular song of some years ago was based on the
Spanish motto *que sera sera.*

If you check a dictionary you will see that *mal de mer*
means *seasickness.*

The Latin motto, *e pluribus unum*, used on U.S. coins,
means "one out of many"—a government formed by
uniting many states.

The term *et al.* is an abbreviation of the Latin words *et alii*,
meaning *and others.*

Note: Many foreign words have been absorbed into English
and no longer need to be italicized. When in doubt, consult
a dictionary.

5. Letters, numbers, and words used out of context

Do you spell *dollar* with an *er* or an *ar*?

He spells *grammar* with an *er.*

Please use the words *obscene* and *immoral* in sentences
which demonstrate both their connotative and
denotative meanings.

A popular current expression is *like wow,* which might
indicate the speaker is impressed, amazed, indignant,

embarrassed, delighted, depressed, or merely speech-
less.
   6. Words or phrases singled out for special emphasis
          Do not (I repeat—*do not*) leave the classroom during the
          test.

   Note: The use of italics or underlining for emphasis is not a
   substitute for strong, clear writing, as the examples suggest:
          He was violently angry.
          (better than)
          He was *very* mad.

          She shrieked her refusal.
          She screamed "no."
          (better than)
          She said *no* very loud.

Exercise 12   Mastery test on italics.

   1.   John bought a paperbound edition of Gone With the Wind.
   2.   The National Observer was a weekly newspaper.
   3.   Their favorite painting is the Mona Lisa; their favorite opera is
        Tosca.
   4.   Be certain to use ibid. and op. cit. correctly when footnoting.
   5.   Will you translate vaya con Dios for me?
   6.   My parents sailed on the last trip of the Queen Elizabeth.
   7.   I suggest that you inquire why it happened, not how it happened.
   8.   One of her Christmas gifts to me was a subscription to the New
        Yorker, a weekly magazine.
   9.   The students waited two hours for the Twentieth Century
        Limited before it finally chugged into the depot.
  10.   Do you distinguish between caught and cot in your dialect?
  11.   Why don't you dot your i's and cross your t's?
  12.   A 6 is an inverted 9.
  13.   His parents were delighted to see the words magna cum laude on
        his diploma.
  14.   One of the new TV shows is The Bold Ones.
  15.   I own a Modern Library edition of the Complete Poems of Keats
        and Shelley.
  16.   One of the new albums is All Things Must Pass.
  17.   He spent all day Sunday reading the New York Times.
  18.   Do you keep a dictionary on your desk?

19. Is the primary stress on may or be?
20. Please use the word reluctant in a sentence.
21. Richard Chamberlain's performance in Hamlet has been highly praised by most critics.
22. Is the Spirit of St. Louis the plane Lindbergh flew across the Atlantic Ocean?
23. The Women's Liberation Front has popularized Women: A Minority Group to the best-seller list.

ANSWER KEY

SECTION
A

Unit 1
Exercise 1

For Smith

Tom Smith has all the attributes of a good Student Body president. He is a moderate, with proven ability to speak with all sides on the divisive issues which confront this college.

His opponent in today's election, Bill Jones, cannot do this—at least his voting record of the past and his recent actions do not give the indication that he would.

To get down to specific cases, Jones is too provincial in his outlook. If he wins the election he will owe too many political debts to his supporters in the Agriculture Department to be an effective representative of the entire student body. Jones is overly optimistic to think he can work with all groups on campus. As an Ag major and a leader in the School of Agriculture, Jones is tied idealogically to the students of that school only.

Smith's voting record as College Union Senator-at-Large has been progressive. It was Smith who explored and recommended the need for construction of a new college union. He has continuously supported the Educational Opportunity Program and other programs which serve the needs of providing a broader education.

Exercise 2

Every society feels the need for an ideal for its collective goals; contemporary civilization, which no longer sees life as a God-ordained, unalterable entity but as something in a state of perpetual change, is critical of itself because of some self-assigned ends that it never succeeds in attaining. And individuals no longer regard the position they occupy in society as definitive—as if there were no other life save the one they lead on this earth. They attach vital importance to the political and economic regime that controls their lives.

The question for us in Africa is which, if any, of the many "isms" of our time is best suited for our needs at this time. Is it possible to evolve something entirely new to serve our ends? A possible answer is given by secular ideology which, as the ideology of the State, is held up as the highest embodiment of truth.

Unfortunately for modern man, whose most obvious instrument of progress is science and technology, the language of science and technology and productivity does not warm the heart, even if it is intellectually convincing. But when the demands and goals of science are expressed in the language of an ideology, everything is altered. Now, it is no longer a matter of working or producing, but of building socialism, a great nation, or of creating a new kind of man in a new kind of Great Society.

Exercise 3

Will machines replace teachers? On the contrary, they are capital equipment to be used by teachers to save time and labor. In assigning certain mechanizable functions to machines, the teacher emerges in his proper role as an indispensable human being. He may teach more students than heretofore, but he will do so in fewer hours and with fewer burdensome chores.

The role of the teacher may well be changed, for machine instruction will affect several traditional practices. Students may continue to be grouped in "grades" or "classes," but it will be possible for each to proceed at his own level, advancing as rapidly as he can. The other kind of "grade" will also change its meaning. In traditional practice, the grade C means that a student has a smattering of a whole course. But if machine instruction assures mastery at every stage, a grade will be useful only in showing *how far* a student has gone. The grade C might mean only that he is halfway through a course.

Differences in ability raise other questions. A program designed for the slowest student in the school system will probably not seriously delay the fast student, who will be free to progress at his own speed. If this does not prove to be the case, programs can be constructed at two or more levels, and students can be shifted from one to the other as performances dictate.

Exercise 4
4, 6, 3, 1, 5, 2

Exercise 5
4, 2, 1, 5, 3

Exercise 6
4, 2, 1, 3, 5

Exercise 7
Paragraph I: 3, 6, 4, 9, 1
Paragraph II: 5, 8, 2, 7

Topic sentence recognition
Example 1: The first sentence is the topic sentence.
Example 2: The third sentence.
Example 3: The last sentence.
Example 4: The first sentence.
Example 5: The last sentence.

Selection 1: Best choice is b).
Selection 2: Best choice is a).
Selection 3: Best choice is c).

Exercise 8

These are only suggestions; there is no one best answer.

1. Original author: "Medicine was what Jack always wanted."
    Student suggestions: Jack always knew what his profession would be./Jack was
        a very determined young man./Jack always wanted to be a physician.
2. Original author: "New York City was full of need and suffering."
    Student suggestions: New York City was in the midst of the great depression.
        New York City was experiencing economic difficulties./New York City was
        confronted with serious economic problems.
3. Original author: "Red China, a nation in the communist camp, is currently in
        striking contrast to the island of Japan."
    Student suggestions: China and Japan represent two different points of view.
        China and Japan have chosen different goals for the future./There is a
        different political orientation in two powerful countries of Asia.

Exercises 9 and 10

Exchange papers with a fellow student and give constructive criticism of each other's
paper.

Exercise 11

Corrections are shown in bold type. Other changes are possible by changing singular
nouns to plural and vice versa.

1. The west coast, which **is** wide and sandy, is different from **the** other side of **the**
    island.
2. This **includes** the holidays of Easter and New Year's.
3. The **streets** are **filled** with people hurrying to pay **a** visit to **friends**.
4. Sun-Moon Lake, which is Taiwan's leading holiday resort, ~~it~~ is occupied by
    local people.
5. But most **of** the **tourists** like to have **a** few pictures taken with **the** natives.
6. As **we** all know. ~~The~~ petroleum is not **a** renewable resource.
7. The **farmers** have to get the best use out of the land.
8. Anyone **who** wants to find a place of total relaxation should go there.
9. The tourists come to my country to **visit** different **parts** of the country.
10. It is one of the best **attractions** for the tourists.
11. Vast numbers of **tourists** come to visit every **year**.
12. Some **students** are **forced** to drop out **of** school.
13. The world must find **a** solution for **its** oil shortage.
14. I saw on TV **that** many **buildings** in the city **were** destroyed.
15. Because of the increase in the price of oil, the cost of fertilizer, which ~~it~~ also uses
    a lot of energy in the manufacturing process, **has** also gone up.

16. Today, it is hard for some countries **to afford** the new, higher prices.
17. In other **words**, the world needs an energy source **which** is ecologically good for **the** environment, yet economical to exploit.
18. This new invention can convert sunlight **into** electricity or **the** sea tides **into** some kind of t~~he~~ usable energy.
19. I truly enjoy helping people, **caring** for them, and **making** them happy.
20. Of course, the middle class has fewer **problems compared** to **the** lower class.

Exercise 12
Corrections are shown in bold type. Other changes are possible by changing singular nouns to plural and vice versa.
(1) One of the newest **buildings** on campus is **the** library. (2) Knowing how the library works **helps** us use **the** facilities more **efficiently.** (3) The library **offers** everything most **students** need, and the people who **work** there are very helpful. (4) This **makes it easy for** the students to study. (5) The study areas, however, which are **supposed** to be quiet **places, seem** to generate a lot of talking by **the students.** (6) I like to read in **the** music library because **it** is so quiet. (7) For the student who **wants** to know what **happened** in **the** year he or she **was** born, there **are** old newspapers to look at.

(8) Another of the **services offered** by the library is **the** Reserved Book Room. (9) It offers some **other** services such as copiers and **typewriters.** (10) All of **these** typewriters are t~~he~~ modern **ones.** (11) I also heard that the new library will **contain** a new computer system for checking out **books** in the future.

(12) The students have free access to the stacks and are **allowed** to look at any of the **periodicals** they wish. (13) The Public Affairs section **contains** various **kinds** of materials, such as books, **pamphlets,** and magazines.

(14) The new library **contains** a number of **books** written in the 15th century. (15) There **are** also a lot of instructional materials that **cover** grades K through 12. (16) I cannot go into more detail to describe **the** library facilities because that would **take** too long.

(17) All in all, I think the new library is a **well-organized,** a~~nd~~ quiet place to study.

Exercise 13
Exchange papers with a fellow student and correct each other's work.

Exercise 14
a. Today, the world continues to use more and more oil despite its high price. But as we all know, petroleum is not a renewable resource. One day in the future we will run out of this energy source, and that day may not be very far off.
b. Exchange papers with a fellow student and correct each other's work.

Exercise 15
1. What John has written is only his opinion.
2. Where the money comes from is not my problem.
3. What the workers are demanding is the right to strike.
4. Why the farmers want more land is not the main issue.

5. Whose advice a young person should take is not an easy question to answer.
6. How (by what means) Jones was able to win the election is a very interesting question.
7. How often one should consult the dictionary depends on the individual.
8. How much time that project will require will depend on several factors.

Exercise 16
1. We still don't know what caused all the excitement.
2. I don't remember whom the secretary told.
3. He asked if I knew what the right to strike means.
4. We must decide which (what kind of) typewriter we want to purchase.
5. We can only guess what the consequences of overpopulation will be.
6. We are often asked to explain why (for what reason) we want a good education.
7. Most people do not realize how difficult the entrance exam is.
8. We must find out where the best opportunities lie.
9. No one seems to realize how serious the situation really is.
10. We all have different ideas as to what being successful in life means.

Exercise 17
1. Mr. Hall told me he was in complete sympathy with my position.
2. Janos was saying he didn't like to work in the lab on weekends.
3. Two students told me they couldn't complete their assignment on time.
4. Mr. Scott indicated he was very satisfied with the result.
5. The clerk told me I had to fill out the application form in duplicate.
6. Susie telephoned to say she had the flu and wouldn't be going to class today.
7. The thief admitted that he had stolen the apple pies.
8. The suspect denied he had done it (doing it) and swore he was innocent.
9. The judge asked Mr. King whether he was willing to testify in the case.
10. The instructor demanded to know why Richard had dropped his course.
11. The principal asked Miss Smith whether her students were well behaved.
12. The teacher asked the students whether they wanted to have their test at a later time.
13. The advisor wanted to know why I had chosen history as my major.

Exercises 20 and 21
Check your work with a friend or fellow student; then show it to the teacher for evaluation.

SECTION
B

Unit 2
Exercise 1
1. I met the man who (that) came. . . .
2. . . . that new book that (which) everyone is talking about.
3. . . . the eye doctor whom you recommended.
4. . . . a new car which (that) cost $6,000.
5. I have a friend who (that) thinks that. . .
6. . . . to your friend whose uncle is a lawyer?
7. That is Mrs. Brown, whose daughter John is engaged to.
8. . . . Mr. Hall, whom everyone has confidence in.
9. . . . to Mr. King, whose advice she had taken.
10. . . . to Professor Dunce, whose ideas on. . .

Exercise 3
The relative pronoun *cannot* be omitted in the following: Nos. 2, 5, 8, 11, 13, 14, 16, and 18.

Exercise 4
The word *that* cannot be substituted in the following: Nos. 1, 3, 8.

Exercise 5
1. . . . in the spring when (at which time) the earth is warm and moist.
2. . . . to California where the father soon found a job.
3. . . . on December 31, when (at which time) everyone will be. . . .
4. . . . in Florida, where he can go fishing. . . .
5. . . . in California, where they can enjoy. . . .
6. . . . in 1982, when (by which time) he will have earned his degree.
7. . . . in April, when the cherry blossoms are in full bloom.
8. . . . in April and May, during which time the monsoon rains fall.
9. . . . open market, where one can find a great variety of tropical fruits.
10. . . . to 210 degrees, at which point the solution exploded.

Unit 3
Exercise 1
I have always wanted to visit the city of Paris, which I have heard so much about, where everyone falls in love, especially in the spring, when the flowers are in bloom and romance is in the air.

Exercise 2
Last night I spoke on the phone with my cousin Janos, who plans to stay in Colorado, where he is currently attending college, until next June, when (at which time) he hopes to graduate in Engineering.

Exercise 3
My friend Enrique, (who is) a foreign student from Bolivia, (which is) a landlocked nation in South America which shares (sharing) a common border with Chile and Peru, is going to show some slides of his country.

Exercise 4
The national soup of India is called *curry*, a hot, spicy dish that looks like stew. Curry is made from beans—black beans, white beans, and some others whose names (the names of which) I cannot remember.

To us, curry is good, tasteful food and people from my country love it. Curry is very hot and spicy, and since many people are only used to rather bland foods, they refuse to eat it. Consequently, they are unable to appreciate its exotic flavor.

Exercise 5
3. The maid washes the ... and bathrooms besides taking care of the baby.
4. She is a good teacher and scholar as well as an excellent administrator.
5. War not only stimulates ... materials but also helps to ...
6. He falsified ... documents besides cheating on his ...
7. We appreciate ... lent us as well as the moral support ...
8. She enjoys ... other sports as well as playing in ...
9. He types ... invoices in addition to running errands ...
10. The old method was not only inefficient ... time but also added to the ...
11. These industries ... plastics and butane rubber, along with oil refinery ...
12. It comprises ... and magazines plus numerous rare books ...

Exercise 6
Show your effort to the teacher or to a friend or fellow student for evaluation.

Exercise 7
1. Because we are opposed to violence, we cannot agree. ...
2. Unless I hear from you soon, I shall assume. ...
3. If you are unable to attend regularly, you should. ...
4. Inasmuch as I have not heard from him, I assume that. ...
5. As long as no one suffered any injury, why don't we. ...
Continue in the same manner.

Exercise 8
1. I never liked to study mathematics until I took a class. . . .
2. I couldn't get a plane reservation for the day I wanted because all the seats were sold out.
3. When I was fifteen, I took a job in a supermarket in order to earn. . . .
4. I couldn't enter the university as I had wanted to even though I. . . .
5. I am not going to speak to Nancy again since it was she who. . . .
6. Billions of aerosol spray cans are endangering our lives because ozone is. . . .

Exercise 9
There are two possibilities for each, as follows:
1. Although the woman called for help, no one. . . .
    The woman called for help, yet no one came. . . .
2. Even though we waited for two hours, the bus never came.
    We waited for two hours, but the bus never came.
3. As much as I would like to please you, I can't say "yes."
    I would like to please you, but I can't say "yes."
Continue in the same manner.

Exercise 10
1. Having studied hard, Susie was confident. . . .
2. Having been disappointed in the past, Mary now. . . .
3. Having been promised a large fee, the lawyer. . . .
4. Having been elected by a huge majority, the new president. . . .
5. Having done everything medically possible to save the patient, the doctor. . . .
Continue the pattern.

Exercise 11
Check with the teacher or a friend for an evaluation of your work.

Exercise 12
The following answers are only representative, since the position of the adverbial is variable.
1. . . . He, furthermore, understands the psychology of the people.
2. . . . The average citizen, however, is unwilling to become involved.
3. . . . The peaceful demonstrations and protests, consequently, continued.
4. . . . Team morale was therefore rather low.
5. . . . There are, nonetheless, certain characteristic stages which are. . . .
6. . . . I should think, moreover, that someone might. . . .
7. . . . I am, accordingly, directing the Executive Committee. . . .
8. . . . off the strike; thus the problem was solved.

Unit 4

Exercise 1

These corrections represent only one way of correcting; other changes are also possible. Check your work with the teacher.

1.   ... five hours mean failure.
2.   ... and take walks.
3.   ... but he plays football as well.
4.   ... no study—only the enjoyment of music.
5.   After I graduated from high school and passed the entrance exam. ...
     After graduating from high school and passing the entrance exam. ...
6.   ... catalog, and where to find certain information.
7.   ... the boys laughing and making remarks.
8.   ... to be friends rather than enemies?
9.   ... and enjoyment in our life. (or) Money can make us happy and help us enjoy our life. (or) ... and an enjoyable life.
10. ... contributes to a stable and prosperous society.
11. ... guilty, and the judge sentenced the man to four years in jail.
12. ... vice-president, and they gave him a substantial salary increase.

Exercise 3a

The weather in this town ... is uncomfortable. It is not uncomfortable because although the temperature. ..

Exercise 3b

For me, the most interesting place ... country, Spain. I would choose Spain because I have always wanted to. ..

Exercise 3c

I ask you now, is that fair? I say no! I say no because that would mean we are paying. ..

Exercise 3d

I like my father very much and ... gets harder each day. The reason it gets harder is that his health is not the best. ..

Exercise 3e

Even if I cannot get admitted to ... with people. I will try to find a major that allows me to work directly with both children and adults in order to. ..

Exercise 3f

Most people would agree that knowing ... enjoyable for the tourist. Knowing the language, he or she will be able to. ..
(or) Things will be easier because he or she will. ..

Exercise 3g

Despite this city's many problems—problems such as pollution, heavy traffic, and others—I would still like to remain here as long as I can. I want to remain here because I think it is one of the most exciting cities I have ever lived in.

Exercise 5
1. ... letter from the White House bearing the President's signature.
2. ... at the airport, smiling and waving to the waiting crowd.
3. ... registrar asking for information on admission requirements.
4. ... call from the registrar directing him to report to the Dean's Office.
5. ... phone call asking his parents to send him some money.
6. ... of State informing him that I will resign my office. ...
7. ... as prime minister, designating Mr. Wilson as acting prime minister.

Exercise 6
1. ... a resolution which condemns/condemning the action of the president.
2. ... of language, which states that/stating that every sentence. ...
3. ... recommendation which urged/urging the Graduate School to. ...
4. ... of State which directs/directing him to break diplomatic. ...
5. ... proclamation which states/stating that Thanksgiving will. ...
6. ... a new law which requires/requiring the universities to. ...
7. ... by mothers who wish/wishing to protect them from. ...
8. ... a diary which will list/listing all the food they eat. ...
9. ... a new technique which eliminates/eliminating the need for. ...

Exercise 7
1. While driving along the highway, Frank hit a bump in the road.
2. Before going home I usually unplug the fan.
3. Looking into the cellblock, the jailer saw that the prisoners. ...
4. Before Helen agreed to get married, Tom had bought an engagement ring.
5. Before paying the bill, Tom would like to have a detailed invoice.
6. After seeing the doctor, Mary began to feel more at ease.
7. After graduating from high school, I went to work for. ...
8. While traveling to the moon, the astronauts were kept busy with. ...
9. After measuring the specific gravity of the fluid, one looks at. ...
10. Looking in the dictionary, we discovered the source of. ...
11. While Mary was getting into the taxi, Helen tripped and fell down.
12. Noticing the man's exhausted condition, Tom and I offered to. ...

Exercise 8
1. Scientists have found many ways to solve this problem.
2. We could put an end to hunger and poverty with more cooperation among countries.

3. Every government looks forward to being able to solve the economic problems of its people.
4. I wish we could put an end to all the fighting and violence now going on.
5. The governor has declared that the people will have to make sacrifices.
6. The fire chief reported that spontaneous combustion had caused the fire.

Exercise 9

1. The car may have been stolen.
2. That law was repealed in 1947.
3. The letter was sent out on May 15.
4. The military government has been overthrown.
5. These facts have been known for a long time.
6. The new chemistry journal is being distributed to most college libraries.
7. A note of pessimism can be detected in Mr. Wilson's article.
8. A man's right to a good education cannot be denied.
9. The new low-cost housing development was built six months ago.
10. Nothing can be left in the exhibit hall.
11. Students are given the choice of staying in school or joining the army.
12. In our system of justice a man is innocent until (he is) proven guilty.
13. All citizens are expected to be scrupulously honest in filling out their income tax declarations.
14. Something has to be done about the high divorce rate.
15. All students are requested to notify the Student Records Office of any change in schedules.
16. In 1790 the United States was not considered a world power.
17. The Constitution was adopted in 1792.
18. The election results have been tabulated.
19. Smoking is not allowed in this room.
20. Parking is prohibited in this area.

Exercise 10

	Circle	Cross out		Circle	Cross out
1.	These articles	them	7.	Those lawyers	them
2.	Sales Company	it	8.	stone statues	them
3.	Medicine (career)	it	9.	the tickets	them
4.	That bicycle	it	10.	other reasons	them
5.	oil	it	11.	the money	it
6.	Those errors	them			

Exercise 11

Cross out	Circle
1. it	that she was in love with Tom
2. it	that we were not notified
3. it	that she was wrong
4. it	that our team won the game
5. it	the heavy traffic
6. it	that the situation will improve
7. it	that there are many

Exercise 12

1. . . . in superstitions are silly.
2. Designing a bridge requires. . . .
3. . . . female doctors who are just. . . .
4. . . . only the students who have. . . .
5. . . . which I thought were important.
6. . . . a handgun can do so very easily.
7. Most of the foreign students have a difficult. . . .
8. . . . in education are caused by. . . .
9. . . . of fertilizer, which uses energy for. . . .
10. . . . in the world today are hungry or. . . .

Exercise 13

These are suggested answers only. There are many other possibilities. Check with the instructor or a fellow student.

1.	it	this bird
2.	it	matrimony
3.	Here	This city
4.	it	this problem
5.	there	in these areas
6.	it	these substances
7.	it	this exploitation
8.	it	this situation
9.	it	this imbalance

Exercise 14

1.	this	4. this	6. this
2.	correct as is	5. this	7. this
3.	this		

Exercise 15

1.	there are	6.	there remain	11.	there has to be
2.	there is	7.	correct as is	12.	it cannot
3.	correct as is	8.	there is	13.	there is
4.	correct as is	9.	it is	14.	it is
5.	there is	10.	there is	15.	correct as is

Exercise 16

Other answers are possible

1. other (toilet) articles, things
2. other crops, products
3. other equipment, items
4. other supplies, groceries, items
5. other sports, games
6. other disasters, calamities
7. other cities, places

Exercise 17

1. I went to buy some bananas, oranges, apples, and some other fruits.
   I went to buy some fruits—bananas, oranges, apples, and some others.
2. We bought some ashtrays, dish towels, coffee mugs, and a few other nice souvenirs.
   We bought some nice souvenirs—ashtrays, dish towels, coffee mugs, and a few others.
3. *Life Magazine, Time, Newsweek*, and many other interesting magazines can be purchased at that newsstand.
   Many interesting magazines—*Life, Time, Newsweek*, and many others—can be purchased at that newsstand.
4. I'm taking math, French, history, and a few other easy subjects.
   I'm taking a few easy subjects—math, French, history, and a few others.
5. That's a good store to buy onions, carrots, lettuce, and many other fresh vegetables.
   That's a good store to buy fresh vegetables—onions, carrots, lettuce, and many others.
6. Relaxation includes playing tennis, reading books, watching TV, and a few other activities.
   Relaxation includes activities such as playing tennis, reading books, watching TV, and a few others.
7. The city has automobile factories, steel plants, textile mills, and some other industrial facilities.
   The city has industrial facilities—automobile factories, steel plants, textile mills, and some others.
8. This region produces vegetables, cherries, cotton, and a few other agricultural products.
   This region produces agricultural products—vegetables, cherries, cotton, and a few others.
9. She has honesty, integrity, patience, and several other good qualities.
   She has good qualities—honesty, integrity, patience, and several others.

Exercise 18

1.	Others	6.	Other religions
2.	Other merchandise	7.	Other knowledge
3.	Other equipment	8.	others
4.	Others	9.	Others
5.	Other chemicals	10.	others

Exercise 19

2. omit "and finish"
3. omit "of the commencement"
4. omit "during the time"
5. omit "to be able to"
6. omit "only" or "no more than"
7. a. The capacity is ... (or)
   b. The library accommodates ...
8. omit "to me"
9. a. omit "of how" (or)
   b. ... I do not know how to go about ...
10. a. omit "in which" (or)
    b. ... taught how to express these ideas.
11. Replace "for the purpose of getting" with "to get"
12. The letter informed Mrs. Levy that ...

Unit 6

Writing Assignment 2

Here are some suggested paraphrases for this exercise.

2. Disposable containers reduce the risk of contamination.
3. Our sales reports sometimes contain confidential information.
4. Please comply promptly.
5. Unlike many people, we fully appreciate careful workmanship.
6. It is reasonable to assume you are interested in our products.
7. This new regulation would require us to conform to the law.
8. The present budget deficit is not entirely unexpected, but the extent of the deficit is rather surprising.
9. It is fairly common for company employees to complain about their salaries.
10. If the number of interoffice phone calls and personal notes becomes so great as to significantly interfere with our employees' normal work, we may have to limit these services in the future.

SECTION

D

Unit 9

Exercise 1

1. Are you not capable of. . . .
2. Is she not worthy. . . .
3. Do you not believe in. . . .
4. Should she not be advised of. . . .
5. Have they not the responsibility. . . .
6. Was he not the injured party. . . .
7. Would you not do the same. . . .
8. Did they not warn you of. . . .
9. Could he not be encouraged to. . . .
10. Had they not announced the plane's departure. . . .
11. Does he not support you. . . .
12. Had he not warned you of the possibility of. . . .
13. Can we not count on your assistance. . . .
14. Must we not be more sure of. . . .
15. Would it not be wise. . . .
16. Would that not be too. . . .
17. Are you not satisfied with. . . .
18. Can we not help each other. . . .

Exercise 2

1. The old man whom there was an article about in the newspaper lives in. . . .
    The old man about whom there was an article in the newspaper lives in. . . .
2. Mr. Smith is the nice man whom I borrowed the money from.
    Mr. Smith is the nice man from whom I borrowed the money.
3. I spoke to some impatient students whom we had ordered those textbooks for.
    I spoke to some impatient students for whom we had ordered those textbooks.
4. Someone contaminated the salt solution which the sample was drawn from.
    Someone contaminated the salt solution from which the sample was drawn.
5. I bought some of those bright blue flowers { which the island is noted for. / for which the island is noted. }
6. Allen West is a philosopher { whom I got my inspiration from. / from whom I got my inspiration. }

7. That is Tom Blonsky, the famous sociologist,
   { whom I went to school with.
   { with whom I went to school.

8. The police interviewed the frightened jeweler
   { whom the diamonds had been stolen from.
   { from whom the diamonds had been stolen.

9. You have to send in an application
   { which you must attach your check to.
   { to which you must attach your check.

10. Sam gave us the answers to some math problems
    { which we are now working on.
    { on which we are now working.

11. The lack of funds caused many problems
    { which I was not prepared for.
    { for which I was not prepared.

12. Mr. Johnson is the man who developed the new program
    { which we have heard so much about.
    { about which we have heard so much.

13. Please indicate below the names of the committees
    { which you are willing to serve on.
    { on which you are willing to serve.

14. Much of the territory in North America had been previously owned by the French
    { whom the British acquired large tracts of land from.
    { from whom the British acquired large tracts of land.

Exercise 3
1. My friend told me about an ugly incident in which a nervous wife shot her husband.
2. For me, the best part of the book was the introduction, in which the author describes the tropical island.
3. A conference on . . . the last week of March, during which time the faculty is requested. . . .
4. . . . serious problem, to which a solution must be found.

5. ... Hawthorne's creative processes, by which the writings of this American novelist came into being.

6. ... an I.D. card, without which no student will be permitted to. ...

7. ... an adequate education, without which it is difficult to. ...

8. ... these four schools, at which new curriculum changes have. ...

9. ... colored tail, by which this beautiful bird can be easily recognized.

10. ... these basic processes by which the economy of the country can be expanded.

11. ... level of income below which one is considered to be poor.

12. ... limits of decency beyond which we should not go.

13. ... new school plan to which we all gave our approval.

14. The dean of the School of Social Sciences, of which the Geography Department is a vital part, cancelled two geography classes for lack of enrollment.

15. ... the various routes by which many new words came into the English language.

Exercise 4

There may be other acceptable word order arrangements. These are the most common:

1. a. Since Aristotle, there has been, and will continue to be, ...
   b. There has been, and will continue to be, much progress in this area since Aristotle.

2. a. (Located) In the suburbs, there are several industries such as light manufacturing and food processing.
   b. There are several industries such as light manufacturing and food processing located in the suburbs.

3. I have dreamed of visiting those places for a long time.

4. a. (In order) to keep the air fresh, they have moved the factories ...
   b. They have moved the factories ... to keep the air fresh.

5. ... of our own to make our family complete.

6. There are a lot of nice places to visit there.

7. I have yet to see a more beautiful beach.

8. I stayed there for two days.

9. The winner has already been decided.

10. Not only did she steal ..., but she also took her job away.
    (..., but she also took away her job.)

11. Some people ... they only look on the bright side of urban life.
    Some people ... they look on only the bright side of urban life.

Exercise 5

The following represent normal, non-emphatic word order.

2. Carl was often late for his appointments.
3. I am presently a student ...
4. I am very much interested in ...
5. The winner has already been decided.
6. I have now earned a total of 13 units.
7. Nancy never comes to school late.
8. My little sister frequently walks to school.
9. If I were suddenly to become rich I would ...
10. I have never been fond of those ...
11. I am now attending Ball State ...
12. Bill has usually studied very hard.
13. Maria has hardly ever been homesick.
14. Albert must have always studied hard.
15. One can seldom find those books ...
16. Automobile exhaust fumes are especially blamed ...
    Automobile exhaust fumes especially are blamed ...

SECTION

F

Unit 11

Exercise 1

1. **Mr. Nelson does not trust young men.**
    Jack is in love with Mr. Nelson's daughter.
    Mr. Nelson considers young men to be foolish and unreliable.
    Perhaps he is influenced by memories of his own youth.
2. **Mr. Morgan married Susie Brown.**
    Mr. Morgan teaches English Literature here in California.
    Susie Brown's father owns that new restaurant on Broadway.
    The restaurant opened just recently.
3. **The Statue of Liberty was a gift from the people of France to the United States.**
    The torch has symbolized freedom and economic opportunity for millions of immigrants.
    Most of the immigrants viewed America as the land of plenty.

4. **America's language has undergone a vigorous growth and development.**
   America itself has undergone a vigorous growth and development.
   This growth has tended to widen the differences between the English of
      England and that of America.
   America's language came from England.
5. **The organization's members were quickly and quietly arrested by the FBI.**
   The members had received orders to launch a strike against the railroad
      company.
   The FBI had been tipped off by an informer.
   The informer had infiltrated the leftist organization.
6. **The Apollo XI astronauts were enthusiastically welcomed aboard the aircraft
   carrier.**
   Two of the astronauts were the first men to set foot on the surface of the
      moon.
   The aircraft carrier had been assigned to the recovery operation to pick up
      the returning space heroes.
7. **The Appeals Court refused to grant an immediate stay against the contro-
   versial underground blast.**
   The underground blast was scheduled to go off within a week.
   The Court said it was dealing only with the legal question of disclosure of
      information.

Exercise 2
1. Mary Wilson, who teaches sixth grade at Kratt Elementary School, won the
   annual teaching award (which is) given for outstanding service to students.
2. Hawaii, (which is) often called the "island paradise," was settled by
   Polynesian people from Tahiti who sailed across the Pacific in large canoes.
3. A hormone (which is) responsible for growth in the human body was
   synthesized for the first time by research scientists at the Medical Center.
4. William Faulkner's *Two Soldiers*, (which is) about an eight-year-old farm boy
   whose older brother goes off to enlist in the army, is one of the finest short
   stories ever written in America.
5. Larry Francis, (who is) a customer service manager in Chicago, where he
   coaches a little league baseball team, won the award for community service
   two years in a row.
6. The new governor of Texas, who, like the previous governor, was confronted
   with a deficit budget, has proposed new legislation to solve the current
   financial crisis.
7. The award for the best short story was won by James Robinson, (who is) a
   young author, who, according to the editor of *Literary Review*, really knows
   how to write a suspenseful tale.
8. Captain Kane, the company commander who claims he gave no unlawful order
   to Lt. Smith, will be asked to testify . . .

(Note: Other ways of combining the above sentences are also possible.)

Exercise 3

1.   Nathaniel Hawthorne, (who was) an American novelist and short-story writer, wrote several novels which, like many of his short stories, deal with the gloomy spirit of Puritanism.
2.   The state of emergency, which was declared after new disorders broke out late this morning, affects the capital city and the provincial area around it, where about a third of the country's nine million people live.
3.   Successful candidates for the job will be chosen by a special committee consisting of seven employees of the company, at least three of whom must be under thirty years of age.
4.   The Suez Canal, which has always been a vital region in peace as in war, is important for both Egypt and other maritime nations because it represents a short route between the Far East and western Europe.
5.   Unlike Soviet subs, which are used to keep track of fishing vessels and to gather strategic information, American submarines are assigned to keep open shipping lanes and to escort convoys.
6.   The university, which, like the community colleges, has no fixed policy regarding part-time instructors, will definitely be affected by the new ruling.
7.   In Spain, as in some parts of the U.S., many people in the small towns are escaping to the cities, hoping to find better economic opportunity there.
8.   The racing cars, which just minutes before had been slowed by the yellow caution flag, were now thundering down the track at speeds in excess of 200 miles per hour, (which is) a rate of speed not thought possible just a few years ago.

(Note: Alternative solutions to the above are possible. Check with the teacher.)

Unit 12

Exercise 1

1. that (which) is	7. who (that) is	11. which (that) is
2. that (which) is	8. who are	12. which (that) is
that (which) is	that (which) is	which (that) is
3. who was	9. that (which) are	13. which (that) is
4. who was	10. who (that) are	
5. that (which) was	which (that) were	
6. who was		

Exercise 2

1. (which is)	6. (who were)	10. whom
2. (which is)	7. (which is)	11. (who were)
3. (who were)	8. (which is)	12. (which is)
4. (which was)	9. (which is)	(which was)
5. whom		

Exercise 3
1. (which is)   (that is)
2. (which is)   (which is)   (which was)
3. The first *which* cannot be omitted.   (which are)
4. (who is)   (which was)   (who was)   (which is)

Exercise 4

This is how the sentence might look after all deletions and changes have been made.
1. Yesterday, Jack Bishop, administrator of social services, approved the new regulations scheduled to go into effect May 1.
2. World-famed Yosemite National Park, whose scenery has inspired poets and nature lovers over the years, will be the site of this year's meeting of the Audubon Society, an organization dedicated to bird watching and conservation.
3. I was pleased to receive your letter dated April 15, forwarded to me by Mr. Johnson, our sales manager, in which you expressed interest in our products.
4. The FBI, tipped off by an informer who had infiltrated the leftist organization, quietly arrested the club members as they arrived for the meeting called by the executive committee.
5. Bill Jones, a promising young author, has written a new novel said to be his best effort so far.

Exercise 5
1. Ted Smith, now at home in Vermont, is able to continue. . . .
   Now at home in Vermont, Ted Smith is able to continue. . . .
2. The history professor, offended by the student's remark, walked. . . .
   Offended by the student's remark, the history professor walked. . . .
3. Dolores Simpson, whom the FBI is now investigating, has been accused. . . .
   (Deletion and front shift not permitted.)
4. Joe Sampson, denied membership in the Sports Club, made a claim of. . . .
   Denied membership in the Sports Club, Joe Sampson made a claim of. . . .
5. John Hunter, sworn in as a deputy sheriff, easily captured. . . .
   Sworn in as a deputy sheriff, John Hunter easily captured. . . .
6. Mr. Snodgrass, educated in London, speaks with a British accent.
   Educated in London, Mr. Snodgrass speaks with a British accent.
7. Mrs. Bluegrass, angered by the remark, got red in the face.
   Angered by the remark, Mrs. Bluegrass got red in the face.
8. The night nurse, alarmed by the great loss of blood, ran quickly. . . .
   Alarmed by the great loss of blood, the night nurse ran quickly. . . .
9. The huge trees, uprooted by the fierce storm, lay on the ground. . . .
   Uprooted by the fierce storm, the huge trees lay on the ground. . . .

Exercise 6

1. Richard H. Wilson, now an ex-president and private citizen, is busy. . . .
   Now an ex-president and private citizen, Richard H. Wilson is busy. . . .
2. The old man, soon forgotten by his old friends and neighbors, continued. . . .
   Soon forgotten by his old friends and neighbors, the old man continued. . . .
3. The new American ambassador to England, speaking with his newly acquired
   British accent, gave his first public speech. . . .
   Speaking with his newly acquired British accent, the new American ambassador to England gave his first public speech. . . .
4. John Coleman, a 1946 graduate of Harvard Law School, was at one time. . . .
   A 1946 graduate of Harvard Law School, John Coleman was at one time. . . .
5. The Greek government, furious over the Turkish invasion of Cyprus, plans
   to expel the 4,000. . . .
   Furious over the Turkish invasion of Cyprus, the Greek government plans to
   expel the 4,000. . . .
6. The government of Greece, powerless to intervene militarily against the
   Turks, took its case to the United Nations.
   Powerless to intervene militarily against the Turks, the government of Greece
   took its case to the. . . .
7. Mr. A. Bishop, now retired from his position as editor-in-chief of *Harper's
   Magazine,* is a contributing editor to the newly created. . . .
   Now retired from his position as editor-in-chief of *Harper's Magazine,* Mr. A.
   Bishop is a contributing editor to the newly created. . . .
8. The champion, wrapped in a heavy blue bathrobe, climbed into the ring with
   the agility of a mountain goat.
   Wrapped in a heavy blue bathrobe, the champion climbed into the ring. . . .
9. Timothy Brown, rescued from a man trying to drown him, had a joyous. . . .
   Rescued from a man trying to drown him, Timothy Brown had a joyous. . . .

Exercise 7

1. In approving the new law just passed by Congress, the President affirmed his
   support of the concept of. . . .
2. In deciding to reduce its military budget, the U.S. government has. . . .
3. In admitting that he lied on the witness stand, Jones has made. . . .
4. In (By) throwing himself on the mercy of the court, the accused man. . . .
5. In (By) proclaiming the wonders of its new micronite filters, the tobacco
   industry. . . .
6. In granting $10 a month to each participant for room and board in 1895, the
   U.S. War Department. . . .

Exercise 8

1. Regarded by many as one of the greatest generals of all time, Hannibal and
   his African armies. . . .

2. Marching his army through the Alps with African war elephants, Hannibal won a. . .

3. Containing (With) more than 35,000 record albums, the music library has a large collection of. . . .

4. At your earliest convenience, but no later than March of next year, please send us your application request for. . . .

5. In order not to waste time and create unnecessary confusion, please send us a complete transcript of. . . .

6. In West Germany's first such case, a divorced husband has sued his former wife for. . . .

7. Angry and upset because he had been denied permission to park in the reserved parking spaces, the disgruntled student drove his red sports car. . . .

SECTION

G

Unit 13

Exercise 1

1. It is assumed that. . . .
2. It is recognized that. . . .
3. It cannot be denied that. . . .
4. It cannot be said that. . . .
5. It is often claimed that. . . .
6. It can be argued that. . . .
7. It is well known that. . . .
8. It has been suggested that. . . .
9. It is often taken for granted that. . . .
10. It is understood that. . . .
11. It is thought that. . . .
12. It can be shown that. . . .
13. It has been reported that. . . .
14. It has been pointed out that. . . .
15. It has been rumored that. . . .
16. It has been demonstrated that. . . .

Exercise 2

1. It is assumed that William is innocent.
   William is assumed to be innocent.

2. It is said that money is the root of all evil.
   Money is said to be the root of all evil.
3. It has always been known that the practice of medicine is an art. . . .
   The practice of medicine has always been known to be an art. . . .
4. It is believed that passive resistance is the only alternative to. . . .
   Passive resistance is believed to be the only alternative to. . . .
5. It is claimed that the manuscript is over six hundred. . . .
   The manuscript is claimed to be over six hundred. . . .
6. It is said that women generally are not mechanically inclined.
   Women are generally said not to be mechanically inclined.
7. It is held that crime prevention costs less than law enforcement.
   Crime prevention is held to cost less than law enforcement.
8. It is felt that passing stricter laws is the only solution to. . . .
   Passing stricter laws is felt to be the only solution to. . . .
9. It has been revealed that cholesterol is injurious to the. . . .
   Cholesterol has been revealed to be injurious to the. . . .
10. It has been found that good eating habits contribute greatly. . . .
    Good eating habits have been found to contribute greatly. . . .
11. It is expected that good citizens will report crimes. . . .
    Good citizens are expected to report crimes. . . .
12. It is required that all citizens owning guns register with. . . .
    All citizens owning guns are required to register with. . . .
13. It is contended that economic frustration is at the root of all crime.
    Economic frustration is contended to be at the root of all crime.
14. It is said that writing exercises like this is a waste of time.
    Writing exercises like this is said to be a waste of time.

The following are only sample paraphrases. There are, of course, many ways to "skin a cat."

Exercise 3
The following are only suggested responses. Many variations are possible. When in doubt, check with the teacher.
2. It is very important to shake the bottle before using.
3. Please leave before the new owner arrives.
4. We ask the chairman to recognize the difficulty of this assignment.
   (or) We would like the chairman to realize this is a very hard assignment.
5. It is very dangerous to predict the impact of these policies. . . .
6. I think you don't have enough units to graduate in the spring.
7. I think we spent more money on that project than was necessary.
   (or) I think we spent too much money on that project.
8. I firmly believe that Mr. Johnson is not realistic.
   (or) I really think Mr. Johnson's goals are not realistic.
9. We ask you to try as hard as you can to finish this job as soon as possible.
10. I will try my best to finish the job on time.

11. We would very much like you to join us in trying to solve the problem.

12. I think I have a lot to say but I don't have a large enough vocabulary to say these things accurately.

Exercise 4

It is clear that the youth's assistance shortened the search and prevented the possible escape of the suspect.

Exercise 5

2. It is hard to refrain from making a guess as to the kind of response some of those middle-aged administrators would make if they were to lose *their* jobs.

3. One can't help guessing the course of action some of those middle-aged administrators would take if someone fired them from *their* jobs.

4. It would be easy to hazard a guess as to what some of those middle-aged administrators would do if they were to suffer the same fate—loss of *their* jobs.

5. One finds it hard not to guess what the reaction would be if some of those middle-aged administrators lost *their* employment.

Exercise 6

1. If you give homework assignments, make them rather challenging because if one reaches one's goal too easily one will lose the thrill of accomplishment.

2. The main purpose of science is to improve man's condition by adding to the advantages he naturally enjoys.

3. The committee put into effect a plan to establish a remedial instructional program in reading.

4. We admit that for some time English courses for foreign students at the university level often do not meet the needs of the graduate students.

5. a. There is very little difference between promoting a product or service in terms of public relations and doing the promoting in the name of marketing.

   b. Whether you call it public relations or marketing, you do practically the same thing when promoting a product or service.

   c. When you are promoting a product or service, no matter whether you call it public relations or marketing there will not be much difference in what you do.

   d. It is difficult to distinguish between what one does to promote a product or service in the field of public relations and what one does in the field of marketing.

6. a. If one finds significant changes in a nation's statistics for life expectancy, then the nature of these changes becomes very important.

   b. If one finds significant changes in a country's life expectancy statistics, then the reason for these changes assumes great importance.

7. People are giving evidence of their great desire for peace. Governments have to do something to carry out the people's will if they do not want to see the world fall into a hopeless situation.

8. No one has ever clearly defined administrative policy with regard to our new sports program.

9. a. We cannot allow any further delay in making our policies regarding this program because we must comply with new federal and state laws.
    b. We have to obey (follow) the new federal and state laws; consequently we have to make our policies affecting this program immediately.

10. As regards Chi Min Ling's research activities, we suggest you limit his access to unpublished or classified work funded by the government.

11. Practically everyone would agree that the average student can understand these instructions.

12. Using the major parameters of time interval and shock intensity it should be possible to advance the genetic analysis of the laboratory animals' avoidance conditioning.

13. a. We cannot afford to neglect the fact that in present-day society women are treated unfairly and irrationally.
    b. We must pay attention to the fact that ...
    c. We can ill afford not to pay attention to the way present-day society treats women unfairly and irrationally.

Exercise 7

According to the author, if we look at success in terms of the number of women who are working, we can say that the changes in the economic position of women amount to a feminist success. After all, there are twenty-four million working women, and this number is too large to be ignored. However, if we consider this change in economic status in terms of quality rather than quantity, then the change is not so remarkable. It is true we can find women employed in every job listed by the Bureau of the Census. In addition the popular press continues to report the success women are having entering what used to be considered men's occupations. For example, three years ago a prize for the mutual fund salesman of the year was awarded to a woman. There is a good representation of women working in the fields of advertising and real estate, and it is no longer unusual to find women working as taxi drivers.

Exercise 8

Paraphrased Version

In this article the author says that the most serious problem that people have now is a crisis of scientific warfare. In his opinion, the continual improvement of science will make mankind disappear from the earth by the next world war. There are, he says, two opinions about this scientific warfare. One of the opinions is about establishing organizations which function to prevent world wars from occurring. The other is about an agreement between fighting countries that both sides will use inefficient weapons.

The author prefers the former solution because he thinks the latter is not realistic. If a war happens, such an agreement will be broken by both sides. He emphasizes that new methods which enable us to prevent a war from starting should be found. Otherwise, he says, human beings will not survive much longer.

Paraphrased by Setsuko Ishimaru

Unit 13
Exercise 10

In his essay published in 1798, English economist Thomas Malthus attempted to explain the poverty and misery among the world's lower classes. His thesis is that a nation's population tends to grow at a faster rate than its capacity to produce the food and fiber it needs to stay alive. Malthus says that population tends to increase at a "constant geometric rate" but that food production grows only arithmetically. These different growth rates will cause the world's population, which is ever growing larger, to inevitably encroach upon the food supply. This, according to Malthus, will result in "subsistence living levels, misery, and perhaps even starvation."

We all well know that the earth's population has been expanding greatly, so much so that one now hears the term "population explosion" quite often. In the last two hundred years, the growth of the world's population has been three times larger than the "accumulated expansion" of the population since the very beginning of history.

The author of this essay thinks it is highly relevant at this time to ask ourselves to what extent Malthus' pessimistic prediction has come true or will come true in the near future. He thinks this because of the unbelievable population growth, its projected continuance, and the fact that the amount of land on this planet is "finite." The author suggests that we ask ourselves whether a limited food supply in the future will mean "bare subsistence living" for people in the twenty-first century.

Exercise 11

a. The giant corporations have been hit by the recession and by competition from smaller companies. As a result, people are no longer afraid of the giant corporations.
b. The recession and the competition from smaller companies have hit the giant corporations. Consequently, the latter no longer produce the fear they used to among the general public.

Exercise 12

The quality of the material people have submitted (for publication) is high, and the papers show variation, as was originally hoped. A look at the specifics of the forthcoming articles listed on the back of this leaflet confirms this.

Exercise 13

Speakers at the 16th Congress of the White Dove Peace Association have again issued a passionate call to uphold peace in the world. They have also made a plea to avert a nuclear war and to halt the senseless but extremely dangerous arms race.

Exercise 14

Situated in one of the industrial centers of Eastern Siberia, Lake Baikal is the world's largest reservoir of fresh water, containing 20 per cent of the global reserves. The value of this beautiful lake increases as the problem of fresh water grows more complex and as the area around the lake becomes increasingly affected by human economic activity.

Exercise 15

Giant multinational corporations operating in some developing countries are prohibited from repatriating any of their profits. Thus, when a company's business is thriving and its profits increasing, the host country may require the corporation to develop facilities which will create more jobs. In this way the host government forces the company to recycle its profits earned in the country, and can utilize still another instrument of control of the multinational corporations.

Exercises 16 and 17

Exchange papers with a fellow student and compare efforts.

SECTION

H

Unit 16

Exercise 1

1. The capital city has a huge, modern airport.
2. Mr. Hill, our chemistry teacher, was at the party last night.
3. In the first course we study essays, poems, and plays.
4. As the story indicates, a man should respect his wife's judgment.
5. I wrote to Mr. Smith several times, but he never answered my brilliant letters.
6. The committee appreciates suggestions of this type, and we hope that more people will contribute their ideas.
7. Before exporting, the goods have to be inspected.
8. A college teacher, for example, has to fill out dozens of forms each semester.
9. Some of the diseases now under control are measles, diphtheria, and smallpox.

10. The courses I take are the ones which you recommend.
11. My doctor is a kind, patient, understanding man.
12. You can send the money to the bank, or you can send it directly to me.
13. Such as it is, this poem was written after days of profound meditation.
14. We have to use the big steel hook.
15. She is a tall, thin, middle-aged woman.
16. My Aunt Susie, whom we all love very much, is coming for a visit.
17. You are, I think, the best man for the job.
18. The shortage of water, from our point of view, is one of the more serious problems.
19. Mary enrolled in a College for women, and her brother went to Harvard.
20. Mr. Brown arrived in town, and when he heard the news about his son he became furious.
21. He was a sad, dejected, suicidal patient.
22. As these statistics indicate, a man is safer in the air than on the highway.

Exercise 2

Rawalpindi, in northeastern Pakistan, has recently developed into a modern city. Its old buildings have been replaced by modern ones, ten to fifteen stories high; its bridges have been widened, and its old system of transport by horse and wagon has been replaced by cars, buses, and trains. Rawalpindi, a name which hardly appeared on Pakistani maps of some years ago, is now one of the most important cities of the country.

Exercise 3

On a cold, windy November morning Harold caught a large catfish with a small steel hook and a white nylon line as he was fishing from an old, deserted boat dock. Margie, the little old woman who kept house for him, cleaned, floured, and fried the fish for his usual mid-morning snack.

Exercise 4

At the time of his death in 1976, Robert Johnson's literary estate, consisting of some four thousand pages of manuscript, notebook sheets, and dozens of letters, lay scattered and almost lost.

However, through the efforts of Helen Johnson, the author's widow, virtually all of this material was recovered—from such places as a Colombian bank vault and the back room of a New York bar—and stored in safe deposit boxes in Newark, New Jersey. It is this complete and irreplaceable collection that Professor King has now systematically sorted and cataloged for publication in his new book—the result of six months spent in detailed analysis, poring over every sheet or scrap of paper that might be of literary value.

Exercise 5

1. It is evident our system of justice works for some, but not for all; in this case it has not worked at all.
2. I recommend that we move toward, in effect, a policy of "direct consultation."
3. Becoming a heart surgeon is like learning to do magic tricks; one has to practice in order to gain proficiency.
4. Two hundred students took the examination; only twenty-two passed.
5. He asked me what I was now studying at school.
6. These men are, I think, the best people presently available for the job.
7. Don't tease that little monkey; he might bite you.
8. The young lady who broke her leg is in the hospital.
9. Mr. Snodgrass, our chemistry teacher, was at the party last night.
10. The child learns to base relationships with others on criteria fixed by the state; other boys and girls can be rated on an objective scale.
11. Acceptance of this report without modification would be, I fear, an invitation to future frustration.
12. A report of this kind must come to grips successfully with the boundaries of consultation; the Blue Ribbon Committee report, in my opinion, does not do this effectively.
13. My girlfriend's brother is a tall, good-looking man.
14. We Chinese are different from Americans. We are hesitant to blurt out the truth for fear of offending others; they are not.
15. John's oldest brother died at the age of eighty-two; his youngest brother died at seventy.
16. This morning Mrs. Johnson got up early, made breakfast for herself and her husband, and washed the dishes; then she got into the car and drove downtown.
17. The Supreme Court's role is to review law; it is not a fact-finding court.
18. This classification is extremely important to a person in our society; it determines almost everything else about his future life.

Exercise 6

1. It is easy for politicians to talk about fighting for one's country; ~~but~~ they are not the ones who have to go to war.
2. One would think that a man with all that money was extremely happy; ~~but~~ as a matter of fact he is miserable.
3. Many people call Mr. Reed a communist; ~~and~~ others call him the poor man's hero.
4. Everyone should take only one piece of chicken; ~~but~~ if you are still hungry, you can come back for seconds.
5. In the olden days the man of the house made all the decisions; ~~and~~ the wife never dared to disagree.

6. Mr. Young was a respected member of the community; ~~and~~ he was also the town's sheriff and dog catcher.

7. Of course I told the sheriff about that crazy woman driver; ~~for~~ how was I to know she was his wife.

8. We all agree that every institution of higher education needs such plans; ~~for~~ without them our day-to-day operation lacks adequate direction.

9. This was the case with my brother; ~~and~~ I have found it to be true with other students as well.

10. A man can stay alive without food for about thirty days; ~~but~~ a man without water will die within one to four days.

11. The hungry student looked in the refrigerator for something to eat; ~~and~~ all he could find was a tiny chicken leg.

Exercise 7
1. ... you please—at 12 midnight. ...
2. ... wanted to be—a trial lawyer.
3. ... Atacama desert—the driest spot on earth—as well as. ..
4. ... for our children—these are the goals. ..
5. All these factors—unity, coherence and organization—are extremely. ..
6. Only five other countries—Peru, Ecuador ... and Paraguay—had a relatively. ..
7. ... for only one reason—to upgrade the. ..
8. ... we plan—especially in ... for the aged—are not yet funded.
9. ... with that philosophy—nonviolently, with. ..
10. ... the obvious—that human beings. ..
11. ... in a single day—winter in the morning. ..
12. ... of the dean—an unexpected move by the new president—caused many. ..
13. ... obtained elsewhere—for its serious. ..
14. ... of character—achievements which. ..

Exercise 8
1. Hoover High School was represented by the following beauty queens: Rose White, sophomore; Helen Blue, senior; and Marie Gold, senior.

2. Here are some steps to take before going abroad: apply for a passport, get the necessary shots from your doctor, and ask him for a stomach remedy just in case.

3. The goals of education are these: to learn about the past, to study the present, and to realize one's full potential in the future.

4. There are three causes for these unfortunate conditions: lack of education, constant poverty, and few job opportunities.

5. The point I want to make is this: let's not be too quick to criticize the *other* guy.

6. Who can forget the words of Neil Armstrong as he set foot on the moon: "One small step for a man; one giant leap for mankind."
7. The Grand Jury outrage amounts to this: It has whitewashed a highly culpable National Guard Unit; it has made a severe attack on the academic community, and it has tried to discredit our students.
8. The future seems reserved for fast, efficient, electronic communication networks.
9. Approaching the end of the decade, (comma optional) our membership had almost tripled, losing some and gaining others.

Exercise 9
Reverend Thomas White   the Alps   the Far East   The University of Minnesota the Twentieth Century Limited   the USA   293 Ocean Avenue, San Luis Obispo, California   the Reverend Thomas   the Rocky Mountains   the Mississippi River Yosemite National Park   New England.

Professor Jones   the Reverend White   a Ford   Coca-Cola   C. and H. sugar Campbell soups.

the Bible   Shakespeare   *the War of the Roses*   *World War II in Retrospect* *The Siege of Leningrad.*

Exercise 10

whose	whose	hers	hers
baby's	babies'	its	- - - -
attorney's	attorneys'	person's	persons'
man's	men's	mother-in-law's	mothers-in-law's
lady's	ladies'	child's	children's
woman's	women's	yours	yours
someone's	- - - -		

Exercise 11

Charles' hat	Robert's friend
Keats' poems	a friend of Robert's
babies' tears	anyone's problem

Exercise 12
1. John bought a paperbound edition of *Gone With the Wind.*
2. *The National Observer* was a weekly newspaper.
3. Their favorite painting is the *Mona Lisa*; their favorite opera is *Tosca.*
4. Be certain to use *ibid.* and *op. cit.* correctly when footnoting.
5. Will you translate *vaya con Dios* for me?
6. My parents sailed on the last trip of the *Queen Elizabeth.*
7. I suggest that you inquire *why* it happened, not *how* it happened.
8. One of her Christmas gifts to me was a subscription to the *New Yorker*, a weekly magazine.

9. The students waited two hours for the *Twentieth Century Limited* before it finally chugged into the depot.

10. Do you distinguish between *caught* and *cot* in your dialect?

11. Why don't you dot your *i's* and cross your *t's*?

12. A *6* is an inverted *9*.

13. His parents were delighted to see the words *magna cum laude* on his diploma.

14. One of the new TV shows is *The Bold Ones*.

15. I own a Modern Library edition of the *Complete Poems of Keats and Shelley*.

16. One of the new albums is *All Things Must Pass*.

17. He spent all day Sunday reading the *New York Times*.

18. Do you keep a dictionary on your desk?

19. Is the primary stress on *may* or *be*?

20. Please use the word *reluctant* in a sentence.

21. Richard Chamberlain's performance in *Hamlet* has been highly praised by most critics.

22. Is the *Spirit of St. Louis* the plane Lindbergh flew across the Atlantic Ocean?

23. The Women's Liberation Front has popularized *Women: A Minority Group* to the best-seller list.

NOTES TO THE INSTRUCTOR

Unit 1

This revised unit is based on Unit 3 of the original edition. This unit has been placed first because the author believes it best to thrust the students into the writing process right from the start, rather than to begin with peripheral matters such as relative clauses.

Exercises 1 to 3

Students sometimes have to be shown that there is a logical structure to paragraph division. These exercises should help in this regard.

Exercises 4 to 7

Although these are fairly easy exercises, they serve to illustrate the logical arrangement of sentences in a paragraph. It might be well to point out to the students the many linking devices used, including the semicolon in exercise 6.

MINI-RESEARCH REPORT

The purpose of this assignment is to see whether students can take various data and transform them into a cohesive report. Students tend to put in too many *and*s or to misuse the expression "and many others." Help for this problem is available in Unit 4.

Exercise 8

Items 1 and 2 are examples of professional writing from a novel by Ruth Soloman.

Exercises 11 to 14

It is a good idea to have students exchange papers and correct errors while individual students are called upon to go over these assignments. Although there is an answer key for most of these exercises, it is best to have students correct each other's errors.

SECTION B

Unit 2, Page 26, Comments on *wh*-words

In a sentence like *I don't know whom she saw* the relative, of course, cannot be deleted. This is a different structure: *whom she saw* is not a relative clause, but rather the complement of *know*. (*I don't know + she saw wh+*.)

Unit 2, Exercise 3

Note that the *wh*-words are all in non-*be* clauses.

Unit 3, Exercise 6

Don't allow your students to produce meaningless sentences here. Ask them to produce a sentence providing a context which shows they really understand the meaning of the various subordinating conjunctions.

Unit 3, Exercise 7

The question may be asked, "What is the point of this exercise?" The main purpose here is not the practice of front shifting or of punctuation, but rather to provide a means of practicing these forms so that students gain more familiarity in their use. The exercise itself is very easy. Each sentence provides a small context for the use of that conjunction. Students have to learn the full range of these forms, and not be limited to the one or two conjunctions they use in speech.

Unit 3, Exercise 8

This exercise is a good opportunity for students to recognize fragments or incomplete sentences.

Unit 3, Exercise 9

Only some students have this problem (e.g., those from Taiwan), but those that do, need some help. This exercise is probably not necessary for most students.

Unit 3, Exercise 10

a. The *have* + -*ing* transformation deletes the tense/aspect marker, thereby losing the formal distinction between present perfect and past perfect. In such cases one must rely on context alone.

b. A sentence like *After visiting the local jail, John went on to the city hall* may appear to have the same meaning as the *having* plus past participle construction, but there is a difference. In the sentence just cited there is no causal relationship between the two clauses. Rather, the *after. . . -ing* construction merely relates the two clauses as a sequence of events; no causal relationship is intended.

Unit 3, Page 43, Sentence adverbials

Note that the connectors in parentheses are not true sentence adverbials. True sentence adverbials exhibit great flexibility in word order; the words in parentheses do not.

Unit 3, Exercise 12

See comment on Exercise 7, Unit 3, and substitute *sentence adverbial* for *conjunction*.

Unit 4, Exercise 1

Nos. 11 and 12: Note the active/passive difference.

Unit 4, Exercises 3a to 3g

These are actual sentences taken from students' essays. While other revisions might be better, the use of this technique, i.e., deliberate repetition, allows students to keep their own phrasing more or less intact.

Unit 4, Exercises 10 and 11

Many students from Iran have this problem, but students from other language backgrounds may or may not need this practice.

SECTION D

Unit 9, Page 124, Nonseparation, preposition + *which*

In clauses where the word *which* replaces the NP of an adverbial phrase, the separated pattern does not ordinarily occur.

Unit 9, Exercise 3

For help with relative clauses, inside modification, see Section E of *Preparation for Writing*.

For help in punctuating these sentences, refer students to Section H of this volume, on the use of the comma. Some of these sentences can be punctuated either as restrictive or as nonrestrictive clauses.

In no. 13, we can also say *approval for* instead of *approval to*.

SECTION F

Unit 12, Page 154, Deletion in nonrestrictive clauses

In nonrestrictive clauses, *wh*-words with object function cannot be deleted. For example, deletion is not permitted in a sentence like, *Mr. King, whom everyone is talking about, used to be the mayor.*

Note also that selectional restrictions apply to definite and indefinite articles in these clauses. For example, indefinite pronouns cannot go here. Note the following: *#Anyone, who was tormented by the memory of his dead wife, . . .*

Unit 12, Exercise 7

Nonrestrictive relative clauses can only be front shifted when the *wh-* word is in subject function. Note that in passive sentences the *wh-* word is the grammatical subject, not the logical subject. This probably accounts for the fact that most clauses in passive form can be front shifted.

SECTION G

Unit 13, Page 163, The passive in technical writing

In the example of the active sentence the use of *the fact that* is obligatory. For an explanation on the use of the factive, see *Preparation for Writing*, Section F.

Unit 13, Exercise 2

No. 14, *writing exercises* is a nominalization of *one write exercises* and derives from *for one to write exercises*. Compare with: *Writing exercises are better than oral exercises.*

Unit 13, Exercise 6

An alternate paraphrase for no. 9 could be as follows:

The urgent need to comply with new federal and state laws demands that we formulate our policies affecting the administration of this program without further delay.

Unit 13, Exercises 16 and 17

Here are sample paraphrases for these two exercises.

Exercise 16

The business monopolist is not interested in selling the greatest possible number of products. In like manner the union members have no interest in creating the largest number of jobs possible. The union members, like the businessman, are interested in earning as much money as possible. A union is not likely to cause union wages to go up so much that many of its own members will be out of a job. However, if there is an increasing demand for a particular industry's product, there may be a theoretical loss of jobs in that industry. These theoretical lost jobs would belong to those workers who might have worked in that industry if the high wage rate had not reduced the demand for labor. We don't expect the union to give a lot of consideration to this vague group of workers.

Exercise 17

History has pointed out to us that the slaves of our ancient civilizations made it possible for the people at the top to indulge in art and literature, which remain as the glory, or great accomplishment, of that era. Present-day mechanization, in a way, duplicates this same condition: the huge development of labor-saving machines, by expanding mankind's capacities, provides the necessary leisure time for man to pursue his extensive cultural pursuits. Our present-day slave owner is mechanization, but with a difference—all groups of the community are able to benefit from its inventions.

Unit 15, "Let 'em Starve"

Make sure the students understand the term "goodies." Here it probably means all the material things enjoyed by rich people in rich countries.

The author invites comments.